ARCHPRIEST AVVAKUM

FOR PAULA

Archpriest Avvakum

The LIFE

written by Himself

WITH THE STUDY OF V. V. VINOGRADOV

TRANSLATIONS, ANNOTATIONS, COMMENTARY,
AND A HISTORICAL INTRODUCTION BY

KENNETH N. BROSTROM
WAYNE STATE UNIVERSITY

MICHIGAN SLAVIC PUBLICATIONS
UNIVERSITY OF MICHIGAN
ANN ARBOR

MICHIGAN SLAVIC TRANSLATIONS, No. 4

International Standard Book Number: 0-930042-33-6
Library of Congress Catalog Card Number: 79–19639
Copyright 1979 by Kenneth N. Brostrom

MICHIGAN SLAVIC PUBLICATIONS

Department of Slavic Languages and Literatures
The University of Michigan, Ann Arbor

CONTENTS

PREFACE

Earnest translators are fond of saying they labor between a rock and a hard place, between the often unduplicable felicities of the original language and the stubborn intransigence of the target language, which so reluctantly and rarely yields a genuinely happy equivalent. There seems in addition to be an inverse relation between the likelihood of success and the stylistic difficulty of the original text. Perhaps the aspiring translator of the stylistically formidable *Life of the Archpriest Avvakum, Written by Himself* should first consider seriously Dostoevsky's possibly clairvoyant observation: "I think that if one were to translate a piece such as the narrative of the Archpriest Avvakum, the result would be nonsense, or better, nothing whatever would come of it." [1]

Yet the need for a good translation exists: the *Life* is generally considered one of medieval Russia's finest literary works as well as an important document from the early history of the schism, which crippled the Russian Church during the seventeenth century; but the two published English translations are inadequate. The more readily available version by Jane Harrison and Hope Mirrlees contains numerous serious errors, while its quaintly archaic, rather elevated manner transmits little of Avvakum's dyadic style and fails to illustrate an observation found in D. S. Mirsky's introduction to this very translation, that "Avvakum's style, archaic in detail, is essentially the same as the (uneducated) spoken Russian of today." [2] The second translation by Helen Iswolsky [3] contains few errors, but its value is vitiated by numerous, seemingly capricious excisions, most of them not signaled by ellipses. The Iswolsky translation is uninteresting stylistically, and it avoids translating with greater determination than its rival instances of indelicate or unseemly language. We need a complete, accurate English translation of Avvakum's *Life* based on the best

vii

available edition, that of A. N. Robinson.[4] It is this need which the present volume primarily seeks to satisfy.

Despite the urgency which sometimes attends defenses of the "art" of translation, it is finally, if not exclusively, a pragmatic activity, and largely pragmatic considerations have shaped the contents of this book. It aims to serve several rather discrete audiences. The function of the annotations on the *Life* is obvious; their content is based primarily on the voluminous, thorough annotations contained in Robinson's book. The Introduction is designed for those who do not know, wish to be reminded of, or need to know the ecclesiastical and historical context within which the *Life* was written; here I am deeply indebted to Serge Zenkovsky for his highly readable, detailed account of the history of the Old Belief. [5] It also summarizes the important textological investigations of N. S. Demkova.[6] A translation of V. V. Vinogradov's seminal analysis of Avvakum's *Life*, "On the Tasks of Stylistics: Observations Regarding the Style of *The Life of the Archpriest Avvakum*,"[7] is also included. Certainly the most influential and probably the best literary study of the *Life* ever published, it nevertheless remains difficult to obtain, having never been reprinted in its entirety. It is in my view a persuasive refutation of the late A. I. Issatschenko's energetic derogation of Avvakum's literary reputation. Arguing that Russia had no genuine literary language before 1750, he sees in Avvakum a striking illustration of the homely ham-handedness allegedly characteristic of literary activity in seventeenth-century Muscovy: "Es ist kein Zufall, dass dieser erzkonservative Obskurant Zitate aus der Heiligen Schrift mit Obszönitäten niederster Sorte vermengt, ohne offenbar die Dishormonie solcher Juxtapositionen zu ahnen."[8] Vinogradov's article is also an important theoretical statement with relevance to his later work; one can detect in it the influence of Saussure's distinction between the synchronic and diachronic levels of analysis and early Formalism's inclination to understand art in terms of unexpected, structured departures from the habitual and normative. The present translation is a careful condensation of the lengthy original; both the specific points and the general shape of Vinogradov's argument have been preserved, while exhaustive lists of examples, many footnotes, and some text have been sacrificed. My own study attempts to extend, supplement, and in part dispute some of Vinogradov's observations concerning the thematic organization of the *Life*; it aims to be a companion piece, although it tends to lay greater emphasis than Vinogradov's study on the conventional aspects of Avvakum's art.

Wherever possible quotations from the Bible have been rendered by the King James Version, because of its familiarity (Avvakum's audience knew these passages well) and its stylistic distinctness from the more colloquial English style used elsewhere.

As always, transliteration is an irritating problem. With minor exceptions the International Linguistic System is used in the annotations and notes on the assumption that this will not confuse the nonspecialist seriously but may assist the Slavist. In the translation of the *Life* and the Introduction, this system was modified in an *ad hoc* manner for the sake of those not knowing Russian (e.g., *Isaiah* rather than *Isaija*). Such readers will find it useful to familiarize themselves with the rough-and-ready guide below, which will help them approximate the pronunciation of Russian words and names:

č – *ch* (church)	x – *ch* (Ba*ch*)	' – palatalization of
š – *sh* (shoal)	i – *i* (machine)	the preceding con-
šč – *shch* (fresh cheese)	ë – *yaw* (yawn)	sonant, i.e., with
ž – *zh* (azure)	u – *u* (chute)	the mid-tongue held
c – *ts* (newts)	j – *y* (yodel, Okay)	near the palate.

With minor changes Avvakum's spelling of names has been retained.

Dates are Old Style unless otherwise indicated. To convert dates here from the Julian to the Gregorian calendar, add ten days.

I am particularly indebted to Ladislav Matejka, who originally suggested this project to me and who contributed substantially to its evolution. I am also grateful to Horace Dewey and Deming Brown for critical readings of the translation in its first version, and to Frank Gladney and Tatjana Cizevska, both of whom read it with care later on. The late Max Hayward played a special role here; I wish it were possible to thank him again for a delightful two hours spent in his Oxford office one spring morning, when he discussed in detail his criticisms of my first draft and treated me to his experienced observations regarding certain general and highly relevant problems of translation. However much I have benefited from the wise counsel of these colleagues, they bear no responsibility for damage done here to Avvakum's literary legacy. My thanks also go to the National Endowment for the Humanities, which supported my work during the summer of 1975, and to Wayne State University, which generously assumed a portion of the costs of printing.

If the translation is deemed worthy of something other than oblivion by its readers, the translator solicites their comments, corrections, and emendations for future reference.

8 July 1979

INTRODUCTION

It is one of the ironies of Russia's ironic history that her greatest religious crisis occurred during the seventeenth century, as she entered an era shaped by forces which were moving her toward a secularized future. One need not be a Marxist, of course, to recognize that great crises frequently erupt during periods of historical transition: the moribund flares into new but ephemeral life, just as a dying star sometimes explodes into a supernova, then fades away forever. Old Muscovy had idealized the political and cultural isolation of her life during the fifteenth and sixteenth centuries: she was the "Third Rome," the final repository after Rome and Constantinople of unsullied Orthodox Christianity, destined to lead a degenerate world to history's culmination in the Second Coming. Significantly, however, this persistent idea never became official doctrine. As was often to be the case in the future, prophetic ardor regarding Russia's historical destiny had to yield to political realities. Visions of the Apocalypse and world spiritual supremacy provided no useful guide to action as Russia began to seek her place among the peoples who were coalescing into modern Europe.

Old habits of mind hold tenaciously to life, however, even among pragmatists. The collapse of Byzantium and the Tatar Golden Horde during the fifteenth century and Moscow's astonishing rise to hegemony in the East Slavic area during the sixteenth had not created, but simply reinvigorated much older dreams of Russia's special destiny. In addition, the chaotic historical hiatus Russia experienced between the death of the house of Rurik and the birth of the Romanov dynasty (the so-called Time of Troubles, 1598–1613) had taught Russians to distrust the Westerners who had repeatedly invaded Russia then, plundering and attempting to impose the "heretical Papist faith." Despite growing admiration of things Western among the elite, this distrust along with the

1

old visions of national grandeur led Tsar Aleksej Mixajlovič (1645–1676) to perceive the natural arena for Russian leadership, within the European context, in the lands of the Greek Orthodox faith. But to assume this position of preeminence, Moscow had to harmonize her religious practices with those of the Greeks, who were willing to humor Muscovite aspirations to gain protection against their overlords, the Turks in particular. Patriarch Nikon's ecclesiastical reforms, however, had implications far transcending the ambitious calculations which gave them birth. The old dream of a purely spiritual supremacy was abandoned for a new one; in order to establish Moscow as first among Orthodox nations, the reforms declared the Third Rome defunct by identifying "errors" in her ancient, sacrosanct, "unsullied" traditions. This revolution in Muscovy's self-image provoked terrible antagonisms between those who would preserve the past inviolate and those equally committed to supremacy who would achieve it without exclusive reliance upon God's national preferences. Avvakum was a mighty spokesman for the conservative opposition. His auto-biography is not only an important historical document and a literary masterpiece, but an imperishable portrait of the mind of an era torn apart by commitments which now seem bizarre and sometimes quaint, for all their tragic, hideous consequences.

Frequently encountered in Soviet historical accounts is the assertion that the ecclesiastical reforms reflected to a considerable degree internal developments in Russia, specifically the centraliza-tion of autocratic power in Moscow: a centralized church was a necessary ideological and institutional bulwark for the state. Certainly the social system in Russia during the seventeenth century can be described as a centralized, hierarchical feudal order based upon serfdom and a service gentry. But this is not very helpful in understanding the reforms. For example, emphasis on the Church's supporting role tends to ignore the fact that Patriarch Nikon's attempt to elevate the Church over the state, thereby setting them against one another, was a manifestation not only of personal ambition but of powerful theocratic impulses evident in all the reformers. Even more to the point, the reforms did not strengthen but seriously weakened both Church and state. Soviet historians are nevertheless correct in part: the reforms were a response to internal conditions in Russia. But there were no hidden, secular "class" motivations behind them at the outset; their purpose was not the centralization but the "churchification" (*ocerkovlenie*) of Russia. Here we are primarily concerned with the reform movement's first phase, which proceeded not "from above," like Nikon's calamitous innovations, but spontaneously "from below." In this the early years of the reform movement were distinct from every effort to achieve a religious revival in the Russian past.

The destruction, the social chaos, the death, the humiliations visited upon Russia during the Time of Troubles left many of the devout in bitter confusion. What had happened to "Radiant Russia" (*svetlaja Rus'*), favored by God and destined for elevation above all the nations of the earth? Contemporary historical accounts predictably fall back on a traditional explanation for misfortune: Russia's agony was punishment sent by God, just recompense for unrepented and proliforating sins. The ignominious depths of Russia's suffering were thus a measure of God's great wrath against his chosen people. What then must be done so that such punishment would never come again? This question became more urgent with the passage of time, for the religious fervor that accompanied the expulsion of foreign rulers from Moscow early in the century soon waned, and age-old abuses of piety returned with irrepressible vitality. What is more, the premonitions of doomsday which had agitated Western Europe during the sixteenth century now began to stir in Russia, and the need for Russians to shoulder their eschatological responsibilities seemed even more pressing. Reports and rumors of repressions visited upon Orthodox believers and churches by the Turks, Lithuanians, and Poles, the constantly shifting configurations of alien religious movements — Islam, Roman Catholicism, Calvinism, Unitarianism — in the regions along Russia's periphery, continuing military weakness, and spreading internal unrest and sporadic revolts, all contributed to the general unease and the belief that Russia was in desperate need of spiritual renewal.

The first stage of the reform movement is generally associated with the activities of a group of energetic spiritual leaders who emerged from the ranks of the married parish, "white" clergy (as opposed to the monastic "black" clergy); they are known as the Lovers of God (*Bogoljubcy*) or the Zealots of the Ancient Piety (*Revniteli starogo blagočestija*). Although certain prelates of the Church were interested in spiritual revival (Zenkovsky shows that publication of religious materials rose dramatically during the period 1631–50; *Staroobrjadčestvo*, p. 93), it was primarily clerics active in the scattered villages and towns of the upper Volga area who sought to work a miracle, to bring the ideal and the real together, making of their land a genuine "Holy Russia," the final earthly repository of undefiled heavenly Truth. Some, and perhaps many, of these stalwarts remain unknown to us. Avvakum mentions numbers of them in his *Life*, and we know others from other sources. The remainder were buried literally and figuratively by Nikon and his heirs, for almost without exception the Lovers of God found themselves in the camp of the Old Believers – those who later would not and could not accept Nikon's innovations, even when the alternative was death.

The odds were against these zealous parish priests from the outset. The Russian episcopate had long been chosen exclusively from the monastic clergy, which had acquired and retained a virtual monopoly on ecclesiastical wealth and education during and after the era of the Tatar Yoke (12th–14th centuries). Not only did parish priests have little influence on an ecclesiastical hierarchy dominated by monks and a powerful contingent of lay administrators, but they were generally patronized and often disdained as the lesser of the brethren of the cloth: they were denizens of ten thousand derelict villages, ignorant, uncouth, and most likely drunken. The Lovers of God were possessed, however, of an enormous ambition for Russia, which meant declaring all-out war on the status quo. They were thus caught between a self-interested ecclesiastical bureaucracy, hoary with ancient prerogatives and privileges, and a secular, simply human world uninterested in heroic spiritual exercises. That they had any success at all is attributable in large measure to the combined efforts of three men: Archpriest Ivan Neronov (see annotation 57), the Tsar's confessor Archpriest Stefan Vonifat'ev (see annotation 56), and the Tsar himself, Aleksej Mixajlovič.

Ivan Neronov was apparently born with the ardor of the prophet and reformer. But his life probably acquired its direction from the teachings of Dionisij, Archimandrite of the St. Sergius-Trinity Monastery (or "Laura"), in the early seventeenth century Russia's greatest center of religious and cultural life. Neronov

St. Sergius-Trinity
Monastery in
Zagorsk

17th-century encolpion,
gold, set with pearls
with silver chain

arrived at the monastery in the early 1620's, and his piety and appealing personality immediately attracted Dionisij's attention. Neronov lived in Dionisij's cell, becoming his personal servant and devoted disciple. This venerable holy man had rendered his beloved Russia great service during the Time of Troubles, and from him Neronov undoubtedly heard much regarding her destiny. At the same time, his sense of the urgency of reform must have been sharpened by the tales told by the many pilgrims who were drawn to the monastery and who kept the monks alive to threats to the faith both within and outside Russia. In his teachings in response to these challenges, Dionisij drew heavily upon the writings of St. John Chrysostum and Maksim Grek ("Maksim the Greek"), two writers who later became favorites among the reformers (see notes 39, 260). John Chrysostum's reforming zeal and timeless sermons in rebuke of human wickedness inspired the Zealots to great works, while Maksim Grek's unwavering affirmation of faith against Rome's systematically elaborated dogmatics and his extensive commentaries on the details of Russian life and faith recommended him to men who wished to remake their world. Around 1630 Neronov left the St. Sergius-Trinity Monastery filled with Dionisij's spirit of personal responsibility for the fate of the Russian land. In this he marked the way for later Zealots, who similarly eschewed the ancient anchoritic ideal of solitary piety; not personal salvation alone but elevation of the spirit of Orthodoxy and its penetration into every corner of Russian life and into the life of every Russian was the vision that moved them.

Neronov began his work in Nižnij Novgorod and soon acquired a reputation as an outspoken moral pedagogue; in 1632 he was exiled to the far north by Patriarch Filaret for publicly criticizing preparations for war with Poland. Filaret's death in 1633 brought Neronov back to Nižnij Novgorod, and in the years following his fame as a preacher spread far beyond his city. In 1647 he was brought to Moscow, where he became a member of Tsar Aleksej Mixajlovič's inner circle; this group included Stefan Vonifat'ev, who was to become Neronov's closest friend and associate. They and a few others such as Fëdor Rtiščev were soon deeply involved in ecclesiastical reform (see annotation 205).

Neronov's previous labor as a reformer was certainly a major reason for his transfer to Moscow. His sermons were a minor revolution in themselves, as the practice of preaching had virtually disappeared in the Russian Church despite the great preachers in her past. Neronov's sermons consisted of readings from Holy Writ followed by a commentary, not in ecclesiastical but in simple, moving vernacular language; their impact was measured by his spreading fame and perhaps by the subsequent popularity of preaching among the Lovers of God. In his sermons Neronov persistently summoned his brothers of the cloth to a life-style which would edify rather than vex or entertain their flocks. Like St. John Chrysostum he preached and practiced a social Gospel, urging clergy and laity alike to labor for the welfare of the poor, the sick, and the downtrodden. He himself established a hospital and a refectory for the needy in Nižnij Novgorod, and a school as well, and during the entirety of his career he devoted substantial energy to such charitable activities. No one including the lords of the realm, the boyars, was beyond the reach of his blunt denunciations and the prescriptive urgency of his summons to renewal.

With regard to liturgical matters, nothing was more vital to Neronov than the principle of so-called *edinoglasie* 'chanting in a single voice.' The Russian Orthodox service was lengthy, in some instances lasting six hours or more. This was a grueling experience for those whose zeal and piety were insufficient to sustain them so long in a standing position (there were no pews). Consequently, the Church had shortened the service by permitting *mnogoglasie* 'chanting in many voices'; that is, various portions of the liturgy, sometimes as many as six or even more, were performed simultaneously. The ensuing cacophony provided a suitable backdrop for the shuffling congregation's conversations, wisecracks, arguments, and jokes. In 1636 a group of militant priests from Nižnij Novgorod led by Neronov submitted a document to Patriarch Ioasaf in which they decried *mnogoglasie* and the spiritual lethargy of most clergy. Existing conditions could only perpetuate the religious ignorance and indifference of the people. The priests described the atmosphere of levity characteristic of worship services and the cursing, drunkenness, and depravity often encountered in Russian villages, the male inhabitants of which often celebrated religious holidays by organizing mass fist-fights in which "many die without repenting."

8

Fistfighters Ermoška (left) and Paramoška the sexton (right), whose vocation was often associated by Russians with the ability to brawl.

Patriarch Ioasaf was not unsympathetic to this appeal, and he soon issued an instruction which directed the clergy to chant in two, or not more than three, voices. This was not the end of the matter, however, for the militants from Nižnij Novgorod had reopened a troublesome question. Their desire to enforce *edinoglasie* reflected not so much a concern for liturgical style and coherence as it did their conception of the nature and purpose of divine worship. In Eastern Orthodox thought the liturgy was understood as a majestic procession toward a genuine, mystical communion of the earthly and heavenly congregations. Just as men encountering a deep ravine will build a bridge over it, so they span the gulf between heaven and earth through the liturgy, completing that solemn task during the triumphal celebration of the Eucharist. In accord with this, the Kingdom of God was viewed metaphorically as an Eternal Eucharist, in which the Elect (the "Pure Bride") commune with the Heavenly Bridegroom by sharing the bread and wine at a joyful wedding feast. Divine worship thus granted erring men a real foretaste of Christ's Second Coming, provided they were in a properly elevated spiritual state. The practice of *mnogoglasie* was therefore self-defeating, as it could not generate the deep emotion and deepened understanding upon which this state depends. Rather than lifting men up to God so they might bear the life of the spirit into the world, the *mnogoglasie* was a worldly intrusion into the Church, reflecting an irreverent desire to get out fast. This principle of spiritual elevation, which shaped the Zealots' defense of *edinoglasie*, was the bedrock of their entire program of reform: all Russians were in duty bound to strive upward toward heaven if the Third Rome was to prepare the way for the approaching Kingdom of God.

Between 1636 and 1647, when Neronov was transfered to Moscow, scattered parishes in the Russian Church voluntarily adopted the practice of *edinoglasie*. By 1649 the number of such successes convinced Vonifat'ev and his friends that the time had come to place this issue before a Council of the Church. The Council, which convened for a single day only (11 Feb. 1649), refused to make *edinoglasie* binding upon every parish, a decision which caused Vonifat'ev to denounce the prelates, including the Patriarch, as "wolves" and "wreckers" of God's Church in Russia. The Tsar ignored the Council's demand that Vonifat'ev be brought to trial, instead pressuring Patriarch Iosif to seek an external liturgical opinion from Parthenios, Patriarch of Constantinople. On 16 February 1650 Parthenios categorically affirmed *edinoglasie*; his position was endorsed a year later by another Russian Council. This victory for the Lovers of God obviously signaled God's approval of their reform efforts. They, and not the hierarchy, were now the preeminent force in the Church, thanks to the Tsar's support. Aleksej Mixajlovič's piety and apparent devotion to their vision of Russia's future became increasingly important as the youthful Sovereign grew in experience and in his ability to enforce his views. During the first seven years of his reign (1645–52), clergy associated with the Lovers of God had gradually begun to occupy a number of important ecclesiastical posts, both in monasteries and in the administrative hierarchy of the national Church. Now a great victory had been won; God's plan was visibly being realized in Russia.

Unfortunately for the reformers, the force that raised them up soon brought them low. The Tsar was deeply impressed by Nikon, who came to Moscow in the same year as Neronov; at that time he was Father Superior of the Koževerskij Monastery in the Far North, but he soon was appointed Archimandrite of the famous Novo-Spasskij Monastery. Owing to his sharp intelligence, strength of will, piety, energy, eloquence, and imposing physical presence, he swiftly became a member of the Tsar's inner circle of religious advisors. In 1649 he became Metropolitan of Novgorod, the highest ecclesiastical rank held by any of the reformers and a measure of the Tsar's esteem. Administrative experience at high levels made the Tsar's favorites, Nikon and Vonifat'ev, the likely candidates to accede to the patriarchal throne, which was vacated suddenly in 1652 by the death of the aged and ineffectual Iosif. Although Vonifat'ev's case was pressed by many including Avvakum, who was living in Moscow at the time, Vonifat'ev humbly declared that he did not wish to be patriarch. In consequence, Nikon's astonishing rise to supreme power in the Church was virtually uncontested.

Nikon's hunger for that power was not immediately evident, as he initially continued the reform program of the Zealots. Indeed, he had enforced *edinoglasie* in his Novgorod eparchy even before the Council of 1651, and he too was convinced the

Church must labor unremittingly to rehabilitate its own spirit and to purify its people. So Nikon gave those people no relief from now familiar demands that they observe all fasts, come to worship services and confession, curtail their drunkenness, cease their gambling, and eliminate the pagan practices and beliefs which were still polluting their souls and distorting their lives.

The Lovers of God had never expected the devil to give up easily, knowing him to be stubborn and slow to yield past gains. In their program of reform, moral suasion was often succeeded by promulgated law; as Avvakum's *Life* shows, both admonitions and law enforcement were frequently answered violently by the laity, and often enough by the clergy as well. But violence is the devil's tool, and it only demonstrated the need for more reforms; Nikon continued to close taverns, to limit, and during fasts to prohibit, the sale of alcohol, to enforce discipline in the monasteries, and so on. Nowhere was his desire to protect his countrymen from the wages of sin more evident than in his efforts to isolate them from foreigners by forcing the latter into a special settlement outside Moscow (later called the "German Quarter" [*Nemeckaja sloboda*]), by forbidding them to hire Russian servants or to wear Russian clothes (facilitating visual identification), and by erasing their previous privileges in matters of trade. But if Nikon was infected by the xenophobia of the Lovers of God, he also practiced their virtues in committing the resources of the patriarchal treasury to charitable activities and to the renovation of churches and monasteries.

An important aspect of the reformers' work involved the details of the liturgy. During the 1640's, the Lovers of God had shown an interest in cleansing the liturgy of uncanonical accretions by returning to the oldest available Slavonic texts. At the same time they wished to correct Russian translations of the works of the ancient Holy Fathers, whose teachings had established the bases of Orthodox doctrine before the Greeks had fallen into "heresy." However, a lack of native scholars knowing Greek made it necessary to invite learned foreign ecclesiastics to Russia to assist in this work. Although the first Greeks to appear on the scene proved to be scholarly mountebanks and Ukrainian monks from Kiev ultimately provided the necessary specialized knowledge, a precedent for looking to the south for specific kinds of information existed prior to Nikon's accession to the patriarchal throne. The first and finally irreconcilable breach between Nikon and the other Lovers of God occurred when he altered fundamentally this limited, controlled relationship with the "heretical" Greek Church.

Quite simply, Nikon decided to accept as authoritative the contemporary Greek liturgy. If the Lovers of God were willing to recognize the gradual accretion over time of minor errors in Russian liturgical practices, they were completely unprepared to recognize the primacy of a tradition "sullied" by constant intercourse with Islam and undermined by its past compromises with Rome (especially the Florentine Union of 1439). After all, they were accustomed to thinking of Russian Orthodoxy as the Truth, as the word "Orthodoxy" itself is a compound (*Pravoslavie*), whose components suggest truth, exactitude, correctness (*prav-*) and praise (*slava*) — that is, the true way to praise God. In short, it was impossible for them to reconcile their vision of the Third Rome with Nikon's revolutionary initiatives.

The first specific hint of those initiatives was contained in a new edition of the Psalter (11 Feb. 1653), which omitted the old instructions regarding the conformation of the hand while making the Sign of the Cross (i.e., with two fingers) and the manner in which obeisances were to be performed during the Prayers of Efrem Sirin. Two weeks later a circular was issued by Nikon in which he proscribed the old practices here and prescribed the contemporary Greek model (in particular, crossing with three fingers; see also annotation 84). Nikon made this unprecedented decision regarding fundamental and very familiar ritualistic gestures on the eve of Lent, the most revered of the great fasts; almost unimaginably, he did so on his own authority, without consulting any officially constituted ecclesiastical body. As Avvakum remarks, "Hearts froze, and legs began to shake."

Nikon's abrupt departure from the path blazed by Neronov and Vonifat'ev can probably be explained by his intoxication with the dream of an Orthodox Empire centered in Moscow. Such an empire, founded upon common religion, would inevitably make Russia's patriarchate *primus inter pares*, and the patriarch himself potentially the most powerful man in Christendom. Thus, the theocratic impulse inherent in the Zealots' efforts to transform their land into a genuine Holy Russia acquired with Nikon a malignant mephitis. His astounding rise from obscurity to the patriarchal throne must have seemed an indisputable proof of the favor he had found in heaven. Feeling the hand of God on his shoulder, this fallible, foolish man began his pursuit of earthly power in the name of heavenly things. His ambitious quest inevitably brought Nikon into collision with his earnest, soon-to-be erstwhile friend Aleksej Mixajlovič, who shared his Pan-Orthodox ambitions.

These ambitions had been fanned, perhaps even kindled, by Greek prelates, who were coming to Russia not only as advisors but as mendicants and supplicants, having discovered in Russian wealth and military potential qualities meriting their serious attention. In their first rank was Paissios, Patriarch of Jerusalem and slyboots *extraordinaire*, who came to Russia in 1649 and seduced both Tsar and Patriarch with his schemes. That he and several colleagues of the cloth turned a neat profit in Moscow is certain; that they overestimated Russian potentials is equally certain and far more unfortunate. Dream as they might, Aleksej Mixajlovič and Nikon lacked the resources to lead the Orthodox world and free fellow believers from their heathen masters, the Turks in particular. Yet in pursuit of this new dream, they forced the "inviolable" Russian ecclesiastical traditions to conform to the Greek, creating thereby the cancer of schism. Their apparently honest belief that the discrepancies between the two traditions resulted from Russian, and not Greek, errors, was the product of ignorance. Neither they nor their Greek confreres knew Orthodox liturgical history: the old Russian liturgy was in fact closer to ancient practice than the modern Greek. But honest conviction could not excuse Nikon's unseemly, careless haste (he made *no use* of the many old Slavonic and Greek texts which were collected and brought to Moscow in these years). More important, neither Nikon nor the conservatives fully realized the secular implications of his reforms: in effect the Church abandoned the Third Rome (making it official during the Council of 1666–67) for the forbidden fruit of earthly power; that is, Russia's heavenly relations were abruptly supplanted by foreign relations.

Certainly a vision of empire would appeal to a tsar, who however pious was still responsible for Russia's security and prosperity. Aleksej Mixajlovič probably took seriously the notion

that the tsar reflected God the Father's active concern and love
for his children; like a priest, he was called "little father" by his
own Russian people. A desire to expand dramatically the arena
of their influence (and his) is the best explanation for his refusal
to abandon the Nikonian reforms, even as he gradually divested
himself of their author. Nikon's position was in fact almost
untenable. While pursuing an ecclesiastical policy congenial to the
secular interests of the throne, he understood that policy in terms
conditioned by the old millennial expectations of the Third Rome:
the Church, the foundation of future empire, is the Body of Christ
and God's instrument in the world; it can be inferior to no earthly
power, as God rules supreme in heaven and on earth. Such ideas,
reminiscent of Innocent III's defense of papal supremacy, were
foreign to the traditions of the Russian Church; Nikon's aggressive
assertion of them in word and arrogant deed gradually alienated
Aleksej Mixajlovič, whose jealousy of his own prerogatives grew
markedly during his personal leadership of military operations
against the Poles and Swedes (1654–57). The Tsar's burgeoning
animosity toward Nikon was rooted not only in his belief in the
divine origin of his own authority but in political realities: the unrest
generated by Nikon's opulent life-style and barbaric enforcement
of his reforms made him a serious liability, especially when
military triumphs in the West were succeeded by reversals during
the summer of 1658. A campaign of slights and increasingly
conspicuous insults was culminated by an extraordinary opportunity to return Nikon to obscurity. In July 1658, the isolated,
frustrated Patriarch abruptly abandoned his ecclesiastical responsibilities and retired to the Voznesenskij Monastery outside Moscow.
Perhaps he did so in imitation of Ivan the Terrible, who in the
sixteenth century had been triumphantly recalled from voluntary
retirement by his previously disgruntled subjects. If this was
Nikon's plan, it was a serious if not surprising miscalculation —
he was always a poor strategist, as his high-handedness had long
since shown. He was left to languish in his monastery for eight
years before being deposed by the Ecumenical Council of 1666–67
and sent into exile (see annotations 20, 221, and 228). Despite his
talents and love for the Church, Nikon culminated his career by
derailing the Russian reformation and placing himself in the ranks
of those vicars of Christ who have too frequently served him by

A church built by Nikon at the Voskresenskij Monastery in imitation
of the Temple in Jerusalem. It was called "New Jerusalem," a term
closely linked to the doctrine of the Third Rome and the millennial
Kingdom of Christ on earth.

nurturing the secular spirit. He had sought a vast extension of his personal power and the power of the Russian Church; he achieved the opposite.

Aleksej Mixajlovič's genial treatment of Avvakum upon his return from Siberian exile in 1664 (see p. 80) reflected not only personal esteem but a calculated effort to forestall new hostilities. The truculent Archpriest had reason to be amiable himself. During the confusing, uncertain patriarchal "interregnum," when recluse Nikon refused to resign his office and the Tsar was in effective control of the Church, a restoration seemed possible. But the amenities were all Aleksej Mixajlovič was willing to offer, as ecclesiastical reform and Orthodox empire were still indissolubly linked in his mind. It is probable in addition that his lengthy wartime exposure to a variety of Orthodox liturgical practices in Poland, the Ukraine, and Lithuania caused him to view his conservative friends' insistence on the letter of the old ritual as a troublesome, frustrating fixation. Restoring to them their former influence would be unwise for another reason as well. Surely the Tsar now understood that Nikon's theocratic pretensions were in principle indistinguishable from the efforts of the Lovers of God to elevate ecclesiastics over traditionally powerful lay officials in Russian towns (cf. Avvakum's conflicts with local officials). And once bitten is twice shy. Finally, Aleksej Mixajlovič was himself changed. The austere and pious life at court during the *incunabula* of his reign had become rather more jaunty. Official receptions were no longer solemn and prayerful but frolicsome and drunken, and musical instruments, forbidden by the Church and once publicly destroyed by Aleksej Mixajlovič himself, were now used to enliven the proceedings. The Tsar had remodeled his living quarters along Western lines, he invited Western specialists to Russia, and he chose Simeon Polockij, a polonized White Russian monk, as his children's tutor. Clever Polockij, one of the founders of Russian poetry, had considerable influence on the Tsar and was himself a walking emblem of Aleksej Mixajlovič's taste for things Western. Above all, Polockij shared with the wily Greek ecclesiastics in Moscow a respect for the primacy of kingly power. Men of such subtlety and apparent acumen must have been convincing advisors, especially as the Tsar compared them with his old Zealot mentors, so out of touch with realities.

But it was he and his advisors who were out of touch with certain realities. Without doubt the Tsar's efforts to placate Avvakum were doomed to failure. Nikon's swift resort to force a decade earlier showed greater understanding; his employment of the instruments of violent repression to destroy the Zealots' collective leadership demonstrated his accurate assessment of their stubborn commitment. Nikon's methods became *de rigueur* in dealing with dissidents, and moderate Aleksej Mixajlovič ultimately felt compelled to follow the same path. He did so with the able assistance of the hierarchs and their lay administrators, who were quick to belabor the upstart archpriests who had wrenched control of the Church from their hands. It is possible the Tsar remembered in this the example of valiant old Neronov, who had escaped from exile to lead from underground the early opposition to Nikon; but even he had finally been cowed, if not broken, by fear of schism and the continuing violence against his friends and followers.

If Nikon displayed a certain proto-Stalinist realism in consolidating his personal power, he like the Tsar was apparently oblivious to certain conditions in Russia which boded ill for his particular brand of reform. It is indeed astonishing that Nikon failed to take into account the mind and mood of the Russian masses from which he himself had emerged. Millions of unlettered Russians, distrustful of an outside world they did not know, could only be suspicious and fearful of apparently arbitrary ritualistic and liturgical changes, which were soon known to be of foreign origin. Their elementary faith made no distinction between doctrine and ritual. Ritual was sacrosanct, the means established by God for communion with him. This being his unquestionable will, any effort to tamper with the ritual must have been conceived in the depths of hell, as Satan alone eternally strives to sever the bond between man and God. In this understanding of simple "reforms" as subversion of the faith, we recognize patterns of thought conditioned by the old pagan beliefs; charms, spells, and conjurations had always been energized by, and only by, specific rituals properly executed. For most Russians, religion was simply magic.

The Tsar and his advisors neglected one other factor, the mood of eschatological foreboding which waxed and waned in Russia during the middle decades of the seventeenth century. The Lovers of God had anticipated the end of the world, but they had been captivated by a vision of Christ's glorious Second Coming, not by fear of the mighty Antichrist, whose advent would signal the final apostasy and whose reign was to precede the Millennium. Others were not so sanguine. The signs of approaching catastrophe were there for him with eyes to see: simmering social unrest which often boiled over in peasant uprisings, the loss of half Moscow's population to the plague in 1654, in the same year a dread-inspiring solar eclipse, and in 1655–56 the prolonged appearance of a comet in the heavens. An expanding literature of eschatological augury and, presumably, a great deal of panicky talk focused attention on the year 1666, which was to begin the terrible end of history (666 is the number of the Beast of the Apocalypse in the Revelation of St. John). Nikon's reforms fell like a match into this tinder; the interdict laid upon the old ritual by the Ecumenical Council of 1666–67 together with the excommunication and imprisonment of Avvakum and other Old Believer leaders seemed to confirm the prophets of doom, furnishing dire proof that the forces of darkness had taken possession of the earth. Justified at last was the long-festering suspicion that the devil had found trustworthy emissaries in Nikon, the Tsar, and their Greek mentors and aides, especially the clerical adventurer and declared heretic Arsenios (see annotation 293). Now inevitably there would be an escalation in the flight of pious pessimists into the trackless forests of the Upper Volga area, away from the corruptions of this doomed and demon-ridden world.

Pursuit of the ancient eremitic ideal is primarily associated during the second and third quarters of the seventeenth century with the so-called Forest Elders, who constituted a movement second in importance only to the labors of the Lovers of God. In their rejection of the world and the flesh, the Forest Elders moved toward a dualistic vision which has frequently surfaced during the history of Christianity, not always with happy results. They were thus at odds with the Lovers of God, who were radical optimists regarding the capacity of Russians to purify their individual and collective spiritual life. But they were also at odds with the dominant traditions of Russian eremitism in their despairing renunciation of sinful mankind, their rejection of human society as irredeemably evil, and their belief that the Church itself was populated exclusively by the devil's minions. The Elders' program

ИВИДѢ ЗВѢРА ИСХОДАЩА ИМОРА, ИМУШАГЛАВЪ · З · ИРОГѠ · І · ИНАРОГА ЕГОВѢ
ИЕЦѢ · Ї · АНАГЛАЗАЕГОИМА ХУЛЫИ ЗВѢРЬ ЕГОВИДѢ БѢПОДОБЕ РЫСИ · ИНОЗѢ ЕМУ
ѤКО МЕѣ ѣ ДИУСТАЕГѠ ѤКѠ УСТАЛБОВА И ДАДЕ ЕМУ ЗМІИ СИЛУ СВОЮ · ИПРЕСТО. ГѢ
ѣВСѢ ИВЛАВВИѤ СМѢДИѤ ЕДИНУ ѠГЛАѤГОѤКО ЗАКОЛЕНУ ВСМРТ ИАЗВА СМЕРТИ
ЕГОИСЦѢЛѢИ И УДНЕАВГА ЗЕМЛА ВСЛѢД ЗВѢРА · ИПОКЛОНИША ЗМІЮ · ИЖЕ ДАЛ
ЕСТЬ ВЛАЗВѢР И ИПОКЛОНИША ЗВѢРЮ ГЛЮЩЕ ХТО ПОДОБЕ ЗВѢРЮ ИХ ТО МОЖЕРАТОВАТИ
ІНИМЪ ГЛАВА · ГІ ·

The two great beasts in Rev., ch. 13. (From the Apocalypse, engraved
on wood by Koren', from sketches by the monk Grigorij, 1696.)

of extreme asceticism and perpetual prayer was epitomized in the life of their most famous leader Kapiton, who carried two great stones on his chest and back, slept suspended from a hook, and wore only a short smock, leaving his legs unprotected against the terrible cold of the Russian winter.

Certainly not every hermit embraced so fully this gloomy exaltation of the spirit, nor was there at all times a distinct boundary between the Elders and the Lovers of God. The Elder Epifanij, for example, was a monk in the famous Soloveckij Monastery before Nikon's reforms drove him into the forests and the ranks of these anchorites. When arrest and conviction followed upon his denunciations of the Tsar-reformer, he became Avvakum's confessor and closest ally during their imprisonment at Pustozersk. For a time, conservatives of every stripe tended to unite in spirit against the Hellenization of the Church. But after the Nikonians' triumph in 1666—67, the Elders and their ideological allies perceived ever more clearly the visage of the Antichrist in Moscow. Each passing year saw a sharper cleavage between the pessimists and the heirs to the Lovers of God, who still proclaimed the inevitable victory of Old Russian Orthodoxy. Inevitably this breach was to prove unbridgeable, quite simply because the two conservative camps could not agree whether this world was in the hands of God or Satan.

Their differences became increasingly bitter as the fierce spokesmen for despair began to preach a diabolical doctrine of mass suicide, often in infernos of stacked logs or within burning wooden churches. As this malignancy spread implacably through the simple, superstitious peasantry, the northern forests were choked again and again with the sluggish black smoke of burning flesh. Thousands—men, women, children, entire families—cast themselves into the flames. They were moved in part, certainly, by the ancient belief that fire, like water, is an agent of purification (many drowned themselves as well). Just as the "refiner's fire" would incinerate the sinful, earthly body, so dying for the true faith meant forgiveness of all sins. And so these orgies of death were often preceded by orgies in fact, nightmarish, hysterical, despairing bacchanals which evoked visions of the hell and hellfire these tragically misguided creatures so longed to escape. To his discredit, Avvakum did nothing to halt these abominations,

Death on a pale horse, from Rev. 6:8 (engraved on wood, Kiev, 1626)

although he had sufficient authority in his last years to discourage them, as many of his own disciples strove to do. In his *Life* he speaks of his follower Avraamij, who was executed by fire and whose soul was yielded up "like sweet bread . . . to the Holy Trinity" (see annotations 252–53). We encounter here an image which was later freakishly deformed in his epistolary magnifications of mass suicide by fire. Thus did eschatological despair in these years often transform a love of life and the faith into a deranged love affair with death.

These hallucinatory episodes represented the extreme Old Believer response to a course of events which had culminated in the two Church Councils of 1666–67. The resolutions of the first, an all-Russian affair (April–June 1666), were generally moderate, as they stressed the legality of the Nikonian reforms and the need to preserve unity in the Church. This deliberate effort to avoid inflammatory repudiation of the Old Belief itself was forgotten during the Ecumenical Council, which met in December 1666 and continued into the late summer of 1667. Two Greek patriarchs, Paissios of Alexandria and Makarios of Antioch, along with thirteen other Greek prelates constituted almost one-half the Council's membership; for many Russians this in itself was enough to invalidate anything the Council might do. Despite their ignorance of Russian traditions, the Greeks viewed themselves as judges of Russia's past and arbiters of her future, and they managed to impose on the Council their venomous attitude toward the old ritual and the doctrine of the Third Rome. In spite of the risks, these fundamental elements in the Russian national identity and religion were placed under interdict. Russians committed to the Old Belief now confronted a terrible choice: to acquiesce and risk eternal damnation or to continue their commitment outside the Church which had been their lifetime spiritual home.

It soon became clear that the choice was not only a grave matter of conscience but perhaps of the grave itself. In 1668 the radically conservative monks of the Soloveckij Monastery rose in revolt agains the reforms and the throne, a rebellion they managed to sustain within the fortress walls of their refuge for eight years. Simultaneously Russia was threatened by Cossack uprisings in the south, her relations with Poland and Sweden remained dangerously uncertain, and resistance to the Nikonian reforms was everywhere evident. External threats and internal instability were an intolerable combination for Aleksej Mixajlovič, and during 1670–71 he launched an increasingly violent campaign of repression against the Old Believers; torture, mutilation, enforced starvation, beheading, burning, and hanging were used where arguments, threats, and ecclesiastical law had failed. It was during this period that the terrible drama of Boyarina Morozova's "passion" and death was enacted (see annotation 219). But Aleksej Mixajlovič failed to impose his will through terror, and his death on 29 January 1676, only one week after the fall of Solovki, was widely viewed as the punishment of God visited upon the devil's chief advocate. Morozova's agonies and scores of similar martyrdoms inspired not submission but stiffened resistance among those in possession of mounting evidence that Christ was not guiding the official Church.

The logical conclusion, that Christ was with those who opposed the reforms, stimulated the growth of schismatic churches. The first seeds of rebellion sown by Neronov at Solovki as early as 1655, during his escape from exile, were being harvested all over Russia by the 1680's. For those unenthusiastic about death either by their own hand or at the hand of the state, there remained the alternative of flight to the geographical periphery of Russia, where their religion could be practiced in relative safety. It must be said that some of these pilgrims still ended their lives on the pyre, especially in the North where the influence of wandering radicals, often ex-monks from fallen Solovki, was especially strong. But most joined the large number of pioneers who gradually spread throughout the Russian North and into Siberia, or made their way to the west along the Polish border, to the Lower Volga, and to the lands of the Cossacks in the south. As they did so the Old Belief began to fragment into a variety of sects. The particulars of their differences are beyond us here; suffice it to say that the fundamental division developed along the breach between the radical pessimists and the conservative optimists. The former concluded that Grace had disappeared from a world governed by the Antichrist. The consecration of priests and celebration of all the sacraments including marriage was thus impossible, as no thing, no person, and no state could be sanctified. Ritual had become powerless to this end, even when performed by a priest who had never wavered in his commitment to the Old Belief. The thrust of such ideas was to transform each man and woman into a celibate monk or nun striving for personal salvation in a world literally God-forsaken.

Opposed to the "Priestless" Old Belief (*Bespopovščina*) were those who believed the Church to be the eternal Body of Christ, against which the powers of hell shall never prevail. Initially the "Priested" Old Believers (*Popovščina*) received the ministrations of priests consecrated prior to Nikon's reforms, but as years and death overtook them the inevitable problem arose. The need for priests was generally met by clerics consecrated after 1653 who, in solemn ceremony, renounced and forswore all allegiance to the Nikonian aberration. In this the Priested Old Believers depended in part upon the authoritative statements of Avvakum, who prior to his death had endorsed this practice. The problem of establishing a hierarchy remained, however, as the old Canons required a bishop or bishops to raise a cleric to the episcopate. For over 150 years these devout conservatives searched for a bishop committed in his heart to the Old Belief; final success led to the creation of a hierarchy still centered in Moscow.

The extreme eschatology which caused the Priestless Old Believers to reject the possiblity of a priesthood or hierarchy led quite naturally to a radical egalitarianism; all members of the flock are equal, and without a shepherd each must decide for himself or all must decide for all, in concert. The likely communal result obtained in most cases: the disintegration of the movement into small, tightly-knit, homogeneous communities, some ruled by forceful patriarchs who aimed to preserve their people from all external contagion. Large numbers of Old Believers continue to exist inside the Soviet Union and some outside it, but the histories of the remote communities are not known, at least in the West. In 1971 the Russian Orthodox Church rescinded the anathemas and interdicts of the seventeenth century and recognized the full validity of the old rites.

During the three decades between Nikon's elevation to the patriarchate (July 1652) and the execution by fire of the prisoners of Pustozersk, including Avvakum (April 1682), the Archpriest's influence and fame grew steadily among those committed to the old rituals. He was thirty-one in 1652, simply one among several outstanding clerics from the younger generation who had impressed Neronov and Vonifat'ev by their piety, force of personality, and devotion to spiritual renewal. Thirty years later he was considered a saint by many; he had become the authoritative doctrinal arbiter among the dissenters and an inspiring example of unflinching defiance no matter the risk or cost.

In reading Avvakum's *Life* we are struck by the astonishing record of his tumultuous existence prior to his final imprisonment. Yet many of his contemporaries could have matched him tale for dramatic tale, had they his narrative gifts. Avvakum's sufferings had little in fact to do with his special destiny. When he returned from his Siberian exile in 1664, the older leaders of the Lovers of God were scattered, discouraged, or dead. Conservatives were understandably attracted by this charismatic and already well-known spokesman for their convictions, especially as his visibility increased in proportion to his growing antipathy for the reformers and their conciliatory blandishments. When Avvakum did not bend under his second exile nor break under the excommunication and anathema heaped upon him by the Ecumenical Council of 1666–67, he was thrust into a position of lasting preeminence. His entire life seems to have been a preparation for this culminating confrontation with the devil's deputies and for his subsequent imprisonment in the arctic village of Pustozersk; it was there in bestial incarceration that he produced the writings which consolidated his place among the schismatics, in the annals of Russian history, and in the cultural consciousness of every literate Russian.

Aleksej Mixajlovič's determination to preserve the reforms obviously overrode his personal regard for Avvakum. But then, he was confronting a difficult situation by 1664: in Moscow, along the Middle and Upper Volga, in the north around Lake Onega and along the shores of the White Sea, in Siberia and in the Don Region to the south centers of religious opposition were growing, living in the hope that the Tsar famed for his piety would come to his senses and return to the rituals of the past. The murky and unprecedented problem of Nikon, retired but still Patriarch, required resolution, while the false hopes of the conservatives had to be quashed. By clarifying the situation in the Church, Aleksej Mixajlovič aimed to bring internal order back to his land;

the Councils of 1666—67 were his instrument.

Those Old Believers who imagined the Councils would realize their dream of restoration should have been disabused by the wave of repression and violence initiated by the Tsar in 1664—65. Intractable Avvakum was arrested and exiled to Mezen (see annotation 227), while military expeditions were sent eastward and northward to "comb" the Forest Elders out of their woodland retreats; many of them were murdered. A quixotic attempt by Nikon to return to his throne led to his "house arrest," which he endured until summoned before the Ecumenical Council more than two years later. Conservative leaders were rounded up for trial or harrassed by constant surveillance. During these months the Tsar's preparations for the Councils were meticulous, and there is little doubt the Russian participants knew in broad terms where their "duty" lay, whatever their private misgivings. As for the Greeks, Aleksej Mixajlovič knew their interests generally coincided with his own.

Meanwhile, efforts to persuade the "mutineers" to recant gradually bore fruit; of the three recalcitrants who stood firm and were finally unfrocked by the Russian Council, two soon relented. Avvakum alone was beyond all persuasion. The Deacon Fëdor soon repented his decision, however, and was rearrested for resuming his denunciatory preaching (see annotation 232). He and Avvakum were excommunicated by the Ecumenical Council in June 1667, together with the newly arrested Epifanij and Nikifor, and the priest Lazar, who had been convicted in 1666 *in absentia* (see annotation 270). The elderly Nikifor died soon thereafter, and the remaining four became the famous prisoners of Pustozersk.

Aleksej Mixajlovič certainly recognized that the incarceration of these men represented a signal failure, and he continued his efforts to cajole them back into the Church. They were now symbols of defiance as well as potential martyrs, and this did not bode well for the future. During the next three years the very limited success of the Councils became obvious. As religious animosities continued to grow and to merge with social discontents, Aleksej Mixajlovič turned once again to the violent methods which now became a permanent part of his internal policy. The major Cossack uprising of Sten'ka Razin (1670—71) drew numerous Old Believers into the fray, insurgent Solovki was supplied and

supported by the northern peasantry, and Old Believer communities had established a "resistance" complete with a communication network centered in Pustozersk.

During their fourteen years of imprisonment at remote Pustozersk, the Old Believer leaders produced an enormous outpouring
of tracts, letters, petitions, and declarations which were recopied
and carried throughout Russia by their followers. Pustozersk was
in fact less isolated than it would seem, as it was frequently
visited by merchants, military personnel, exiles, and others traveling
in the north. These wayfarers brought news and sometimes supple-
mented the labors of Old Believer pilgrims and messengers by
delivering new manuscripts to the faithful. If the Cossack guards
were sympathetic, they too occasionally assisted in these and
other matters. If not, it was still possible to smuggle materials out
in wooden crosses made by Epifanij, a craft he continued to ply
despite his loss to the axe of the four fingers on his right hand.

Initially most of the manuscripts were taken to Mezen, a settlement on the Mezen river where a group of Old Believers had gathered
around Avvakum's exiled wife and children. There these materials
were recopied for dispatch elsewhere. The Mezen community was
in constant contact with Old Believers in Moscow, whose activities
were based in Boyarina Morozova's home until her arrest in late
1671. Morozova's household now differed radically from those
typical of the elite, as she had converted it into a kind of private
convent, and she herself secretly took the veil. Her close collabor-
ator and Moscow's principal Old Believer ideologue and agitator
was the monk Avraamij, who was the first major figure to be
arrested (Feb. 1670) during the purge of 1670–71 (see annotation
252). The Tsar hesitated at this point to touch Morozova, despite
her obvious determination to continue her opposition. Instead
he sent a force commanded by Ivan Elagin to Mezen to destroy
this vital communications link. Avvakum tells us that Elagin
"buried" (i.e., imprisoned) his loyal wife Anastasija Markovna and
his oldest sons in a covered pit, while one of his beloved disciples,
the fool in Christ Fëdor, was hanged (see annotation 222).

Elagin moved on to Pustozersk, where in April 1670 he
subjected three of the four unyielding prisoners to public punishment for the second time. Their tongues, or rather the stumps
remaining after their mutilation in Moscow, were cut out, and

portions of their right hands were chopped off. Only Avvakum escaped this barbaric penalty as he had in Moscow, perhaps because Aleksej Mixajlovič never forgot their past association, perhaps because the Archpriest aroused in him his recurring superstitious fears. After completing his assignment in Pustozersk, Elagin again passed through Mezen during his return to Moscow and hanged Luka, another of Avvakum's followers and a friend of his children.

Prior to 1670 the prisoners had lodged with local inhabitants in Pustozersk and had moved about freely. But Elagin changed all that. Now they were imprisoned in individual log frames set in the earth and covered over, with only one small window for the passage of food, smoke, and excrement. (Later their solitary confinement was eased when the windows were enlarged and lenient guards allowed the prisoners to visit one another occasionally.) In these dark, abominable cages, often described as "graves" by their inhabitants, the writing went on year after year, as the insects and suffocating humidity of the brief summers were succeeded by the bitter winds of winter, which swept ceaselessly over the barren arctic landscape. But intimidation and brutal punishments were useless against these men, who knew with certainty that God was with them and approved their endurance.

The first major work to emerge from Pustozersk was a collective endeavor compiled and recorded by Deacon Fëdor. Called *The Answer of the Orthodox*, it was for a time the fundamental doctrinal guide for Old Believers; its intransigence almost certainly figured importantly in the new mutilations visited upon the prisoners in 1670. As time passed, Lazar ceased to write altogether, while Epifanij was always less prolific than either Avvakum or Fëdor. Conflict was probably bound to erupt between the latter two, considering Avvakum's pride and sense of personal mission and Fëdor's logical patterns of thought, so different from the Archpriest's. Disappointing as it is to read about the growing acrimony between these two stalwarts who shared to the end the same bitter fate, their differences vividly reflect the dilemma they faced: the eternally true faith they served had been declared heretical and they, heretics; deprived of a hierarchy, of churches, of all the institutional supports of the past, these archconservatives were compelled to become innovators in their instructions to their followers. Doctrinal disagreements were inevitable, especially

A monk's vision of the hellish punishments awaiting moneygrubbers
(*lixoimcy*); a tree rises from the bowels of Judas, that great lover of
silver, and on it hang in hellfire both men and women whose lives
were ruined by this sinful obsession.

when courageous self-assurance above all else made life bearable. Avvakum became particularly testy. But then, opposition for him was always traceable to the devil.

Struggle with the forces of evil was the single vital commitment which impelled the bellicose Archpriest to write his polemical, didactic autobiography. This must be emphasized despite numerous scholarly efforts to see in the *Life* a refraction of the seventeenth century's growing literary interest in this world and real people, or to connect it with quasi-autobiographical traditions in medieval Russian literature and among Old Believers. The written word was Avvakum's only potent weapon at Pustozersk, so his new devotion to the pen represented no qualitative change in the general direction of his life. He understood that this undertaking smacked of hubris, that it violated the obligatory medieval literary norm of humble self-deprecation. He justified himself through his confessor Epifanij's "charge" at the outset of the *Life* and by references to autobiographical fragments in the Christian literary heritage. But this was little more than eyewash. The peril of eternal damnation hung like a Damoclean sword over every true Christian, and this was reason enough. "Had things been different, there would be no need for me to talk about my life," he remarks in conclusion.

Whether Avvakum considered himself a saint, that is, whether he was the author of his own *vita* (i.e., the life of a saint), is an important question discussed elsewhere in this volume. Whatever his self-understanding, his repetitive revision of the *Life* suggests he considered it highly effective, both as a polemical weapon and as a guide to living. Yet the history of these revisions has remained problematical until the recent textological studies of N. S. Demkova. Her ordering of the existing redactions of the *Life* is accepted here as correct. Although Demkova describes the creative evolution of the work in six rather complex stages, we are concerned first of all with the relationships in time of the three principal redactions frequently discussed in the critical literature. The version translated in the present volume has always been considered the first. Set against the other two, it is longer than the so-called second redaction and shorter than the third. Strange as it may seem, scholars have accepted the notion that Avvakum first condensed his original text, producing an action-oriented, dynamic narration with very little digressive material, and then expanded it greatly, reintroducing and expanding his religious commentaries and producing a text aesthetically more finished. Demkova's careful study of the available manuscripts demonstrates what instinct divines, that the shorter "second redaction" in fact precedes the "first." The traditional ordering of the redactions A, Б, B (in the cyrillic alphabet) should be Б, A, B. Thus, Redaction A translated here represents a late stage in the development of the *Life* (the fifth of Demkova's six stages); it is also the most interesting, above all because the human is not yet submerged by the saintly, as is the case with the third redaction. In the present volume, the redactions are referred to simply as the first, second, and third, always on the basis of Demkova's reordering.

Demkova dates the development of Avvakum's *Life* as follows: Between 1669 and the beginning of 1672 Avvakum wrote the earliest version, preserved only in the faulty Prjanišnikovskij Copy (available in N. K. Gudzij's edition of the *Life*). Redaction 1 was written during the first half of 1672, Redaction 2 in the middle 1673, and Redaction 3 near the beginning of 1675. It is a paleo-graphical miracle that the holographs of the latter two have been discovered and are preserved in archives in the Soviet Union.

These holographs do not exist in isolation; they are parts of larger volumes commonly called Pustozersk Compilations (Pusto-zerskie sborniki), which contain the autobiographies of both Avvakum and Epifanij along with tracts, petitions, and other materials. Redaction 2 is found in the *Družinin Compilation* (*Družininskij sbornik*), while Redaction 3 is contained in the *Zavoloko Compilation* (*Sbornik Zavoloko*); Družinin was the first to describe in print (1914) that particular collection, while Zavoloko owned the other volume and donated it in 1966 to the Soviet Academy of Sciences. These compilations were colla-borative efforts by Avvakum and Epifanij, who were in frequent consultation on matters both literary and doctrinal. Certainly the two men intended their autobiographies to be read together, an expectation soon frustrated by Old Believers themselves, who cherished the Archpriest's work and made copies of it alone for distribution. Despite the inherent interest of Epifanij's *Life*, this separation was inevitable, and only Robinson's book honors the authors' original intent by printing both works.

Avvakum indeed stands apart from other writers of his era

by virtue of his special genius for narration in the vernacular. Those reading him in the original are not surprised that numerous Russian writers have found in his work a valuable stylistic model (among them Tolstoy, Turgenev, Dostoevsky, Gorky, Goncharov, and Garshin). In historical perspective, Avvakum's revolutionary use of the vernacular to traditional literary ends (didactic and polemical) is symptomatic of the disintegration of the norms which had long shaped Russian literature. One can hardly suppose that the conservative Archpriest wished to dismantle the literary edifice of the past; he was simply moved by a pragmatic desire to communicate effectively. But the urgency of this desire moved him away from the lofty, abstract, involute, and archaic language and style of the Church, scarcely understood by his audience but traditional in the *vita*. A new style and manner both fractured and, in a sense, resusitated an ancient, honored, but moribund genre.

In time Avvakum came to view the vernacular as a special literary style; one of its important products was clearly the accentuation of the authorial voice. This too was a significant break with the past. The rigid norms of the Church language had long had a leveling effect on individual style, reflecting the value placed on Truth expressed rather than on authorial individuality and originality (texts were unstable in that they were frequently rewritten and "improved" over time by several anonymous authors). Avvakum's uniquely expressive style was thus a harbinger of the authorial individuality (and stable texts) characteristic of the modern period. Similarly, his self-depiction bears within it the seeds of a much later commitment to verisimilitude in characterization, in contrast to the abstract, repetitious character types normal to medieval Russian literature.

Analogous if less striking manifestations of these tendencies can be found in the works of other writers from this period. But it would be incorrect to suggest that Avvakum participated directly in the literary changes associated with the processes of secularization during Russia's seventeenth century. He looked backward, not forward; he desired the "churchification" of Russia, not her secularization; he established no lasting school, and his *Life* was long the secret property of fugitive religious dissenters, not of the entire literate population. Yet the secular historical forces evident in the schism were certainly instrumental in pressing Avvakum toward his personal literary revolution, and in this sense his work is a direct reflection of his era. Indeed, the baffling mix of the old and the new in Avvakum's work makes of him an archetypal representative of a complex and contradictory period in Russian history.

According to Old Believer historians, the four prisoners of Pustozersk were brought from their sunken cages of rotting logs to a place of execution on 1 April 1682. The Church Council of 1681–82 had decided to intensify the battle with the schismatics, and the unabating dissemination of inflammatory materials from Pustozersk, especially by Avvakum, was finally deemed intolerable. Besides, the insufferable Archpriest had made no secret of his belief that Aleksej Mixajlovič was now burning in hell. The prisoners' long-held hope of martyrdom and assured sainthood among the faithful was to be fulfilled at last. Legend has it that Avvakum gave away his possessions, including his precious old books, beforehand, and that someone provided clean smocks for the four bent, enfeebled old men, whose grey skin and mattery, half-blind eyes bore witness to years spent in smoky darkness. They were bound and placed in the four corners of a pit filled with logs and birch bark. On this occasion it is unlikely anyone asked them to recant.

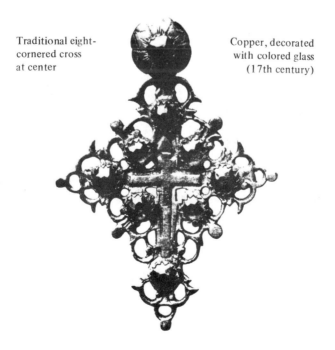

Traditional eight-cornered cross at center

Copper, decorated with colored glass (17th century)

Old-Believer icon of "St. Avvakum" (wood and tempera, c. 1693)

THE LIFE

OF THE ARCHPRIEST AVVAKUM

WRITTEN BY HIMSELF

✝

Though the cause of evil prosper,
Yet 'tis truth alone is strong;
Though her portion be the scaffold,
And upon the throne be wrong;
Yet that scaffold sways the future,
And behind the dim unknown,
Standeth God within the shadow,
Keeping watch above his own.

James Russell Lowell

The Archpriest*   1
Avvakum hath been charged
to write his *Life* by the monk Epifanij
(as this monk is his confessor), so that the   2
works of God shall not pass into oblivion;
and to this end hath he been charged by
his confessor, to the glory of
Christ our God.
Amen.

All-holy Trinity, O God and Creator of all the world! Speed
and direct my heart to begin with wisdom and to end with the good
works about which I, an unworthy man, now desire to speak.
Understanding my ignorance and bowing down I pray to thee; and
as I beseech thee for aid, govern my mind and strengthen my
heart to prepare for the fashioning of good works, so that illumined
by good works I may have a place at thy right hand with all thine
Elect on Judgment Day. And now, O Master, bless me so that
sighing from my heart I might proclaim Dionysios the Areopagite   3
on the divine names which are the eternally connatural and true
names for God, those which are proximate and those which are   4
consequent, that is to say, laudatory. These are the connatural: He
is that is, Light, Truth, Life. Only four are of the essential, but of
the consequent there are many. These are: Lord, the Almighty,
the Unfathomable, the Unapproachable, the Thrice-radiant, the
Trisubstantial, the King of Glory, the Omnipresent, Fire, Spirit,   5
and God; understand others after this manner.

From this same Dionysios on Truth: For the falling away of
Truth is repudiation of self, for Truth is connatural; for if Truth
is connatural, the falling away of Truth is repudiation of the
connatural. But God cannot fall away from the connatural, and
that which cannot be, is not.   6

And we say this: the novelty lovers have lost the substance of
God by falling away from the true Lord, the holy and life-giving
Spirit. According to Dionysios, as soon as they fall away from the
Truth, they at once repudiate the connatural. But God cannot fall
away from his own substance, and that which cannot be is not in
him: omnipresent and everlasting is our true God. It would be

*Numbers in margins refer to the annotations, beginning on page 207.

better for them in the Creed not to say "Lord," a consequent name, than to cut out "the true," for in it is contained the substance of God. But we, the true believers, confess both names; we believe "in the Holy Spirit, the true Lord and our life-giving Light," who   7 is worshiped together with the Father and the Son, for whom we suffer and die with his lordly help. Dionysios the Areopagite comforts us, for he writes thus in his book: Therefore, such a man is in truth a true Christian, inasmuch as having through Truth understood Christ and by this gained knowledge of God, denying himself, he succumbeth not to their seductions and worldly ways and knoweth himself to be sober and liberated from all seductive unbelief; not only doth he live in tribulations even unto death for the sake of the Truth, but passing away in ignorance [of the world], he liveth forever in wisdom. In this are Christians witnessed.   8

This Dionysios was instructed in the Christian faith by the Apostle Paul; earlier, living in Athens, before coming to the Christian faith, he possessed the art of reckoning the movement of heavenly bodies; but when he believed in Christ, he counted all this as dung. He writes in his book to Timothy, speaking thus: 9, 10 "My child, dost thou not understand that all this outward whoredom is nothing, only temptation, and corruption, and perdition.   11 Through these things have I passed, and I found nothing, only vanity." Let him who reads understand. The perishing love to reckon the movements of heavenly bodies, as "they received not the love of the Truth, that they might be saved. And for this cause God shall send them strong delusion, that they should believe a lie; and judgment shall come to those who believed not the Truth, but had pleasure in unrighteousness." (Read the Apostle, 275.)   12

Before he had come to the Christian faith, this Dionysios was in the City of the Sun [Heliopolis] with his disciple during the   13 Crucifixion of the Lord. And he saw how the sun "turned into darkness and the moon into blood"; at midday the stars in the   14 heavens appeared, shining darkly. And he said unto his disciple, "Either the end of the age hath come, or the Word is suffering in the flesh." For he saw creation changed contrary to its wont, and because of this he was in confusion.   15

This same Dionysios writes about the signs of the sun when it is darkened. There are in the heavens five wandering stars which are called moons. These moons God placed not within boundaries as other stars, for they move over all the heavens, making signs either of wrath or of favor, moving according to their wont. When a wandering star, that is, a moon, moves to the sun from the west and covers the sun's light, then the darkening of the sun shows God's wrath against men. But when it happens that the moon approaches from the east, then moving according to its wont it covers the sun.   16

And in our Russia there was a sign: the sun was darkened in 7162 [1654], a month or so before the plague. Simeon, the Archbishop of Siberia, was sailing along the river Volga about two   17 weeks before St. Peter's Day, and at midday there was darkness.   18 For about three hours they waited by the shore weeping. The sun grew dim, and from the west a moon approached. According to Dionysios, God was revealing his wrath against men: at that time   19 Nikon the Apostate was defiling the faith and the laws of the   20 Church, and for this God poured forth the vials of his wrathful fury upon the Russian land; a mighty plague it was, there's been no time to forget, we all remember. Afterwards, about fourteen   21 years having passed, there was a second darkening of the sun. During the Fast of St. Peter, on Friday during the sixth hour, there was darkness. The sun grew dim and a moon approached from the west, revealing the wrath of God. And at that time in a cathedral   22 church the bishops were shearing the Archpriest Avvakum, that   23 poor, miserable soul, along with some others, and after damning them they cast them into a dungeon at Ugreša. The true believer   24 will understand what is happening in our land because of the turmoil in the Church. Enough talk of it. On Judgment Day it will be understood by everyone. Let us endure to that time.

This same Dionysios writes about a sign from the sun that happened in Israel, in the time of Joshua, son of Nun. When Joshua was slaying the enemy and the sun was over Gibeon, that is, at midday, Joshua stood in cruciform, that is, he stretched out his arms, and the sun's movement was stayed until he destroyed the enemy. The sun receded unto the east, that is, it went backwards, and again moved on. And there were in that day and night thirty-four hours, as it went backwards in the tenth hour. So ten hours were added to the day. And in the time of King Hezekiah there was a sign: the sun went backwards in the twelfth hour of the day, and in the day and night were thirty-six hours. Read Dionysios' book; there will you learn of it at length.   25

That same Dionysios also writes about the Heavenly Powers,   26

and describes in discoursing how they bear praise unto God, their
nine orders dividing into three trinities. The Thrones, Seraphim,
and Cherubim receive sanctification from God and cry out after
this manner: "Blessed be the glory from the place of the Lord!"   27
And through them sanctification passes to the second trinity,
which is of the Principalities, Virtues, and Dominions. This trinity,
glorifying God, cries out: "Alleluia, Alleluia, Alleluia!" According
to the *Alphabet*, "All" is for the Father, "el" is for the Son, and
"uia" is for the Holy Spirit. Gregory of Nyssa interprets Alleluia as   28, 29
praise to God, but Basil the Great writes, " 'Alleluia' is the speech   30
of angels, and spoken as men do it means 'Glory be to thee, O
God!' " Before St. Basil the words of the angels were chanted in   31
church: Alleluia, Alleluia, Alleluia! But when Basil was alive he
decreed chanting twice in the words of angels and once in those of
men, in this manner: Alleluia, Alleluia, glory be to thee, O God!
It was agreed by the saints, by Dionysios and by Basil: in threefold
laudation we glorify God with the angels, but not in fourfold,
like the whore of Rome; repulsive to God is a fourfold laudation
of this sort, "Alleluia, Alleluia, Alleluia, glory be to thee, O God!"
Let him who chants in this way be damned.

Let's get back to the subject again. Receiving sanctification
through the middle trinity, the third trinity – the Powers, Archangels, and Angels -- chants, "Holy, holy, holy is the Lord God of
Sabaoth, Heaven and earth are full of his glory!" See – this lauda-   32
tion is threefold too. The most immaculate Mother of God inter-
preted the Alleluia at length when she appeared to a disciple of
Efrosin of Pskov named Vasilij. Great is the praise to God in the   33
Alleluia, but great too is the vexation caused by the sophists; in
the Papist way their speech turns the Holy Trinity into a tetrad,
and they show the Holy Spirit issuing forth from the Son as well.   34
Wicked and damned by God and the saints is this sophistry! O God,
deliver thou true believers from this wicked endeavor, in the name
of Jesus Christ our Lord. Glory be to him now and forever and to
all eternity. Amen.

Athanasius the Great hath said: "Before everything it is incum-   35
bent on him who would be saved to cleave to the catholic faith;
but if a man keepeth not this faith whole and pure, without confusion, he will perish forever. For this is the catholic faith, that we
revere one God in Trinity and the Trinity in unity, neither conjoining the persons nor dividing the substance. For one person is

St. Basil the Great, from *Conversations of John Chrysostum*,
published in Moscow, 1664

of the Father, another of the Son, another of the Holy Spirit, but that of the Father, and of the Son, and of the Holy Spirit are one Godhead; equal is the glory, coeternal and universal is the majesty. As is the Father, so is the Son, so too is the Holy Spirit; eternal is the Father, eternal is the Son, eternal too is the Holy Spirit; uncreated is the Father, uncreated is the Son, uncreated too is the Holy Spirit. God is the Father, God is the Son, God is also the Holy Spirit: not three gods but one God, not three uncreated beings but one uncreated Being, one eternal Being. Similarly, almighty is the Father, almighty is the Son, almighty too is the Holy Spirit. Equally, unfathomable is the Father, unfathomable is the Son, unfathomable too is the Holy Spirit. However, they are not three almighty beings, but one almighty Being, not three unfathomable beings, but one unfathomable Being, one universal Being. And nothing in the Holy Trinity is first or last, nothing is greater or lesser; the three persons are whole, coeternal and universal, and equal to one another." As the nonbirth of the Father is parti- 36
cular, so too are the birth of the Son and the issuing forth of the Holy Spirit; to all in common are deity and dominion.

(Here it is also necessary to speak about the Incarnation of the Word for your salvation.) In the abundance of his grace, when the time was come, the Son, the Word of God, came forth from the bosom of the Father into a pure maid, the Virgin Mother of God, and was incarnate by the Holy Spirit of the Virgin Mary, and having become man he suffered for our sake, and rose on the third day, and ascended into heaven, and sat at the right hand of Majesty on high; and he will come again to judge, repaying each according to his works, and to his kingdom there is no end. And foreknowledge of 37
this was in God earlier, before Adam was created, before he was given form. (*The Father's Council*) The Father said unto the Son: 38
"Let us make man in our image and in our likeness." And the other answered, "Let us create, O Father, and lo, he will transgress." And again he said unto him: "O my Only-begotten! O my Light! O Son and Word! O Radiance of my Glory! If thou dost trouble thyself over thy creation, thou shalt be in duty bound to array thyself in the perishable flesh of man, in duty bound to walk the earth, to gather disciples, to suffer, and to accomplish all things." And the other answered, "Father, thy will be done!" And after this was Adam created. If you desire to learn of this at length, read *Marguerite*, "Sermon on the Incarnation"; there you will find it. But I have 39

mentioned it briefly in showing God's foreknowledge. Thus, every man who doth believe in this shall not be ashamed, but he who doth not believe shall be condemned and shall perish forever, according to the above-mentioned Athanasius. Thus do I, the Archpriest Avvakum, believe, thus do I confess, and with this do I live and die.   40

I was born in the Nižnij Novgorod area, beyond the Kudma River, in the village of Grigorovo. My father was the priest Pëtr, my mother Marija, as a nun Marfa. My father was given to hard drink, but my mother fasted and prayed zealously and was ever teaching me the fear of God. Once I saw a dead cow at a neighbor's, and that night I arose and wept much over my soul before the icon, being mindful of death and how I too must die. And from that time I grew accustomed to praying every night. Then my mother was widowed and I, still young, orphaned, and we were driven out, away from our kin. My mother deigned to have me married. And I prayed to the most holy Mother of God that she might give me for a wife a helpmate to salvation. And in the same village there was a girl, also an orphan, who was accustomed to going to church unceasingly; her name was Anastasija. Her father was a blacksmith by the name of Marko, very rich, but when he died everything dwindled away. And she lived in poverty and prayed to God that she might be joined with me in marital union; and so it was, by the will of God. Afterwards my mother went to God amidst great feats of piety. And being banished I moved to another place. I was ordained a deacon at the age of twenty-one, and after two years I was made a priest. I lived as a priest for eight years and was then raised to archpriest by Orthodox bishops. Since then twenty years have passed, and in all it is thirty years that I have been in holy orders.   41 42 43 44 45 46

And when I was a priest I had many spiritual children; up to now it would be about five or six hundred. Never slumbering I, a sinner, was diligent in churches and in homes, at crossroads, in towns and villages, even in the capital and in the lands of Siberia, preaching and teaching the Word of God, this for about twenty-five years.   47

When I was still a priest, there came to me to confess a young woman, burdened with many sins, guilty of fornication and self-abuse of every sort; and weeping she began to acquaint me with it all in detail, standing before the Gospel there in the church. But I, thrice-accursed healer, I was afflicted myself, burning inwardly with

Church, the village of Grigorovo

a lecherous fire, and it was bitter for me in that hour. I lit three candles and stuck them to the lectern, and raised my right hand into the flame and held it there until the evil conflagration within me was extinguished. After dismissing the young woman, laying away my vestments, and praying awhile, I went to my home deeply grieved. The hour was as midnight, and having come into my house I wept before the icon of the Lord so that my eyes swelled; and I prayed earnestly that God might separate me from my spiritual children, for the burden was heavy and hard to bear. And I fell to the ground on my face; I wept bitterly, and lying there sank into forgetfulness. Nothing could I ken, as I was weeping, but the eyes of my heart beheld the Volga. I saw two golden boats sailing gracefully, and their oars were of gold, and the masts of gold, and everything was of gold; each had one helmsman for the crew. And I asked, "Whose boats are these?" And they answered, "Luka's and Lavrentij's." They had been my spiritual children; they set me and my house on the path to salvation, and their passing was pleasing to God. And lo, I then saw a third boat, not adorned with gold but motley colored – red, and white, and blue, and black, and ashen; the mind of man could not take in all its beauty and excellence. A radiant youth sitting aft was steering. He raced toward me out of the Volga as if he wanted to swallow me whole. And I shouted, "Whose boat is this?" And he sitting in it answered, "Your boat. Sail in it with your wife and children if you're going to pester the Lord." And I was seized by trembling, and sitting down I pondered: "What is this vision? And what sort of voyage will it be?"

And lo, after a little while, as it is written, "The sorrows of death compassed me, and the afflictions of hell gat hold upon me; I found trouble and sorrow." An official carried off a widow's daughter, and I besought him that he should return the orphan to her mother. But scorning our entreaty he raised up a storm against me; coming in a multitude they trampled me to death near the church. And I lay dead for more than half an hour, and returned to life with a sign from God. And being terrified he yielded up the young woman to me. Afterwards he was instructed by the devil; he came into the church and beat me and dragged me by the legs along the ground, still in my vestments. But I was saying a prayer the while.

Later, another official at another time raged savagely against me. He rushed into my house, and having beaten me he gnawed the

48

49

50

51

52

53

fingers of my hand with his teeth like a dog. And when his throat filled with blood, he loosed my hand from his teeth, and leaving me he went home. But I, thanking God and having wrapped my hand with a kerchief, I went to Vespers. And when I was on the way he leaped out at me again with two pistols, and being close to me he fired one. By God's will the powder flared in the pan, but the pistol didn't shoot. He threw it on the ground and again he fired the other in the same way, but God's will brought this to pass in the same way — that pistol didn't shoot either. And walking 54
along I prayed earnestly to God, and with one hand I signed him with the Cross and bowed down before him. He was barking away at me, but I said unto him, "Let grace be upon thy lips, Ivan Rodion-ovič!" Afterwards he took away my home and kicked me out, robbing me of everything, and he gave me no bread for the road.

At that same time my son Prokopij was born, who is now locked up, buried with his mother in the earth. And I took up my staff, and his mother the unbaptized child, and we wandered whither God might direct, and we baptized him on the way, just as Phillip baptized the eunuch long ago. When I had trudged to Moscow, to 55
the Tsar's confessor, Archpriest Stefan, and to Neronov, Arch- 56
priest Ivan, they both announced me to the Tsar, and the Sovereign 57
came to know me at that time. The fathers sent me again to my 58
old place with a mandate, and I dragged myself back. And sure enough, the walls of my dwelling had been torn down. So I set to work there again, and again the devil raised up a storm against me. There came to my village dancing bears with tambourines and dom-ras, and I, sinner that I am, being zealous in Christ I drove them out; one against many I smashed their masks and tambourines in a field and took away two great bears. One of them I clubbed, and he came to life again; the other I set loose in the fields. 59

Because of all this Vasilij Petrovič Šeremetev, who was sailing 60
along the Volga to his governorship in Kazan, took me onto his boat, and blistering me plenty he commanded that his shaven-faced son Matvej be blessed. But I, seeing that lechery-loving countenance, I did not bless but rebuked him from Holy Writ. The Boyar, being mightily angered, ordered me thrown into the Volga; and afflicting me much they shoved me overboard. But later they were good to 61
me. We forgave one another in the antechambers of the Tsar, and his lady, the Boyarina Vasilevna, was the spiritual daughter of my

From Adam Olearius, *Vermehrte Moscowitische und Persianische Reisebeschreibung* (1656)
  Top: *Skomoroxi* entertainment with puppets and dancing bears
  Bottom: 17th-century Muscovite dress

younger brother. Thus doth God fashion his people!   62
    Let's get back to my story. Afterwards another official raged
savagely against me; coming to my home with others he attacked,
shooting with bows and pistols. But I locked myself in, and with a
great cry I prayed to God, "Lord, subdue and reconcile him by the
means that thou knowest!" And he ran away from my home, driven
off by the Holy Spirit. Later that same night they came running
from him and called to me with many tears: "Father! Master!
Evfimej Stefanovič is near death and his shouting is past bearing;
he beats himself and groans, and he says, 'Bring me Father Avvakum!
God is punishing me because of him.' " And I expected they were
tricking me, and my spirit was terrified within me. And lo, I besought God after this manner: "O Lord, thou who didst deliver
me from my mother's womb, who broughtest me from nothingness   63
to life! If they strangle me, number me with Filipp, the Metropolitan
of Moscow. If they stab me, number me with Zacharias the prophet.
And if they try to drown me, release me from them again, as thou
didst Stefan of Perm." And praying I rode over to Evfimej, to his   64
house. When they brought me into the yard, his wife Nionila ran
out and grabbed me by the hand, herself saying, "Please come,
our Lord and Father! Please come, our light and benefactor!" And I
said in answer to this: "Will wonders never cease! Yesterday I was
a son of a whore, and now, Father! It's Christ that has the crueler
scourge; your husband owned up in no time!" She led me into his   65
room. Evfimej jumped out of the featherbed and fell at my feet
with a howl beyond words to describe: "Forgive me, my lord, I
have sinned before God and before you." And he was shaking all   66
over. And I answered, "Do you wish to be whole from this time
forth?" And lying there he answered, "Yea, venerable father."
And I said, "Arise! God will forgive you!" But he had been mightily
punished and couldn't rise by himself. And I lifted him and laid
him on the bed, and confessed him, and anointed him with holy
oil, and he was well. Christ deigned it so. And in the morning he
sent me home in honor. He and his wife became my spiritual
children, praiseworthy servants of Christ. Thus it is that "God
scorneth the scorners, but he giveth grace unto the lowly."   67
    A little later others again drove me from that place for the sec-
ond time. And I dragged myself to Moscow, and by God's will the   68
Sovereign ordered that I be appointed archpriest in Jur'evec-on-the-
Volga. I lived here only a little, just eight weeks. The devil instructed   69

Jur'evec-on-the-Volga

Eight-cornered copper cross
(17th century)

Angel on copper cross
(16th-17th centuries)

the priests and peasants and their females; they came to the 70
patriarchal chancellery where I was busy with church business,
and in a crowd they dragged me out of the chancellery (there
were maybe fifteen hundred of them). And in the middle of the
street they beat me with clubs and stomped me, and the females
had at me with stove hooks. Because of my sins, they almost beat
me to death and they cast me down near the corner of a house.
The Commandant rushed up with his artillerymen, and seizing me 71
they raced away on their horses to my poor home. And the
Commandant stationed his men about the yard. But people came
up to the yard, and the town was in tumult. Most of all, as I had
cut short their fornicating, the priests and their females were
howling, "Kill the crook, the son of a whore, and we'll pitch
his carcass in the ditch for the dogs!"

After resting, two days later at night I abandoned wife and
children and with two others headed along the Volga toward
Moscow. I escaped to Kostroma — and sure enough, there they'd
driven out the Archpriest Daniil too. Ah, what misery! the devil 72
badgers a man to death! I trudged to Moscow and presented myself
to Stefan, the Tsar's confessor, and he was troubled with me.
"Why did you abandon your cathedral church?" he says. Again
more misery for me! The Tsar came to his confessor that night to
be blessed and saw me there — again more heartache. "And why,"
he says, "did you abandon your town?" And my wife and children
and the help, some twenty people, had stayed in Jur'evec, no
telling if they were living or dead. Still more misery.

After this, Nikon, our good friend, brought the relics of the
Metropolitan Filipp from the Solovki Monastery. But before his
arrival the Tsar's confessor Stefan, along with the brethren (and I
there with them), fasted for a week and besought God concerning
the patriarchate, that he might give us a shepherd for the salvation 73
of our souls. Together with Kornilij, the Metropolitan of Kazan, we 74
wrote and signed a petition concerning the Tsar's confessor Stefan,
that he should be patriarch, and we gave it to the Tsar and Tsarina.
But Stefan didn't want it himself and mentioned Metropolitan Nikon.
The Tsar listened to him and sent a message to meet Nikon: "To
Nikon, the most reverend Metropolitan of Novgorod and Velikie
Luki and of all Russia, our greetings," and so on. When he arrived 75
he played the fox with us — all humble bows and howdy-do's!

Patriarch Nikon (from *The Titulary*, 1672)

He knew he was going to be patriarch and wanted no hitches along
the way. Much could be said about his treachery! When he was   76
made patriarch, he wouldn't even let his friends into the Chamber
of the Cross! And then he belched forth his venom.   77
    During Lent he sent an instruction to St. Basil's, to Ivan 78
Neronov. He was my confessor; I was with him all the time and
living in the cathedral. When he went anywhere, then I took charge
of the cathedral. There had been talk that I might go to a post at
Our Savior's in the palace to replace the late Sila, but God didn't 79
will it. And little enough zeal there was on my part anyway. This
was just right for me. I stayed at St. Basil's and read holy books to
the folk. Many people came to listen. In the instruction Nikon 80
wrote: "Year and date. According to the tradition of the Holy
Apostles and the Holy Fathers it is not your bounden duty to bow
down to the knee, but you are to bow to the waist; in addition,
you are to cross yourself with three fingers." Having come together 81
we fell to thinking; we saw that winter was on the way – hearts
froze and legs began to shake. Neronov turned the cathedral over
to me and went himself into seclusion at the Čudovskij Monastery; 82
for a week he prayed in a cell. And there a voice from the icon
spoke to him during a prayer: "The time of suffering hath begun;
it is thy bounden duty to suffer without weakening!" Weeping 83
he told this to me and to Pavel, the Bishop of Kolomna, the same 84
that Nikon afterwards burned by fire in the Novgorod region.
Next he told Daniil, the Archpriest of Kostroma, and later he told
all the brethren. Daniil and I wrote down excerpts from Holy
Writ about the conformation of the fingers and obeisances and
gave them to the Sovereign; much was written there. But he hid 85
them, I don't know where. It seems he gave them to Nikon.
    Soon after this Nikon grabbed Daniil, and in the Convent
outside the Tver Gates sheared his head before the Tsar, ripped off 86
his surplice, and cursing, led him off into the bakery of the Čudovskij Monastery. And after afflicting him much, he exiled him to 87
Astrakhan. There a crown of thorns was laid on his head; in a pit
in the earth he was abused until dead. After the shearing of Daniil
they seized another Daniil, Archpriest of Temnikov, and jailed him 88
in the Novospasskij Monastery. Next came the Archpriest Ivan Nero- 89
nov; in church Nikon took away his *skuf'ja* and jailed him in the 90
Simanov Monastery, and afterwards banished him to Vologda, to 91

St. Basil's Cathedral
(17th-century, before
addition of covered
gallery)

the Spasov Kamennoj Monastery, then to the Kola fortress. But in   92, 93
the end, after much suffering, the poor soul gave out; he accepted
the three fingers, yes, and died in that state. Ah, woe is me! "Let
him that thinketh he standeth take heed lest he fall." The times   94
are savage, according to the Word of God, "if it is possible for the
spirit of the Antichrist to deceive the very Elect." It much behooves   95
us to pray to God with all our strength, that he might save and
have mercy upon us, for he is good and loves mankind.

Later on Boris Neledinskij and his musketeers seized me during
a vigil; about sixty people were taken with me. They were led off   96
to a dungeon but me they put in the Patriarch's Court for the night,
in chains. When the sun had risen on the Sabbath, they put me in a
cart and stretched out my arms and drove me from the Patriarch's
Court to the Andronikov Monastery, and there they tossed me in   97
chains into a dark cell dug into the earth. I was locked up three
days, and neither ate nor drank. Locked there in darkness I bowed
down in my chains, maybe to the east, maybe to the west. No one   98
came to me, only the mice and the cockroaches; the crickets chirped
and there were fleas to spare. It came to pass that on the third day
I was voracious, that is, I wanted to eat, and after Vespers there   99
stood before me, whether an angel or whether a man I didn't
know and to this day I still don't know, but only that he said a
prayer in the darkness, and taking me by the shoulder led me with
my chain to the bench and sat me down, and put a spoon in my
hands and a tiny loaf, and gave me a dab of cabbage soup to sip –
my, it was tasty, uncommonly good! And he said unto me, "Enough,
that will suffice thee for thy strengthening." And he was gone.
The doors didn't open, but he was gone! It's amazing if it was a
man, but what about an angel? Then there's nothing to be amazed
about, there are no barriers to him anywhere.   100

In the morning the Archimandrite came with the brethren and
led me out; they scolded me: "Why don't you submit to the
Patriarch?" But I blasted and barked at him from Holy Writ. They
took off the big chain and put on a small one, turned me over to
a monk for a guard, and ordered me hauled into the church. By the
church they dragged at my hair and drummed on my sides; they
jerked at my chain and spit in my eyes. God will forgive them in
this age and that to come. It wasn't their doing but cunning Satan's.
I was locked up there four weeks.

At this time, after me, Login, Archpriest of Murom, was 101
seized; he sheared him at Mass in the Cathedral Church, in the 102, 103
presence of the Tsar. During the Transposition of the Host the
Patriarch took the paten with the Body of Christ from the head of
the Archdeacon and put it on the altar, but Ferapont, the Archi- 104
mandrite of the Čudovskij Monastery, was still outside the sanctuary
with the chalice, standing by the royal gates! Alas, a sundering of
the Body of Christ worse than the work of the Jews! When they 105
had shorn him, they ripped off his surplice and kaftan. But Login
blazed with the zeal of the fire of holiness, and rebuking Nikon
he spat across the threshold into the sanctuary, in Nikon's face.
Unbelting himself, he tore off his own shirt and threw it into the
sanctuary, in Nikon's face. And wonder of wonders! − the shirt
spread out and covered the paten on the altar like it was a communion cloth. And at that time the Tsarina was in the church. 106
They put a chain on Login, and dragging him from the church
they beat him with brooms and whips all the way to the Bogojav-
lenskij Monastery and tossed him naked into a cell, and musketeers
were stationed to stand strict watch. But that night God gave him
a new fur coat and a cap. In the morning Nikon was told, and having
roared with laughter, he said, "I know all about those sham saints!"
And he took away the cap but left him the coat.

After this they again led me on foot out of the monastery to
the Patriarch's Court, as before stretching out my arms, and having
contended much with me they led me away again the same way.
Later, on St. Nikita's Day, there was a procession with crosses,
but me they again carried in a cart, meeting the crosses on their 107
way. And they carried me to the Cathredal Church to shear me,
and kept me at the threshold for a long time during the Mass.
The Sovereign came down from his place, and approaching the
Patriarch he prevailed upon him. They didn't shear me, but led
me off to the Siberia Office and handed me over to the secretary
Tret'jak Bašmak, now the Elder Savatej who also suffers in Christ, 108
locked up in a dungeon pit at Novospasskij. Save him, O Lord!
And at that time he was good to me.

Later they exiled me to Siberia with my wife and children. And
of our many privations on the road there is too much to tell, but
maybe a small portion of them should be mentioned. The Archpriestess had a baby, and we carried her sick in a cart to Tobol'sk.
For three thousand versts and about thirteen weeks we dragged

along in carts, and by water and sledges one-half the way.   109

The Archbishop in Tobol'sk appointed me to a post. Here in   110
this church great troubles overtook me. In a year and a half the
Word of the Tsar was spoken against me five times, and one person   111
in particular, the Secretary of the Archbishop's court Ivan Struna,
he shook my soul. The Archbishop left for Moscow, and with him
gone, because of the devil's instruction, he attacked me. For no
reason at all he took it into his head to afflict Anton, the Secretary
of my church. But Anton fled him and came running to me in the
church. That same Ivan Struna, having gotten together with some
other people another day, came to me in the church (I was chanting
Vespers). He leaped into the church and grabbed Anton by the
beard in the choir. At the same time I shut and locked the church
doors and didn't let anyone in. All alone Struna whirled about the
church like a devil. Leaving off Vespers Anton and I sat him down
on the floor in the middle of the church and I lashed him up one side
and down the other for rioting in church. The others, some twenty
people, all fled, driven off by the Holy Spirit. After receiving
Struna's repentance, I let him go again.   112

But Struna's kinswomen, the priests, and the monks, they stirred
up the whole town in hopes of doing away with me. At midnight
they pulled up to my place in sledges and broke into my house,
wanting to take me and drown me. And they were driven away by
the fear of God, and again they fled. Nearly a month was I tormented, escaping from them on the sly; sometimes I bedded down
in a church, sometimes I went to a commander's house, and some-   113
times I tried to beg my way into the prison – only they wouldn't
let me in. Often Matvej Lomkov went with me, he whose monastic
name is Mitrofan. Later on he was Steward of Church properties
in Moscow for the Metropolitan Pavel, and in the Cathedral Church,   114
along with the Deacon Afanasij, he sheared me. He was good before,   115
but now the devil's swallowed him whole.

Later the Archbishop came back from Moscow, and as just
chastisement he put him, Struna, in chains for this reason: a certain
man committed incest with his daughter, but after taking fifty
kopecks, he, Struna, let the peasant off without punishing him.
And his Grace ordered him fettered and made mention too of that
affair with me. But that one, Struna, he went off to the commanding
officers in their chambers and spoke the Word and Deed of the Tsar

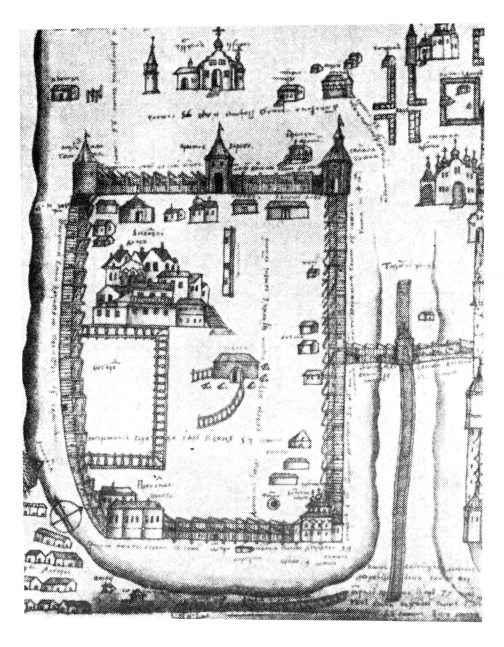

Map of fortress in Tobol'sk, where vast numbers of pelts from the fur
trade were stored. Tobol'sk, the capital of Siberia, was located high
on the hills above the Irtysh river.

against me. The officers turned him over to Pëtr Beketov, the best son   116
of the boyars, as his guardian. Alas, calamity came to Pëtr's household! And it still brings grief to my soul. The Archbishop thought
things over with me, and in accordance with the Canons he started
to damn Struna for the sin of incest in the main church on the first
Sunday in Lent. This same Pëtr Beketov came into the church, blistering the Archbishop and me. And in that hour, after leaving the   117
church, he fell into a frenzy while going home and died a bitter death.
And his Grace and I ordered his body thrown in the middle of the
street for the dogs, that the citizens might lament his transgression.
For three days we entreated the Deity most diligently that Beketov
might be absolved on Judgment Day. Pitying Struna he brought such
perdition on himself. And after three days his Grace and I buried his
body ourselves with honor. But enough talk of this lamentable affair.

Then a decree arrived. It was ordered that I be taken from
Tobol'sk to the Lena river because I was blasting from Holy Writ
and blistering the Nikonian heresy. During those times a short letter   118
came to me from Moscow. Two of my brothers lived up in the
Tsarina's apartments, and both died during the plague along with
their wives and children. And many of my friends and kinsmen
died off. God poured forth the vials of his wrath upon the kingdom!   119
And still those poor souls didn't come to their senses, and kept
right on stirring up the Church. Then Neronov spoke, and he told
the Tsar the three pestilences that come of schism in the Church:
plague, the sword, and division. So it has come to pass now in our   120
time. But the Lord is merciful. Having punished he has mercy on
us in our repentance; having scattered the diseases of our bodies
and souls he gives us peace. I hope and trust in Christ, I await his
compassion, and I tarry in hope for the resurrection of the dead.

So then I climbed into my boat again, the one that had been
shown to me, of which I have spoken previously, and I journeyed
to the Lena. But when I came to Yeniseisk another decree arrived;   121
it ordered us to carry on into Daurija — this would be more than
twenty thousand versts from Moscow. And they handed me over   122
into the troop of Afanasij Paškov; the people there with him numbered six hundred. As a reward for my sins he was a harsh man; he
burned and tortured and flogged people all the time. I had often   123
tried to bring him to reason, and here I had fallen into his hands
myself. And from Moscow he had orders from Nikon to afflict me.

After we had traveled out of Yeniseisk, when we were on the great Tunguska River, my prame was completely swamped by a   124
storm; it filled full of water in the middle of the river, the sail was ripped to shreds, only the decks were above water, everything else had gone under. My wife, bareheaded, just barely dragged the chil-   125
dren out of the water onto the decks. But looking to Heaven I shouted, "Lord, save us! Lord, help us!" And by God's will we were washed ashore. Much could be said about this! On another prame two men were swept away and drowned in the water. After putting ourselves to rights on the bank, we traveled on again.

When we came to the Šamanskij Rapids we met some people sailing the other way. With them were two widows, one about sixty and the other older; they were sailing to a convent to take the veil.   126
But Paškov started to turn them around and wanted to give them in marriage. And I said to him, "According to the Canons it is not fitting to give such women in marriage." What would it cost him to listen to me and let the widows go? But no, being enraged he decided to afflict me. On another rapids, the Long Rapids, he started   127
to kick me out of the prame. "Because of you," he says, "the prame don't go right! You're a heretic! Go walk through the mountains, you're not going with Cossacks!" Ah, misery came my way! The mountains were high, the forests dense, the cliffs of stone, standing like a wall – you'd crick your neck looking up! In those mountains are found great snakes; geese and ducklings with red plumage, black ravens, and grey jackdaws also live there. In those mountains are eagles and falcons and gerfalcons and mountain pheasants and pelicans and swans and other wild fowl, an endless abundance, birds of many kinds. In those mountains wander many wild beasts, goats and deer, Siberian stags and elk, wild boars, wolves, wild sheep – you'll lay your eyes on them but never your hands! Paškov drove me out into those mountains to live with the   128
beasts and the snakes and the birds.

So I wrote him a short little epistle; the beginning went like this: "Man! Fear God, who sitteth above the Cherubim and gazeth into the abyss; before him the heavenly Powers do tremble and all creation together with mankind. Thou alone dost scorn and exhibit unseemliness" – and so on. A good bit was written there, and I sent it to him. And lo, about fifty men ran up, seized my prame, and rushed   129
off to him (I was camped about three versts away from him). I

cooked the Cossacks some porridge, and I fed them. The poor souls, they both ate and trembled, and others watching wept for me and pitied me. A prame was brought up, the executioners seized me and brought me before him. He stood there with a sword, all atremble, and started to speak to me. "Are you a frocked or unfrocked priest?" And I answered, "Verily, I am Avvakum the Archpriest. 130 Speak! What is your business with me?" And he bellowed like a savage beast and hit me on one cheek, then on the other, again on top of my head, and knocked me down. Grabbing his commander's 131 axe, he hit me three times on the back as I lay there, and stripping 132 me, he laid seventy-two blows across that same back with a knout. But I was saying, "O Lord, Jesus Christ, Son of God, help me!" And I kept on saying the same thing, the same thing without let-up. So it was bitter for him that I was not saying "Have mercy!" At every blow I said a prayer, but in the middle of the beating I cried out to him, "That's enough of this beating!" So he ordered it stopped. And I managed to say, "Why are you beating me? Do you know?" And he again ordered them to beat me, now on the ribs, and then they let me go. I began to tremble and fell down. And he ordered me dragged off to the ammunition prame; they chained my hands and feet and tossed me against the mast bracing.

It was autumn, rain was falling on me, and all night long I lay in the downpour. When they were beating, it didn't hurt then, what with the prayers, but lying there a thought strayed into my head: "O Son of God, why did you let him beat me so hard that way? You know I stood up for your widows! Who will set a judge between me and thee? You never shamed me this way when I thieved in the night! And this time I don't know how I've sinned!" There's a good man for you! — another shit-faced Pharisee wanting to drag the Lord to court! If Job spoke in this way, he was righteous and pure, 133 and moreover had not fathomed Holy Writ; he was outside the Law, in a barbarous land, and knew God from his creation. But I, firstly, am sinful; secondly, I find repose in the Law and am supported in all things by Holy Writ, as "we must through tribulation enter into the Kingdom of God" — but I fell into such madness! 134 Alas for me! Why wasn't that prame swamped by the water with me in it? And in those moments my bones started to ache, and my veins went stiff, and my heart gave out, yes and I started to die. Water splashed in my mouth, so I sighed and repented before God.

The Lord our Light is merciful; he doth not recall against us our former transgressions, rewarding repentance. And again nothing was hurting.

In the morning they tossed me into a small boat and carried me onwards. When we reached the Padun Rapids, the biggest of them all – the river around that place is near a verst in width – they brought me right up to the rapids. Three cascades run across the whole river, fearfully steep; find the gates or your boat will be kindling! Down came the rain and snow, and only a poor little kaftan had been tossed across my shoulders. The water poured down my belly and back, terrible was my need. They dragged me out of the boat, then dragged me in chains across the rocks and around the rapids. Almighty miserable it was, but sweet for my soul! I wasn't grumbling at God a second time. The words spoken by the Prophet and Apostle came to mind: "My son, despise not thou the chastening of the Lord, nor faint when thou art rebuked of him. For whom God loveth he chasteneth, and scourgeth every son whom he receiveth. If ye endure chastening, God dealeth with you as with sons. But if ye partake of him without chastisement, then are ye bastards, and not sons." And with these words I comforted myself.

Afterwards they brought me to the Bratskij fortress and tossed me into the dungeon, and gave me a little pile of straw. And I was locked up till St. Philip's Fast in a freezing tower. Winter thrives there at that time, but God warmed me even without clothes! Like a little dog I lay on my lump of straw. Sometimes they fed me, sometimes not. The mice were plentiful, and I swatted them with my *skuf'ja* – the silly fools wouldn't even give me a stick. I lay on my belly all the time; my back was rotting. Plentiful too were the fleas and lice. I wanted to shout at Paškov, "Forgive me!" But the power of God did forefend it; it was ordained that I endure. He moved me to a warm hut, and there I lived the winter through in fetters along with hostages and dogs. But my wife and children were sent about twenty versts away from me. Her peasant woman Ksen'ja tormented her that whole winter long, all the time yapping and scolding. After Christmas my son Ivan, still a little boy, trudged over to stay with me awhile, and Paškov ordered him tossed into the freezing dungeon where I had been locked up. He spent the night, the little love, and almost froze to death. In the morning he

62

Tower of Bratskij fortress
(see annotation 137)

Location of the former Irgen fortress (see annotations 141–43)

ordered him thrown out, back to his mother. I didn't even get to see him. He dragged himself back to his mother – and frostbit his hands and feet.

In the spring we traveled on again. Not much space was given to supplies. One store was looted from top to bottom, books and extra clothes were taken away. But some other things still remained. On Lake Baikal I was swamped again. Along the river Xilok he made me haul on the tow-rope. The going was bitter hard on that river – there wasn't time for eating, much less for sleeping. All summer long we suffered. People keeled over and died from hauling in water, and my legs and belly turned blue. For two summers we tramped around in water, and in the winters we dragged ourselves over portages.

On that same Xilok River I was swamped for the third time. The little barge was torn away from the bank by the water; the other people's stayed there but mine was snatched up and away we went! My wife and children were left on the bank, and only the helmsman and I were swept away. The water was fast and it whirled the barge gunnels high and bottom-side up, but I kept crawling up on it, and myself shouted, "Queen of Heaven, help us! Our Hope, don't drown us!" Sometimes my legs went under, sometimes I crawled up on top. We were carried more than a verst, then some people snared us. Everything was smashed to bits! But what could be done if Christ and the most immaculate Mother of God deigned it so? I was laughing after coming out of the water, but the people there were oh'ing and ah'ing as they hung my clothes around on bushes, satin and taffeta coats and some other trifles. We still had a good bit left in chests and sacks. After this everything rotted through, and we were left naked. But Paškov wanted to flog me again: "You're making a laughing-stock of yourself," he said. So once again I pestered our Light, the Mother of God: "Queen of Heaven, calm that fool!" So she, our great Hope, she calmed him down: he started to take pity on me.

Then we moved to Lake Irgen. A portage is there and during the winter we started hauling. He took away my workers but wouldn't order others hired in their places. And the children were little – many to eat but no one to work. All alone this poor, miseried old Archpriest made a dogsled, and the winter long he dragged himself over the portage.

In the spring we floated down the Ingoda river on rafts. It was the fourth summer of my voyage from Tobol'sk. We were herding logs for houses and forts. Soon there was nothing to eat; people started dying off from hunger and from tramping about and working in water. The river was shallow, the rafts heavy, the guards merciless, the cudgels big, the clubs knotty, the knouts cutting, the tortures savage — fire and the rack! — people were starving, they'd only start torturing someone and he'd die! Ah, what a time! I don't know why he went off his head like that! The Archpriestess had an overdress from Moscow that hadn't rotted. In Russia it'd be worth more than twenty-five rubles, but here, he gave us four sacks of rye for it. And we dragged on for another year or two, living on the Nerča River and eating grass to keep body and soul together. He was killing everyone with hunger. He wouldn't let anyone leave to get a living, keeping us in a small area. People would roam across the steppes and fields and dig up grasses and roots, and we right there with them. In the winter it was pine bark, and sometimes God gave us horse meat; we found the bones of beasts brought down by wolves, and what the wolf hadn't eaten, we did. And some of those near frozen to death even ate wolves, and foxes, and whatever came their way, all sorts of corruption. A mare would foal and on the sly the starving would eat the foal and the foul afterbirth. And when Paškov found out, he would flog them half to death with a knout. And a mare died. Everything went to waste because the foal had been dragged out of her against nature; he only showed his head and they jerked him out, yes and even started eating the foul blood. Ah, what a time!

And in these privations two of my little sons died, and with the others we somehow suffered on, roaming naked and barefoot through the mountains and over sharp rocks, keeping body and soul together with grasses and roots. And I myself, sinner that I am, I both willingly and unwillingly partook of the flesh of mares and the carrion of beasts and birds. Alas for my sinful soul! "Who will give my head water and a fountain of tears that I might weep for my poor soul," which I wickedly sullied with worldly pleasures? But we were helped in the name of Christ by the Boyarina, the Commander's daughter-in-law Evdokija Kirillovna, yes and by Afanasij's wife Fekla Simeonovna too. They gave us relief against starvation secretly, without his knowing. Sometimes they sent a little piece of meat, sometimes a small round loaf, sometimes a bit

143

144
145

146

147

148

149

150

151

of flour and oats, as much as could be scraped together, a quarter pood and maybe a pound or two more, sometimes she saved up a good half pood and sent it over, and sometimes she raked feed 152 out of the chicken trough. My daughter Agrafena, the poor little love, on the sly she would wander over under the Boyarina's window. And we didn't know whether to laugh or cry! Sometimes they'd drive the little child away from the window without the Boyarina's knowing, but sometimes she'd drag back a good bit. She was a little girl then, but now she's twenty-seven and still unmarried. My poor, dear daughter, now she lives in tears at Mezen with her younger sisters, keeping body and soul together somehow. And her mother and brothers sit locked up, buried in the earth. But what's to be done? Let those broken hearts suffer 153 for the sake of Christ. So be it, with God's help. For it is ordained that we must suffer, we must suffer for the sake of the Christian faith. You loved, Archpriest, of the famed to be friend; love then to endure, poor wretch, to the end! It is written: "Blessed is not he that begins, but he that has finished." But enough of this. Let's 154 get back to my story.

We lived in great need in the land of Daurija for about six or seven years, but now and then we found relief. But Afanasij kept on 155 blackening my name and sought a death for me without let-up. In this time of want he sent me from his household two widows named Mar'ja and Sof'ja (his favorite house servants), who were possessed of an unclean spirit. He had conjured and worked many charms over them, and he "saw that he could prevail nothing but that rather a tumult was made." That devil was uncommonly savage 156 in afflicting them, they'd beat themselves and scream. He summoned me, bowed to me, and said, "Maybe you could take them home and look after them, praying to God: God listens to you." And I answered him, "Master, you ask too much, but after the prayers of our Holy Fathers all things are possible to God." And I took them, the poor things. Forgive me! But it happened during my trials in Russia that three or four lunatics were brought one time or another into my home, and after the prayers of the Holy Fathers the devils departed from them by the command and action of the living God and of our Lord Jesus Christ, the Son of God our Light. I sprinkled them with tears and holy water and anointed them with oil, chanting supplications in Christ's name, and the

power of God cast out the devils from these men and they were
made whole, not because of my merit – no way in the world! –
but because of their faith. In ancient times a blessing was accomplished through an ass with Balaam, and through a lynx with Julian
the Martyr, and through a deer with Sisinnius; they spoke with   157
the voices of men. "For wheresoever God desireth, there is the
order of creation overcome." Read the *Life* of Theodore of Edessa,   158
there you will find it, how even a harlot resurrected the dead. In
The Christian's Pilot it is written: "Not all are ordained of the Holy   159
Spirit, but any man, save a heretic, may be his instrument."

Later the madwomen were brought to me. I myself fasted
according to custom and didn't let them eat either, I made supplication, anointed them with oil, and what I know, I did. And in Christ
the women became whole in body and in mind. I confessed them
and gave them the Sacrament. Afterwards they lived in my household and prayed to God; they loved me and didn't go home. He
found out they had become my spiritual daughters and again raged
against me worse than ever – he wanted to burn me at the stake!
"You're rooting out my secrets," he said. Yes, only tell me, good
sir, how to give the Sacrament without confession? And without
giving a madman the Sacrament there's no way you'll cast out a
devil. That devil's no peasant, he's not afraid of a club. He's afraid
of the Cross of Christ, and of holy water, and of holy oil, and he
plain cuts and runs before the Body of Christ. Except by these Mysteries I am unable to heal. In our Orthodox faith there is no Sacrament without confession; in the Papist faith they do it this way,
they are not vigilant about confession. For us who observe the
Orthodox rite this is not fitting, but rather that we seek each time
after repentance. If because of privations you can't come by a   160
priest, declare your transgressions to a brother tried and true, and
God will forgive you, having seen your repentance. And then with   161
a brief little Office partake of the Eucharist. Keep some of the
Host with you. If you're on the road or about your work, or how-   162
ever it may be, except in church, having first sighed before the Lord
and confessed to your brother in accordance with the above, partake of the precious Mystery with a clear conscience. This way all
will be well! After fasting and after your Office, spread out a bit of
cloth on a small box before the icon of Christ, and light a little
candle, and put a dab of water in a little bowl. Ladle out some with

a spoon and with a prayer place a portion of the Body of Christ in the spoonful of water. Cense it all with a censer and having wept say: "I believe, O Lord, and confess that thou art the Christ, Son of the living God, who came into the world to save sinners of whom I am the first. I believe that this is in truth thy most immaculate Body and that this is thy most virtuous Blood. For its sake I pray to thee that thou wouldst have mercy on me and forgive and diminish my transgressions for me, both voluntary and involuntary, those in word and in deed, those in knowledge and in ignorance, those in intention and in thought, and enable me to partake blamelessly of these thy most immaculate Mysteries for the remission of sins and for life eternal, as thou art blessed forever. Amen." Then 163 fall to the ground before the icon and ask forgiveness, and having arisen kiss the icon and cross yourself, and with a prayer partake of the Sacrament, sip a little water, and again pray to God. Well then, glory be to Christ! Though you die right after this, all is well. But enough talk about this. You yourselves know what's good is good. Now I'll talk about the two women again.

Paškov took the poor widows away from me and blistered instead of blessing me. He expected Christ would accomplish this thing simply, but they began to rave even worse than before. He locked them in an empty hut, and no one could get in to see them. He summoned the priest of darkness to them, and they drove him 164 out with logs. So he dragged himself away. I was at home weeping, but what to do, that I didn't know. I didn't dare go near his place, he was no end riled at me. Secretly I sent them some holy water and commanded them to wash and drink abundantly, and they were somewhat eased, the poor souls. They trudged over secretly to see me themselves, and I anointed them with oil in Christ's name. So with God's leave they again became whole, and they went home again. And at night they came running to me to pray to God. Praiseworthy little ones they turned out to be, ceased their merrymaking and observed a goodly rule. In Moscow they moved into the Voznesenskij Convent with their lady. Glory be to God in this! 165

Later we turned back from the Nerča River towards Russia. 166 For five weeks we traveled by dogsled over naked ice. He gave me two miserable old nags for the little ones and for our pitiful belongings, but the Archpriestess and myself trudged along on foot, stumbling and hurting ourselves on the ice. The land was barbarous, the natives hostile. We dared not leave the horses at length; keeping up with them was outside our strength — starving and weary people we were. The poor Archpriestess tottered and trudged along, and then she'd fall in a heap — fearfully slippery it was! Once she was trudging along and she caved in, and another just as weary trudged up into her and right there caved in himself. They were both ashouting, but they couldn't get up. The peasant was shouting, "Little mother, my Lady, forgive me!" But the Archpriestess was shouting, "Why'd you crush me, father?" I came up, and the poor dear started in on me, saying, "Will these sufferings go on a long time, Archpriest?" And I said, "Markovna, right up to our very death." And so she sighed and answered, "Good enough, Petrovič, then let's be getting on."

We had a good little black hen. By God's will she laid two eggs a day for our little ones' food, easing our need. That's how God arranged it. During that time she was crushed while riding on a   167 dogsled, because of our sins. And even now I pity that little hen when she comes to mind. Not a hen nor anything short of a miracle she was — the year round she gave us two eggs a day! Next to her a hundred rubles aren't worth spit, pieces of iron! That little bird was inspired, God's creation. She fed us, and there at our side she'd peck the pinebark porridge right out of the pot, or if some fish came our way, then she'd peck at a little fish. And against this she gave us two eggs a day! Glory be to God, who hath arranged all things well! And we came by her in no ordinary way. All the Boyarina's hens went blind and started to die, so she gathered   168 them into a basket and sent them to me in hopes that "the good Father might favor us and pray for these hens." Well sir, I thought some on it: to us she'd been a real benefactress, she had little ones, and she needed those hens. I chanted prayers of supplication, blessed some water, and sprinkled and censed the hens. Then I tramped around in the forest and built them a trough to eat from. I sprinkled it with the water and sent the whole kit and caboodle back to her. And with a sign from God the hens were cured and made whole, because of her faith. It was from that flock that our little hen came. But enough talk about this. It wasn't today that such became the usual thing with Christ; Cosmas and Damian performed good deeds and healed for both man and beast in Christ's name. All things are needful to God; every little beast and   169

Silver gilt censer (15th-century)

bird lives to the glory of him, who is our most immaculate Lord, and for the sake of man as well.

Later we dragged ourselves back again to Lake Irgen. The Boyarina showed us her favor: she sent us a frying pan full of wheat, and we filled up on wheat porridge. Evdokija Kirilovna was my benefactress, but the devil made me squabble even with her, in this way. She had a son Simeon; he was born there, I gave the prayer and baptized him, she sent him to me every day for a   170 blessing, and I blessed him with the Cross, sprinkled him with holy water, kissed him, and sent him off again. He was a healthy, good child. Once I wasn't at home and the youngster fell ill. She lost heart, and fuming at me sent the baby to a peasant wizard. Hearing about this I flared up at her too, and great strife began between us.   171 The youngster got even sicker, his right arm and leg dried up like little sticks. She brought this shame on herself, she didn't know what to do, and God oppressed her even worse. Her sweet little baby was near death. Nurses came to me weeping, but I said, "If a woman's an evil thorn, let her stick to herself!" But I was expecting her repentance. I saw how the devil had hardened her heart; I fell down before the Lord that he might bring her to her senses.

And the Lord, our most merciful God, softened the soil of her heart. In the morning she sent her son, the younger Ivan, to me;   172 with tears he begged forgiveness for his mother, all the while moving around my stove and bowing. And I was lying naked under birch bark on top of the stove, and my wife was right in the stove, and the children wherever. Rain had set in, our clothes were gone, the shelter leaked – no rest from vexations! To humble her I said, "Command your mother to beg forgiveness from Orefa the sorcerer." Afterwards they brought the sick child; she had ordered him laid down before me. And they were all weeping and bowing. Well sir, I got up, pulled my stole out of the mud, and found the holy   173 oil. All the while entreating God and censing, I anointed the youngster with oil and blessed him with the Cross. With God's leave the baby got well again, both the arm and the leg. I gave him aplenty of holy water to drink and sent him back to his mother. You see, my listener, what power was created by the mother's repentance: she doctored her own soul and healed her son! But why not? It's not nowadays only there's a God for penitents! In

the morning she sent us some fish and pies, just what we needed,
hungry as we were. And from that time we made our peace. After
traveling out of Daurija she died in Moscow, the dear soul, and I
buried her in the Voznesenskij Convent. Paškov himself found out
about the youngster – she told him. Then I went over to see him.
And he bowed nice and low to me and himself said, "God save
you! You act like a real father, you don't remember our wicked-   174
ness." And at that time he sent food enough.

But after this he soon wanted to torture me – hear what for.
He was sending his son Eremej off into Mongolian territory to
make war; the Cossacks with him numbered seventy-two men and   175
the natives twenty. And he made a native shamanize, that is,   176
tell their fortune: Would they be successful and return home in
victory? And that evening this peasant sorcerer brought out a live
ram close by my shelter and started conjuring over it, twisting it
this way and that, and he twisted its head off and tossed it aside.
Then he started galloping around and dancing and summoning
devils, and after considerable shouting he slammed himself against
the ground and foam ran out of his mouth. The devils were crushing him, but he asked them, "Will the expedition be successful?"
And the devils said, "You will come back with a great victory and
with much wealth." The leaders were happy, and rejoicing all the
people were saying, "We'll come back rich!"

Ah, it was bitter for my soul then, and it's not sweet even now.
This bad shepherd destroyed his sheep, from bitterness he forgot
what is said in the Gospel when the sons of Zebedee gave advice
concerning the hardhearted villagers: " 'Lord, wilt thou that we
speak, that fire might come down from Heaven and consume them,
even as Elias did?' But Jesus turned and said to them, 'Ye know
not what manner of spirit ye are of. For the Son of Man is not
come to destroy men's souls but to save them.' And they went to
another village." But I, accursed man, I didn't do it that way.   177
There in my little pen I shouted out in lamentation to the Lord:
"Hear me, O God! Hear me, O King of Heaven, our Light! Hear
me! Let not one of them return here again, and prepare thou a
grave for them all in that place. Bring evil down upon them,
O Lord, bring it, and lead them to destruction, that the prophecy
of the devil shall not come to pass!" Plenty more along this line was
said, and in secret I entreated God about it too. Paškov was told I

was praying like this, but he only barked and bayed at me. Then he sent his son off with his troops. It was night and they traveled by the stars. I was sorry for them then. My soul saw they would be beaten, but I kept right on calling destruction down upon them. Some came up and said good-bye to me, and I said to them, "You will perish there." When they moved out, the horses under them suddenly began to neigh and the cows to bellow, the sheep and goats started bleating, the dogs were howling, and the natives themselves started howling like dogs. Terror fell upon everyone. With tears Eremej sent me a message, "that my father and master might pray for me."

And I started feeling sorry for him. Here he'd been a secret friend to me, and he'd suffered on my account. When his father was flogging me with a knout, he started to talk his father out of it, so that he chased after him with a sword. And when they arrived after me at one of the rapids, the Padun, forty prames had all made it through the passage, but as for Afanasij's prame, her rigging was good and all six hundred Cossacks put their backs into it, but they couldn't get her up through. The water took away their strength, or to put it better, God was punishing them! They were all dragged off into the water, and the water threw the prame onto the rocks; it poured over the boat but not into her. It's a miracle – somehow or other God teaches the witless! He himself was on the bank, the Boyarina in the prame. And Eremej began to speak: "Father, it's for your sin that God is punishing us. You flogged the Archpriest with that knout for no reason. Time to repent, my lord!" But instead he bellowed at him like a beast. Ducking behind a pine tree Eremej stopped, his hands folded, and standing there himself said, "Lord, have mercy!" And Paškov grabbed an attendant's wheel-lock rifle – it never tells lies – aimed at his son, and pulled the trigger. And by God's will the rifle misfired. So he fixed the powder and again pulled the trigger, and again the rifle misfired. He did the same thing for the third time, and the rifle misfired for the third time. So he threw it down on the ground. The attendant picked it up and put it down, off to the side – and then it went off! But the prame was lying all by itself on the rocks, half under water. Paškov sat down on a chair, and leaning on his sword he fell to thinking, then to weeping, and himself said, "I have sinned, accursed man, I have spilled innocent blood. I flogged the Archpriest for no

reason. God is punishing me for it." It was a miracle! A miracle!
According to Holy Writ: God is slow to anger but swift to hearken.   178
Because of his repentance the prame floated off the rocks by itself
and stood bow against the current. They gave a tug, and she flew
up into quiet water then and there. Then Paškov summoned his
son and said to him, "Eremej, forgive me, please, you speak the
truth!" And Eremej leaped over to him, fell down, bowed before
his father, and said unto him, "God will forgive you, my lord!
I am guilty before God and before you." And taking his father by
the arm, he led him away. An exceedingly sensible and good man
was Eremej; he already had a grey beard of his own, yet exceedingly
did he honor his father and fear him. And according to Holy Writ,
so it should be: God loves those children who honor their fathers.   179
See then, my listener, didn't Eremej suffer for our sake, and even
more for the sake of Christ and his Truth? But all this was told me
by Grigorij Telnoj, the helmsman of Afanasij's prame – he was
there. Let's get back to my story.   180
   After leaving us they rode off to war. I started feeling sorry for
Eremej and started pestering the Lord that he should have mercy
on him. We waited for them to return from war, but they didn't
turn up at the appointed time. And during this time Paškov wouldn't
let me in to see him. One day he set up a torture chamber and built
a fire; he wanted to torture me. And I recited the prayers for the
dying. I knew all about his hash-slinging, how few came out of
his oven alive. I was waiting for them in my hut, and sitting there
I said to my weeping wife and my children, "The will of the Lord
be done! 'For whether we live, we live unto the Lord; and whether
we die, we die unto the Lord.' " And lo, two executioners came   181
running for me. But marvelous are the works of the Lord, and
inexpressible are the designs of the Most High! Eremej, wounded,
and another man rode along the little road past my hut and yard;
he hailed the executioners and took them back with him. And
Paškov, he left his torture chamber and walked toward his son
looking drunk from grief. And exchanging bows with his father
Eremej informed him of everything in detail: how his troop was
wiped out to a man, how a native had led him away from the
Mongolians through empty regions, how he had strayed for seven
days without eating through the forests on rocky mountains – he
ate just one squirrel – and how a man in my image had appeared

to him in a dream, and blessing him had shown him the road, in what direction to journey. And leaping up he had rejoiced and trudged out onto the way. While he was telling this to his father I came up to bow to them. But laying eyes on me, Paškov – the spitting image of a polar bear he was! He would have gulped me   182 down alive, but the Lord didn't let him; he only sighed and said, "Is this how you carry on? Look how many people you've done in!" But Eremej said to me, "Father! Get out, my lord! Go home! Keep quiet, for the love of Christ!" And I did get out.

Ten years he tormented me, or I him – I don't know. God will sort it out on Judgment Day.   183

A transfer came for him and a document for me: I was ordered to journey to Russia. He moved on, but he didn't take me – he had a scheme in mind: "Just let him travel alone and the natives will kill him." He was sailing in the prames with both weapons and men, but I heard while traveling that they were trembling and afraid because of the natives. But not I – a month passed after he   184 left, and I gathered together the old and the sick and the wounded, those of no use there, about ten men, and with my wife and the children and myself there were seventeen of us in all – we climbed in a boat, and hoping in Christ and placing a Cross in the bow we journeyed wherever God might direct, fearing nothing. I gave *The Christian's Pilot* to the adjutant and he gave me a peasant pilot   185 in return. And I ransomed my friend Vasilij, who used to fill Paškov's ear with lies about people, who spilled blood and was after my head too. Once after beating me he was about to impale me, but God preserved me still! But after Paškov left, some   186 Cossacks wanted to flog him to death. Pleading with them to turn him over for Christ's sake and giving the adjutant a ransom, I carried him to Russia, from death to life. Let him be, poor soul – maybe he will repent his sins.

Yes, and I carried away another loose fish of the same sort. This one they didn't want to give up to me. And he ran into the forest, away from death, waited for me along the way, and weeping flung himself into my boat. But then the hounds were behind him and no place to hide! And I, sir – forgive me – I was a thief in the night: like the harlot Rahab of Jericho who hid the agents of Joshua, son of Nun, so I hid him away. I put him on the bottom of the boat and covered him with a sleeping mat, and I ordered the Archpriestess and my daughter to lie on top of him. They searched everywhere, but they didn't budge my wife from her place. They only said, "You go to sleep, little mother, and you too, Lady, you've stomached a lot of grief." And I – forgive me for God's sake! – I lied then and said, "He's not here with me" – not wanting to hand him over to death. They searched awhile and then rode off empty-handed, and I carried him back to Russia. Elder and you, servant of Christ! Forgive me for lying then. How does it seem to you? Was my sin a small one? With the harlot Rahab, it seems she did the same thing and the Scriptures praise her for it. You judge, for God's sake. If I arranged this business sinfully, then you forgive me, but if it was not contrary to the traditions of the Church, then all is well. Here I've left a place for you; write down with your own hand either forgiveness or a penance for me, my wife, and my daughter, since we all played the thief for one reason: we buried a man away from death, seeking his repentance before God. Judge us in such a way for this business that Christ won't on Judgment Day. Write something down, Elder. 187 188

God doth forgive and bless thee in this age and that to come, together with thy helpmate Anastasija, and thy daughter, and all thy house. Ye have acted rightly and justly. Amen.

Good enough, Elder. God save you for your charity! Enough of this!

The adjutant gave us about thirty pounds of flour, and a little cow, and five or six little sheep, and a bit of dried meat; we lived the summer on this as we sailed. The adjutant was a good man; he helped baptize my daughter Ksen'ja. She was born when we were with Paškov, but he gave me no myrrh nor holy oil, so she went unbaptized a long time; after he left we baptized her. I myself said the prayer for my wife, and with the godfather, the adjutant, I baptized my children; my oldest daughter was godmother, and I was the priest. Likewise I baptized my son Afanasij, and while saying Mass at Mezen I gave him the Sacrament. And I confessed my children and gave them the Sacrament myself, excepting my wife; it's all in the Canons and decreed that it be done so. As for that interdict of the apostates, I trample it in Christ's name, and 189 190, 191 192

that anathema – to put it crudely – I wipe my ass with it! The Holy
Fathers of Moscow bless me, Pëtr and Aleksej and Iona and Filipp.   193
I believe in and serve my God according to their books with a
clear conscience. But I reject and curse the apostates! They are
the enemies of God! I fear them not while I live in Christ! If they
pile stones on me, then with the traditions of the Holy Fathers will
I lie even under those stones, and not only under that lowdown,
harebrained Nikonite anathema of theirs! But why go on and on?
Just spit on their doings and on that ritual of theirs, yes, and on
those new books of theirs too, and all will be well. Let us talk now
about pleasing Christ and the most immaculate Mother of God,
and enough talk about their thievishness. Dear Nikonians, forgive
me, please, for blistering you – live as you like. I'm going to talk
again about my grief, how you've favored me with your lovingkindness. Twenty years have passed already; were God to sustain
me in suffering from you again as long, then so for my part it
would be, in the Lord our God and our Savior Jesus Christ! And
after that, as long as Christ gives, that long will I live. Enough of
this, I've wandered a long way. Let's get back to my story.

We journeyed out of Daurija, and the food ran low. And with
the brethren I entreated God, and Christ gave us a Siberian stag,
a huge beast. With this we managed to sail to Lake Baikal. Sable
hunters, Russians, had gathered in a camp by the lake; they were
fishing. The good souls were glad to see us; dear Teren'tij and his
comrades took us and our boat out of the lake and carried us far up
the bank. Looking at us they wept, the dear souls, and looking   194
at them we wept too. They heaped us with food, as much as we
needed; they carted up about forty fresh sturgeon in front of me,
and themselves said, "There you are, Father, God put them in our
seines for you; take them all!" Bowing to them and blessing the
fish, I commanded that they take them back again: "What do
I need so many for?"

We stayed with them awhile and then, taking a small provision
near our need, we fixed the boat, rigged up a sail, and set out across
the lake. The wind quit us on the lake, so we rowed with oars – the
lake's not so almighty wide there, maybe eighty or a hundred versts.   195
When we put into shore, a squall blew up and it was a hard pull
finding a place to land because of the waves. Around it the mountains were high and the cliffs of rock, fearfully high; twenty thousand versts and more I've dragged myself, and I've never seen their

St. Aleksej, Metropolitan of Moscow (early 17th-century icon)

like anywhere. Along their summits are halls and turrets, gates and
pillars, stone walls and courtyards, all made by God. Onions grow   196
there and garlic, bigger than the Romanov onion and uncommonly
sweet. Hemp grows there too in the care of God, and in the courtyards are beautiful flowers, most colorful and good-smelling.
There's no end to the birds, to the geese and swans – like snow they
swim on the lake. In it are fish, sturgeon and taimen salmon, sterlet
and amul salmon, whitefish, and many other kinds. The water is
fresh, but huge seals and sea lions live in it; in the great ocean sea I
never saw their like when I was living at Mezen. The lake swarms   197
with fish. The sturgeon and taimen salmon are fat as can be; you
can't fry them in a pan – there'd be nothing but fat left! And all
this has been done for man through Jesus Christ our Light, so that
finding peace he might lift up his praise to God. "But man is like
to vanity; his days are as a shadow that passeth away." He cavorts   198
like a goat, he puffs himself out like a bubble, he rages like a lynx,
he craves food like a snake; gazing at the beauty of his neighbor
he neighs like a colt; he deceives like a devil; when he's gorged
himself he sleeps, forgetting his office; he doesn't pray to God;
he puts off repentance to his old age and then disappears. I don't
know where he goes, whether into the light or into the darkness.
Judgment Day will reveal it for each of us. Forgive me, I have
sinned worse than all men.   199

    After this I sailed into Russian towns, and I meditated about
the Church, that I "could prevail nothing, but that rather a tumult
was made." Sitting there feeling heavy at heart, I pondered: "What
shall I do? Preach the Word of God or hide out somewhere? For I
am bound by my wife and children." And seeing me downcast,
the Archpriestess approached in a manner most seemly, and she
said unto me, "Why are you heavy at heart, my lord?" And in detail
did I acquaint her with everything: "Wife, what shall I do? The
winter of heresy is here. Should I speak out or keep quiet? I am
bound by all of you!" And she said to me, "Lord a'mercy! What
are you saying, Petrovič? I've heard the words of the Apostle – you
were reading them yourself: 'Art thou bound unto a wife? seek
not to be loosed. Art thou loosed from a wife? seek not a wife.'   200
I bless you together with our children. Now stand up and preach
the Word of God like you used to and don't grieve over us. As long
as God deigns, we'll live together, and when we're separated, don't

forget us in your prayers. Christ is strong, and he won't abandon us. Now go on, get to the church, Petrovič, unmask the whoredom of heresy!" Well sir, I bowed low to her for that, and shaking off the blindness of a heavy heart I began as before to preach and teach the Word of God about the towns and everywhere, and yet again did I unmask the Nikonian heresy with boldness.

I wintered in Yeniseisk, and after a summer of sailing, I again wintered in Tobol'sk. And on the way to Moscow, in all the towns 201 and villages, in churches and marketplaces I was ashouting, preaching the Word of God, and teaching, and unmasking the mummery of the godless. Then I arrived in Moscow. Three years I journeyed from Daurija, and going there I dragged along five years against the current. They carried me ever to the east, right into the middle of 202 native tribes and their camps. There's much could be said about this! Time and again I was even in the natives' hands. On the Ob, that mighty river, they massacred twenty Christians before my eyes, and after thinking over me some, they let me go altogether. Again on the Irtysh River a group of them was lying in ambush for a prameful of our people from Berëzov. Not knowing this I sailed toward them, and drawing near I put in to shore. They leaped around us with their bows. Well sir, I stepped out and hugged them like they were monks, and myself said, "Christ is with me, and with you too." And they started acting kindly towards me, and they brought their wives up to my wife. My wife likewise laid it on a bit, as flattery happens in this world, and the womenfolk warmed up too. We already knew that when the womenfolk are pleasant, then everything will be pleasant in Christ. The men hid their bows and arrows and started trading with me. I bought a pile of bearskins, yes and then they let me go. When I came to Tobol'sk I told about this; people were amazed, since the Tatars and Bashkirs were warring all over Siberia then. And I, not choosing my way and hoping in Christ, I had journeyed right through the middle of them. I arrived in Verxoturie, and my friend Ivan Bog- 203 danovič Kamynin was amazed at me: "How did you get through, 204 Archpriest?" And I said, "Christ carried me through, and the most immaculate Mother of God led me. I fear no one; only Christ do I fear."

Afterwards I journeyed to Moscow; like unto an angel of the Lord was I received by the Sovereign and boyars – everyone was

glad to see me. I dropped in on Fëdor Rtiščev; he leaped out of his   205
chamber to greet me, received my blessing, and started talking on
and on -- three days and nights he wouldn't let me go home, and
then he announced me to the Tsar. The Sovereign commanded
that I be brought then and there to kiss his hand, and he spoke
charitable words: "Are you living in health, Archpriest? So God
has ordained that we see one another again." And in answer I
kissed and pressed his hand and said myself, "The Lord lives and
my soul lives, my Sovereign and Tsar, but what's ahead will be as
God deigns." And he sighed, the dear man, and went where he
had to. And there were some other things, but why go on and on?
That's all past now. He ordered me put in the monastery guest
house in the Kremlin, and when his train passed my lodging, often
he'd bow nice and low to me, and himself say, "Bless me and pray
for me." And another time on horseback he took his cap off to
me -- a murmanka it was – and he dropped it. He used to lean out   206
of his carriage to see me. Later all the boyars after him started
bowing and scraping too: "Archpriest, bless us and pray for us!"
How, sir, can I help but feel sorry for that Tsar and those boyars?
It's a pity, yes it is! You see how good they were. Yes, and even
now they're not wicked to me. The devil is wicked to me, but all
men are good to me. They were ready to give me a place wherever
I wanted, and they called me to be their confessor, that I might
unite with them in the faith. But I counted all this as dung and I   207
gain Christ, being mindful of death, even as all this doth vanish away.

For lo, most terribly was it announced to me in Tobol'sk, in a
light sleep: "Beware, lest thou be sundered from me." I leaped up   208
and fell down before the icon in great fear, and myself said, "O
Lord, my God, I won't go where they chant in the new way." I
had been at Matins in the Cathedral Church on the Tsarevna's
nameday, and there, in that church, I had played along with their
fool's tricks before lords of the realm. What's more, after my
arrival in Moscow I had watched the division of the Host two or
three times while standing by the credence table in the sanctuary,
and I had cursed them, but as I got used to going I left off cursing.   209
I was just about stung by that stinger, the spirit of the Antichrist!
And that's why Christ our Light scared me, and said unto me,
"After so great a suffering, dost thou wish to perish? Take heed
lest I cut thee asunder!" So I didn't go to the service, but was

served dinner at a prince's instead, and I acquainted them with all this in detail. The Boyar, that good soul Prince Ivan Andreevič Xilkov, started to weep. And was it for me, accursed man, to forget the abundance of God's benefactions?

Once during the winter in Daurija I was hurrying along on ice spurs across the ice of a lake toward a fishing spot, to my children. Snow's not found there, but the great frosts thrive, and the ice freezes thick, close to the thickness of a man. I was thirsty, and so almighty wearied was I from thirst I couldn't walk any more. It was in the middle of the lake – about eight versts wide it was – and no way to get any water. Lifting my eyes to Heaven I began to speak: "O Lord, who brought forth water from a rock in the desert for thy people, for thirsting Israel, then and now thou art! Give me to drink by those means which thou knowest, my Master and my God!" Ah, woe is me! I don't know how to pray! For the sake of the Lord, forgive me! Who am I? A dead dog! The ice started to crack in front of me; it parted this way and that across the entire lake, and then came back together again. A great mountain of ice rose up, and as everything was settling down I stood in the customary place, and lifting my eyes to the east I bowed down twice or thrice, calling upon the name of the Lord in sparing words from the depths of my heart. God left me a small hole in the ice, and falling down I drank my fill. And I wept and rejoiced, thanking God. Then the icehole closed and I arose, bowed to the Lord, and again hurried off across the ice where I had to go, to my children.

And it was often that way with me at other times during my wanderings. On the move, whether I was dragging a dogsled, or fishing, or cutting firewood in the forest, or doing something else, at those times I still recited my Office, Vespers and Matins or the Canonical Hours – whatever. But if it was awkward around other people and we had made camp, and my comrades weren't getting along with me and didn't like my rule, and I hadn't managed it on the move, I'd step away from them, down a mountain or into a forest, and do it short and sweet. I would strike the earth with my head, and sometimes there were tears, and that's how I supped. But if the others were getting along with me, I'd place the folding icons against their props and say a short little Office; some prayed with me, others boiled their porridge. And traveling by sledge on Sabbath days I chanted the entire church service at resting places,

210

211

212

Folding Icons

Top: (left) Bowing to the Virgin are Metropolitans Pëtr, Aleksej, and Iona (see p. 76).
(right) Maksim the Greek is located to the left below Christ.
Bottom: Carved wooden icons of the Virgin and Christ

and on ordinary days I chanted riding in a sledge. And there were times I chanted while riding on the Sabbath too. When it was most awkward, I still grumbled some, if only a bit. For as the hungering body desireth to eat and the thirsting body to drink, so doth the soul desire spiritual sustenance, my Father Epifanij. Neither famine of bread nor thirst for water destroys a man; but a great famine it is for a man to live, not praying to God.   213

There was a time in the land of Daurija, Father – if you and that other servant of Christ will not be wearied by the listening, sinner that I am, I will acquaint you with these things – there was a time that I broke down in my rule from feebleness and terrible hunger. Hardly any was left, only the evening psalms and the Compline and the Prime. But more than that there wasn't. So I   214 dragged along like a little old beast, grieving about my rule but not able to hold to it. You see how weak I'd got! Once I went to the forest for firewood, and with me gone my wife and children sat on the ground by the fire, my daughter with her mother – both were weeping. Agrafena, my poor, suffering darling, was still a little girl then. I came back out of the forest. The babe was crying her heart out. Her tongue was tied, she couldn't get a word out, just sat there mewling at her mother. Her mother was looking at her and weeping. I caught my breath and with a prayer stepped up to the child, and said unto her: "In the name of the Lord I command you: speak with me. Why are you weeping?" And jumping up and bowing she started speaking plainly: "I don't know who it was locked up inside me, Father, a bright little thing, but he held me by the tongue and wouldn't let me talk to Mommy, and that's why I was crying. But he said to me, 'Tell your father that he'd better keep his rule like before, so you'll all journey back to Russia. But if he doesn't start keeping his rule – and he's been pondering this himself – then you'll all die here, and he'll die with you.' " Yes, and a few other things were said to her at that time too: how there'd be an edict about us, and how many of our old friends we'd find in Russia. And thus did it all come to pass.

And I was commanded to tell Paškov that he should chant Matins and Vespers; then God would give dry weather and the grain would grow, for there had been endless rains. A small area had been sown with barley a day or two before St. Peter's Day; it sprouted right away, and then was near ready to rot from the

rains. I told him about Vespers and Matins, and he set right to it.   215
God sent dry weather, and the grain ripened right away. A miracle
even so! Sown late and ripened early! Yes, and he again started
cheating in godly concerns, poor man. The next year he was about
to begin a big planting, and a most uncommon rain poured down;
the river overflowed and flooded the fields, and everything was
washed away, even our dwellings it washed away. There'd never
been a flood there before, even the natives were amazed. So you
see: as he cursed the affairs of God and lost his way, so God weighed
him in the scales of his awful wrath. He had started to laugh at
that first message later on. "The baby wanted to eat, so it cried,"
he said. But I, sir, from that time on I held to my rule, and up to
now I've gotten on little by little. But I've chatted enough about
this; let's get back to my story. It is needful for us to remember
and not to forget all these things, nor should we be negligent in
godly concerns; and we simply must not barter them for the
seductions of this vain age.

    I will speak again about my life in Moscow. They saw that I
was not joining them, so the Sovereign ordered Rodion Strešnev   216
to convince me to keep quiet. I eased his mind: "The Tsar is
invested by God, and here he's been good as gold to me" – I
expected he might come around little by little. And lo and behold,
on St. Simeon's Day they vowed I would be placed in the printing   217
house to correct books. And I was mighty happy; for me this was
needful, better even than being a confessor. He showed his favor
and sent me ten rubles, the Tsarina likewise sent ten rubles,
Luk"jan the Confessor also sent ten rubles, Rodion Strešnev sent
ten rubles too, while our great and good old friend Fëdor Rtiščev,
he ordered his treasurer to slip sixty rubles into my bonnet. About   218
others there's nothing more to say – everyone pushed and pulled
something or other over. I lived all this time in the household of
my light, my dear Feodos'ja Prokop'evna Morozova, as she was my
spiritual daughter; and her sister Princess Evdokija Prokop'evna
was also my spiritual daughter. My lights, Christ's martyrs! And I   219
was always visiting the home of our dear departed Anna Petrovna
Miloslavskaja. And I went to Fëdor Rtiščev's to wrangle with the   220
apostates.

    And so I lived this way near half a year, and I saw that these
ecclesiastical triflings "could prevail nothing but that rather a

tumult was made," so I started grumbling again, and even wrote a little something to the Tsar, that he should seek after the ancient piety and defend from heresies our common mother, the Holy Church, and that he should invest the patriarchal throne with an Orthodox shepherd instead of that wolf and apostate Nikon, the villainous heretic! And when I had prepared the letter, I fell 221 grievously ill, so I sent it to the Tsar in his carriage by my spiritual son Fëdor, the fool in Christ, that Fëdor later strangled by the apostates at Mezen, where they hanged him on the gallows. With 222 boldness he stepped up to the Tsar's carriage with the letter, and the Tsar ordered him locked up in the Red Terrace, still with the 223 letter. He didn't know it was mine. But later, after taking the letter from him, he ordered him released. And Fëdor, our dear departed, after staying with me awhile, he came before the Tsar again in a church, and there that blessed fool started in with his silly pranks. And the Tsar, being angered, ordered him sent to the Čudovskij Monastery. There Pavel the Archimandrite put him in irons, but 224 by God's will the chains on his legs fell to pieces, before witnesses. And he, our light, our dear departed, he crawled into the hot oven in the bakery after the bread was taken out and he sat there, his bare backside against its bottom, and gathered the crumbs and ate them. So the monks were in terror, and they told the Archimandrite, who is now the Metropolitan Pavel. And he acquainted the Tsar with this, and the Tsar came to the monastery and ordered him set free in honor. And again he came back to me.

And from that time the Tsar started grieving over me. It wasn't so nice now that I had started to speak again; it had been nice for them when I kept quiet, but that didn't sit right with me. So the bishops started to buck and kick at me like goats, and they schemed to banish me from Moscow again, as many servants of Christ were coming to me, and comprehending the truth they stopped going to their worship with its seductive snares. And there was a judgment from the Tsar for me. "The bishops are complaining about you," he said, "you've started to empty the churches. Go into exile again!" The Boyar Pëtr Mixajlovič Saltykov told me this. 225, 226 And so we were taken off to Mezen. Good people started to give us a plenty of this and that in the name of Christ, but it was all left behind. They only took me with my wife and children and the help. But passing through towns I again taught the people of God, and those others I exposed for what they are, the motley beasts! And they brought us to Mezen.   227

    After keeping us there a year and a half, they took me to Moscow again alone. My two sons Ivan and Prokopij also journeyed   228 with me, but the Archpriestess and the rest all stayed at Mezen. After bringing me to Moscow they took me under guard to the Pafnut'ev Monastery. And a message came there; over and over   229 they kept saying the same thing: "Must you go on and on torment- ing us? Join with us, dear old Avvakum!" I spurned them like devils, but they wouldn't stop plaguing me. I blistered them good in a statement I wrote there and sent along with Kozma, the Deacon of Yaroslavl and a scribe in the patriarchal court. But Kozma, I don't know of what spirit that man is. In public he tried   230 to win me over, but on the sly he encouraged me, speaking so: "Archpriest! Don't abandon the ancient piety! You'll be a great man in Christ when you endure to the end. Don't pay attention to us, we are perishing!" And I said in answer that he should come again to Christ. And he said, "It's impossible. Nikon's tied me hand and foot!" Putting it simply, he'd renounced Christ before Nikon and just that fast he couldn't stand on his own two feet, poor man. I wept and blessed him, the miserable soul. More than that there was nothing I could do for him. God knows what will become of him.

    After keeping me in Pafnut'ev for ten weeks in chains, they took me again to Moscow, and in the Chamber of the Cross the bishops disputed with me, then led me into the great cathedral,   231 and after the Transposition of the Host they sheared the Deacon Fëdor and me, and then damned us, but I damned them in return.   232 Almighty lively it was during that Mass! And after keeping us awhile in the Patriarch's Court, they carried us away at night to   233 Ugreša, to the Monastery of St. Nikola. And those enemies of God   234 cut off my beard. But what do you expect? They're wolves for a fact, they don't pity the sheep! Like dogs they tore at it, leaving me one tuft on my forehead like a Pole. They didn't take us to the monastery by the road but through marsh and mire so no one would get wind of it. They saw themselves they were acting like fools, but they wouldn't abandon their folly. Befogged by the devil they were, so why grumble at them? If they hadn't done it, someone else would have. The time of which it is written has come;

according to the Gospel: "It must needs be that offenses come."
And another apostle hath said: "It is impossible but that offenses
will come; but woe unto him through whom they come!" Look   235
you, listener: Our misery is unavoidable; we cannot pass it by! To
this end doth God suffer the visitation of offenses, so there might
be an Elect, so they might be burned, might be purified, so those
tested by tribulation might be made manifest among you. Satan
besought God for our radiant Russia so he might turn her crimson
with the blood of martyrs. Good thinking, devil, and it's good   236
enough for us – to suffer for the sake of Christ our Light!

They kept me at St. Nikola's for seventeen weeks in a freezing   237
cell. There I had a heavenly visitation; read of it in my letter to the
Tsar, you'll find it there. And the Tsar came to the monastery. He   238
walked around my dungeon some, groaned, and left the monastery
again. It seems from this he was sorry for me, but God willed it so.
When they sheared me, there was great turmoil between them and the
late Tsarina. She stood up for us then, the dear soul, and later on she
saved me from execution. Much could be said about this! God will   239
forgive them! I'm not asking that they answer for my suffering now,
nor in the age to come. It behooves me to pray for them, for the
living and for those resting in eternity. The devil set the breach
between us, but they were always good to me. Enough of this!

And Vorotynskij, our poor Prince Ivan, journeyed there without
the Tsar to pray, and he asked to come into the dungeon to me, but
they wouldn't let the poor soul in. Looking out the little window I
could only weep for him. My dear, sweet friend! He fears God, the
little orphan in Christ! And Christ won't abandon him. Come what
may, he's our man and Christ's man forever! And all those boyars   240
were good to us, only the devil was wicked. But what can you
do if Christ suffered it to be so? They flogged our dear Prince
Ivan Xovanskij with canes when Isaiah was burned. They ruined   241
Boyarina Feodos'ja Morozova altogether, killed her son, and
tortured her. And they flogged her sister Evdokija with canes,
separated her from her children, and divorced her from her husband.
And him, Prince Pëtr Urusov, they married off to another woman.   242
But what's to be done? Leave them be, the dear souls! In suffering
they will gain the Heavenly Bridegroom. God will surely lead them
through this vain age, and the Heavenly Bridegroom will gather
them to himself in his mansions, he who is the Sun of justice, our

Light and our Hope! Once again, let's get back to my story.

Later they bore me away again to the Pafnut'ev Monastery, where they kept me locked up in a dark cell and in fetters nigh onto a year. Here the cellarer Nikodim was good to me at first. 243 But then, it seems the poor man used some of that tobacco, sixtý poods of which were afterwards seized in the house of the Metropolitan of Gaza, along with a domra and other secret monastic doodads used in merrymaking. Forgive me, I have sinned, it's none 244 of my business. And he knows, "to his own master he standeth or falleth." This was said only in passing. And then, well-beloved 245 teachers of the Canons were there with them.

On Easter I begged respite for the festival from this cellarer Nikodim, that he order the doors opened for me to sit a spell on the threshold. But he heaped curses on me and refused savagely, for no reason. Afterwards, coming into his cell, he was taken mortally ill. He was anointed with oil and given the Sacrament, and once and for all he stopped breathing. That was on Easter Monday. During the night, towards Tuesday, a man in my image and in radiant vestments came to him with a censer and censed him, and taking him by the hand raised him up, and he was healed. And that night he rushed to me in the dungeon with the servitor, and as he came he was saying, "Blessed is this cloister, for such are the dungeons it possesses! Blessed is this dungeon, for such are the sufferers it possesses! And blessed are the fetters!" And he fell down before me, clutched my chain, and said, "Forgive me! For the sake of the Lord, forgive me! I have sinned before God and before you; I gave you offense, and God punished me for it." And I said, "How punished? Tell me of it." And he again, "But you yourself came and censed me, you showed me your favor and raised me! Why hide it?" The servitor standing there too said, "My lord and father, I led you out of the cell by the arm and then bowed down to you, and you came back this-away." And I charged him not to tell people of this mystery. And he asked of me how he should live henceforth in Christ: "Or do you order me to abandon everything and go into the desert?" I chastened him a bit and didn't order him to abandon his stewardship, only that he should keep the ancient traditions of the Holy Fathers, even if on the sly. And bowing he went away to his own cell, and in the morning at table he told all the brethren. Fearlessly and boldly did people trudge over to visit me, and they begged for my blessings and prayers. But I taught them from Holy Writ and healed them with the Word of God. At that time some few enemies made peace with me there. Alas! When will I leave this age of vanity? It is written: "Woe unto you when all men shall speak well of you." In truth I do not know how to live to the end; there are no good works in me, but God glorified me! But this he knows, it's as he wills. 246

Our dear departed Fëdor, my poor strangled one, journeyed to me there on the sly with my children, and he asked of me, "How do you say I should go about, the old way in a long shirt, or should I don other clothes? The heretics are hunting for me and want to put me to death. I was in Riazan, under guard in the court of the Archbishop," he said, "and he, Ilarion, he tortured me no end -- it was a rare day he didn't flog me with whips; he kept me fettered in irons, forcing me toward that new Sacrament of the Antichrist. I got weak, and at night I'd weep and pray, saying, 'O Lord, if thou dost not deliver me, they will defile me and I will perish. What then wilt thou do for me?' " And much did he weep as he talked. "And lo," he said, "suddenly, Father, all the irons fell from me with a crash, and the door unlocked and opened of itself. So I bowed down to God and got out of there. I came up to the gates, and the gates were open! And I headed along the highroad straight for Moscow. When it started to get light, here came the hunters on horses! Three men raced past, but they didn't catch sight of me. I was hoping in Christ and kept trudging along. Pretty soon they came riding back toward me barking, 'He took off, the son of a whore! Where can we nab him?' And again they rode past without seeing me. So now I've trudged over here to ask whether I should go on back there and be tortured or put on other clothes and live in Moscow?" And I, sinner that I am, I directed him to put on the clothes. But I didn't manage to bury him outside the reach of the heretics' hands; they strangled him at Mezen, hanging him on the gallows. Eternal remembrance to him, together with Luka Lavrent'evič. My sweet, good little children! You have suffered for Christ! In them, glory be to God! 247 248

Uncommonly stern was the ascetic life of that Fëdor. During the day he played the blessed fool, but all night long he was at prayer with tears. I knew many a good person, but never had I seen such an ascetic! He lived with me about half a year in

Angel on cross, copper, for personal wear (16th-century)

Iron chains and weights for mortification of the flesh

Moscow – I was still feeble – the two of us stayed in a little back room. Most the time he'd lie down an hour or two, then get up; he'd toss off a thousand prostrations and then sit on the floor, or sometimes stand, and weep for maybe three hours. But even so I'd be lying down, sometimes asleep, but sometimes too feeble to move. When he had wept his fill and even more, he'd come over to me: "How long are you going to lie there like that, Archpriest? Get your wits about you, you're a priest, you know! How come you're not ashamed?" And I was very feeble, so he'd lift me up, saying, "Get up, sweet Father of mine, well come on, just drag yourself up somehow!" And he'd manage to stir some life into me. He'd tell me to recite the prayers sitting down, and he'd make the prostrations for me. A friend of my heart for certain! The dear soul was afflicted by this great over-straining. One time seven feet of his innards came out of him, and another time twelve feet. Ailing like that and still he kept on measuring those entrails – with him you didn't know whether to laugh or cry! For five years without let-up he froze barefoot in the frost in Ustiug, wandering around in just a long shirt. I myself am his witness. There he became my spiritual son as I was coming back from Siberia. In the church vestry, he'd come running in for prayer and say, "When you first come out of that frost into the warm, Father, it's no end burdensome just then." And his feet clattered across the bricks like frozen blocks. But by morning they didn't hurt once again. He had a Psalter from the new printings in his cell then; he still knew only a little bit about the innovations. And I told him about the new books in detail. He grabbed the book and tossed it into the stove then and there, yes, and he damned all innovation. No end fiery was that faith of his in Christ! But why go on and on? As he began, so he ended. He didn't pass his radiant life in story-telling, not like me, accursed man. There's why he passed away in the odor of sanctity.

A fine man too was dear Afanasij, the good soul. My spiritual son he was; as a monk he was called Avraamij. The apostates baked him in their fire in Moscow, and like sweet bread was he yielded up to the Holy Trinity. Before he took the cowl he wandered about both summer and winter barefoot, wearing just a long shirt. Only he was a little gentler than Fëdor, and a wee bit milder in his asceticism. He was a great lover of weeping – he'd walk and he'd weep. And if he was talking with someone, his words were quiet and even, like he was weeping. But Fëdor was most zealous and active no end in the business of God. He endeavored to destroy and expose untruth no matter what. But leave them be! As they lived, so they passed away in our Lord Jesus Christ.

I will chat with you some more about my wanderings. When they brought me from the Pafnut'ev Monastery to Moscow, they put me in a guesthouse, and after dragging me many a time to the   254 Čudovskij Monastery, they stood me before the Ecumenical Council of Patriarchs. And all of ours were sitting there too, like foxes.   255, Much from Holy Writ did I say to the patriarchs; God opened my sinful lips and Christ put them to shame! They said to me at last,   257 "Why are you so stubborn? All ours from Palestine – the Serbs, and Albanians, and Rumanians, and Romans, and Poles – they all cross themselves with three fingers, but you stand there all alone   258 in your stubbornness and cross yourself with two fingers. This is not seemly!" But in Christ did I answer them, after this manner: "Teachers of Christendom! Rome fell long ago and lies never to rise. The Poles perished with her; to the end were they enemies of Christians. And Orthodoxy has become motley in color even with you, from violation by Mahmet the Turk. We can't be surprised at you, you are enfeebled. Henceforth, come to us to learn! By the   259 Grace of God we have autocracy. In our Russia before Nikon the Apostate, the Orthodox faith of devout princes and tsars was always pure and spotless, and the Church was not mutinous. That wolf Nikon, in league with the devil, betrayed us through this crossing with three fingers. But our first shepherds, just as they crossed themselves with two fingers, so did they bless others with two fingers according to the tradition of our Holy Fathers, Meletius of Antioch, and Theodoret the Blessed, Bishop of Cyrrhus, and Peter of Damascus, and Maksim the Greek. What is more, the wise   260 Moscow Council during the reign of Tsar Ivan charged us to cross   261 ourselves and to bless others by conforming our fingers in the manner taught by the Holy Fathers of the past, Meletius and the others. At that council in the time of Tsar Ivan were the Bearers of the Sign Gurij and Varsonofij, the miracle workers of Kazan,   262 and Filipp, the Abbot of Solovki – all Russian saints!

And the patriarchs fell to thinking, but like a bunch of wolf whelps our Russians bounced up howling and began to vomit on

their own Holy Fathers, saying, "They were stupid, our Russian saints had no understanding! They weren't learned people – why believe in them? They couldn't even read or write!" O holy God, how didst thou bear such great mortification of thy saints? As for me, poor man, it was bitter, but nothing could be done. I blistered them, I blistered them as much as I could, and at last I said unto them: "I am clean, and I shake off the dust clinging to my feet before you; according to that which is written: 'Better one who works the will of God than a multitude of the godless!' " 263
So they started shouting at me even worse: "Seize him! Seize him! 264
He has dishonored us all!" And they started to shove me around and beat me – even the patriarchs threw themselves on me. There were about forty of them there, I expect – a mighty army for the Antichrist had come together! Ivan Uarov grabbed me and dragged me around some, and I shouted, "Stop it! Don't beat me!" So they all jumped back. And I began to speak to the Archimandrite interpreter: "Say to the patriarchs: the Apostle Paul writes, 'For 265
such an high priest became us, who is holy, harmless,' and so on; 266
but you, after beating a man, how can you perform the liturgy?" So they sat down. And I walked over toward the doors and flopped down on my side: "You can sit, but I'll lie down," I said to them. So they laughed, "This archpriest's a fool! And he doesn't respect the patriarchs!" And I said to them, "We are fools for Christ's sake! Ye are honorable, but we are despised! Ye are strong, but we are weak!" Then the bishops again came over to me and started to 267
speak with me about the Alleluia. Christ gave me the words; I shamed the whore of Rome within them through Dionysios the Areopagite, as was said earlier in the beginning. And Evfimej, the Cellarer of the Čudovskij Monastery, said, "You're right. There's 268
nothing more for us to talk to you about." And they led me away in chains.

Afterwards the Tsar sent an officer with some musketeers, and they carried me off to the Sparrow Hills. There too they 269
brought the priest Lazar and the monk and elder Epifanij. Shorn 270
and abused like peasants from the village they were, the dear souls! Let a man with sense take a look and he'd just weep looking at them. But let them endure it! Why grieve over them? Christ was better than they are, and he, our Light, he got the same from their forefathers Annas and Caiaphas. There's no reason to be surprised 271

at men nowadays – they've got a pattern for acting so! We should grieve a bit for them, poor souls. Alas! you poor Nikonians! You are perishing from your wicked, unruly ways!

Then they led us away from the Sparrow Hills to the Andreevskij Monastery, and later to the Savvin Settlement. The troop of musketeers guarded us like brigands, even went with us to shit! Remember it, and you don't know whether to laugh or cry. How Satan had befogged them! Then to St. Nikola at Ugreša; there the Sovereign sent Captain Jurij Lutoxin to me for my blessing, and we talked much about this and that.

Afterwards they brought us again to Moscow, to the guesthouse of St. Nikola's, and took still more statements from us concerning Orthodoxy. The gentlemen of the bedchamber Artemon and Dementij were sent to me many a time, and they spoke to me the Tsar's words: "Archpriest, I know your pure and spotless and godly life, and I with the Tsarina and our children beg your blessing. Pray for us!" The messenger said this, bowing the while. And I will always weep for the Tsar; I'm mighty sorry for him. And again he said, "Please listen to me. Unite with the ecumenical bishops, if only in some little thing." And I said to him, "Even if God deigns that I die, I will not unite with the apostates! You are my Tsar," I said, "but what business do they have with you? They lost their own tsar, and now they come dragging in here to swallow you whole. I will not lower my arms from the heights of heaven," said I, "till God gives you over to me!" And there were many such messages. This and that was said. Finally he said, "Wherever you may be, don't forget us in your prayers!" Even now, sinner that I am, I entreat God on his behalf as much as I can.

Later, after mutilating my brethren but not me, they banished us to Pustozersk. And I sent the Tsar two letters from Pustozersk; the first was short but the other longer. I talked about this and that. I told him in one letter about certain signs from God shown me in my dungeons. He who reads it there will understand. Moreover, a small boon for true believers was sent to Moscow, the Deacon's gleanings from the brethren and me, a book *The Answer of the Orthodox* with an unmasking of the whoredom of apostasy. The truth about the dogmas of the Church is written in it. And then two letters were also sent by the priest Lazar to the Tsar and the Patriarch. And in return for all this some small boons were sent our way: they hanged two people in my house at Mezen, my spiritual children — the above-mentioned fool in Christ Fëdor and Luka Lavrent'evič, both servants of Christ. This Luka was 279 a Muscovite, his widowed mother's only child, a tanner by trade, a youth of twenty-five. He journeyed with my children to Mezen, to his death. And when ruin had fallen everywhere upon my house, Pilate questioned him: "How do you cross yourself, peasant?" And he made answer with humble wisdom: "I believe and cross myself, conforming my fingers in the manner of my confessor, the Archpriest Avvakum." Pilate ordered him shut away in a dungeon. Later he placed a noose on his neck and hanged him from a gibbet. So he passed from earthly to heavenly things. What more could they do to him than this? If he was a youngster, he acted like an elder: went straight off to the Lord, he did! If only an old man could figure things out like that!

At that same time it was ordered that my two sons Ivan and Prokopij be hanged. They misreckoned, poor souls, and didn't figure out how to seize the crown of victory. Fearing death they owned their fault. So with their mother for a third they were buried alive in the earth. Now there's a death without death for you! Repent you two locked up there, while the devil thinks up something else! Death is fearsome — that's no surprise! Once denial was made by that close friend Peter too, "and he went out and wept bitterly." And because of his tears he was forgiven. There's 280 no reason to be surprised at these little ones; it's for my sinfulness that Christ suffered them such feebleness. And it's to the good, so be it! Christ is strong enough to have mercy and save us all!

Afterwards that same Captain Ivan Elagin was with us in 281 Pustozersk too, having journeyed from Mezen. And he took a statement from us. Thus was it spoken: year and month, and again, "We preserve the ecclesiastical tradition of the Holy Fathers inviolate, and we curse the heretical council of the Palestinian Patriarch Paisij and his comrades." Quite a little else was said there, and a small part of it fell to the lot of Nikon, that breeder of heresies! So they took us to the scaffold, and after an edict was read they led me away to a dungeon without mutilating me. The edict read: "Imprison Avvakum in the earth, in a log frame, and give him bread and water." And I spat in answer and wanted to starve myself to death. And I didn't eat for about eight days or more, but the brethren directed me to eat again.

Later they took the priest Lazar and cut his entire tongue from his throat. Just a bit of blood there was, and then it stopped. And he again spoke even without a tongue. Next they put his right hand on the block and chopped it off at the wrist, and lying there on the ground, of itself the severed hand composed its fingers according to tradition, and it lay that way a long time before the people. Poor thing, it confessed even in death the unchanging sign of the Savior. And that, sir, was a miracle that amazed even me: the lifeless convicted the living! On the third   282
day after, I felt and stroked inside his mouth with my hand; it was all smooth, no tongue at all, but it didn't hurt. God granted him this speedy healing. They had sliced away at him in Moscow. Some of the tongue remained then, but now everything was cut out, nothing left. But he spoke plainly for two years, as if with a tongue. When two years had passed there was another miracle: in three days his tongue grew back complete, only a little bit blunt, and again he spoke, praising God and rebuking the apostates.

Later they took the Solovki hermit, the Elder Epifanij, a monk of the angelical image, and they cut out the rest of his tongue.   283
And four of his fingers were chopped off. At first he snuffled his words. Later he entreated the most immaculate Mother of God, and both tongues, from Moscow and from here, were shown him on a communion cloth. He took one and put it in his mouth, and from that time he started to speak plainly and clearly. And he had a whole tongue in his mouth. Wonderful are the works of the Lord and inexpressible are the designs of the Most High! He suffers punishment, but he has mercy and heals again. But why go on and on? God's an old hand at miracles, he brings us from nonexistence to life. And surely he will resurrect all human flesh on the last day in the twinkling of an eye. But who can comprehend this? For God is this: he creates the new and renews the old. Glory be to him in all things!

Later they took the Deacon Fëdor and cut out all the rest of his tongue. But they left a little piece in his mouth, cut slantwise across his throat. It healed then at that size, but afterwards it again grew back about like the old one. And when it stuck out of his lips it was a little blunt. They chopped off his hand across the palm. God granted him healing in everything. And he spoke

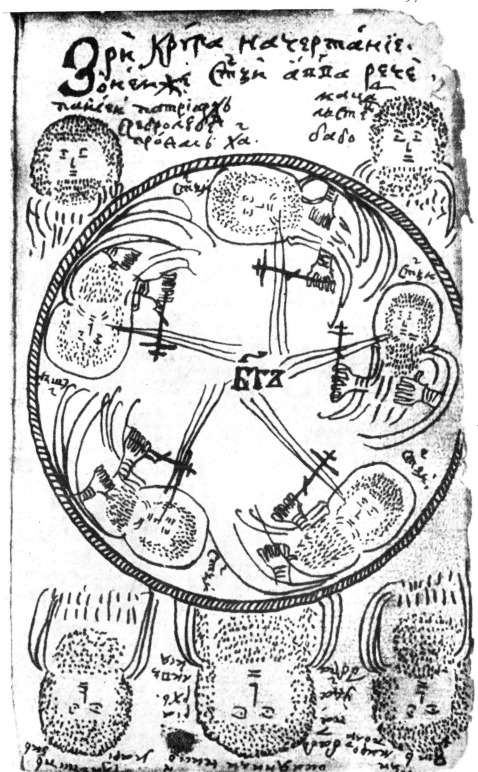

This sketch is found in Redaction 3 of the *Life*.
The five saints inscribed in the circle centered
on God apparently represent the Elect; the
figures outside are certainly the damned. They
are (top, left and right) Patriarchs Paissios and
Makarios (see annotation 255) and (bottom,
left to right) Archbishop Ilarion, Patriarch Nikon
and Metropolitan Pavel (see annotations 114
and 247 regarding Pavel and Ilarion). Avvakum
refers in his marginalia here to Paissios as a
"lover of silver" who "betrayed Christ"; Makarios is a "flatterer," and Nikon is "the accursed
Patriarch who has separated himself from God."
In addition, he seems to allude disparagingly to
Makarios' and Nikon's relations with women;
an incomplete but almost certainly pejorative
appellation (*babo–*) is attached to both (the
ending of the word may be effaced beside the
caricature of Nikon, while the edge of the page
is missing beside Makarios). *Baba* is the disdain-
ful vernacular word Avvakum characteristically
uses in referring to wayward women, and Nikon
and Makarios are here apparently alleged to
be their admirers. A possible word is *baboljub*,
"skirt-chaser" in contemporary English.

clearly and plainly compared to before.   284

Afterwards they covered us up with earth: a log frame was set
in the earth [for each of us], and around this another log frame,
and again around all of them a common palisade with four bolts.
"The keepers before the door kept the prison." And locked up in   285
dungeons here or anywhere we sing before our Lord Jesus Christ,
Son of God, the Song of Songs, the same to which Solomon lifted
up his voice as he gazed upon his mother Bathsheba: "Behold,
thou art fair, my lovely one, behold thou art fair, my beloved.
Thine eyes burn as the flame of fire, thy teeth are white more than
milk; thy countenance is more than the rays of the sun, and thou
shinest ever in beauty, as the day in its strength." (Laud of the
Church)   286

Later Pilate left us, and after finishing up in Mezen he returned
to Moscow. And in Moscow others of ours were roasted and baked.
Isaiah was burned, and later Avraamij was burned, and a great
multitude of other champions of the Church was destroyed; God
will reckon their number. It's a miracle, somehow they just don't
want to gain true understanding! They want to strengthen the faith
with fire, the knout, and the gallows! Now which of the apostles
taught them that? I don't know. *My* Christ never commanded our
apostles to teach this way, that we should bring people to the faith
by fire, the knout, and the gallows. Thus was it spoken to the
apostles by our Lord: "Go ye into all the world and preach the
Gospel to every creature. He that believeth and is baptized shall be
saved; but he that believeth not shall be damned." You see, listener,   287
Christ calls us to come freely; he did not command the apostles
to burn the rebellious in the fire or hang them from the gallows.
The Tatar god Mahmet wrote in his books after this manner:
"It is our charge that the heads of those rebelling against our tradition and law be bowed down by the sword." But our Christ never   288
charged his disciples in this way. And these teachers are brazenfaced,
like imps of the Antichrist who in bringing people to the faith
destroy and give them over to death. As they believe, so do they
act. It is written in the Gospel: "A good tree cannot bring forth
evil fruit, neither can a corrupt tree bring forth good fruit; where-
fore by its fruit shall each tree be known."   289

But why go on and on? If there were no champions, there
would be no crowns. For him who wants to be crowned, there's

no point in going to Persia, Babylon's right here at home. So speak   290
out the name of Christ, you true believers, stand in the middle of
Moscow and cross yourselves with the Sign of our Savior Jesus Christ,
with two fingers as we have received it from the Holy Fathers.
That's how the Kingdom of Heaven was born for you here at home!
God will bless; just you suffer for the conformation of the fingers
and don't reason overmuch. And I'm ready to die with you for
this in Christ. If I be witless twice over, a man without schooling,
still I know that everything in the Church handed down from
the Holy Fathers is holy and spotless. I will keep it to my death
just as I received it. I will not move the eternal boundaries established before our time! Let them lie thus forever and ever! Cease   291
your debauchery, heretic, not only with Christ's Sacrament and
his Cross, but don't so much as stir the altar cloths! But no, they've
finagled with the devil to reprint the books, to change everything: the Cross on the Church and the Host is changed; they've
tossed away the Prayers of Priestly Confession recited within the
sanctuary; they've changed the General Prayer of Petition; during
Baptism they brazenly command us to pray to the Tempter — I'd
like to spit in his face and theirs! And the Tempter leads them
around the baptismal font against the path of the sun, just as they
go against the sun in consecrating churches, and after solemnizing
marriage the procession is again led against the sun! They act in   292
brazenfaced defiance — and in Baptism they don't even renounce
Satan! But what do you expect? They're his children — as if they
would want to renounce their own father! But why go on and on?
Ah, woe to the true-believing soul! Everything lofty has entered
the vale. What Nikon said, that hound from hell, that's what he
did: "Arsen, you print the books any way you want, just so it's   293
not the old way!" Well sir, that's what he did. And there's no way
to change things more than that. It behooves each of us to die for
these things. Let them be damned, accursed men, along with all
their cunning schemes, but threefold eternal remembrance for
those suffering from them!

    After this, I beg forgiveness from every true believer. It seems
that, had things been different, there would be no need for me to
talk about my life. I have read the Acts of the Apostles and the
Epistles of Paul; the apostles made report concerning themselves
when God was at work within them: "Not to us, but to our God

be the glory!" But I am nothing. I have said, and will say anew: 294
"I am a sinful man, a whoremonger and a plunderer, a thief and
a murderer, a friend to publicans and sinners, an accursed hypocrite
before every man." Forgive me and pray for me, as I must for
you who read and listen to me. I know nothing about living more
than this, but what I do, I tell people about; may they pray to God
for me! On Judgment Day everyone there will learn of my deeds,
whether they be good or evil. But still, I am unschooled in words
but not in understanding. I am unschooled in dialectics and
rhetoric and philosophy, but I have Christ's understanding within
me. As even the Apostle hath said: "Though I be rude in speech,
but not in understanding." 295

Forgive me, I will chat with you a bit more about my ignorance.
Once I did a stupid thing, so help me; I transgressed the commandment of my confessor, and because of this my house was punished.
For the sake of the Lord, hearken to how it happened. When I
was still a priest, the Tsar's confessor, the Archpriest Stefan Vonifat'ev, blessed me with an icon of the Metropolitan Filipp and the
book of St. Efrem Sirin, to heal myself in reading, and others as 296
well. But I, accursed man, scorning his fatherly blessing and
instruction, I traded that book for my cousin's horse, because of
his pestering. My brother Evfimej was living in my house with me;
he had a good head for learning and great zeal for the Church.
Later on he was taken into the apartments of the Elder Tsarevna as
a psalmister, but he and his wife passed away in the plague. Evfimej 297
fed and watered that horse and was most zealous about her, many
a time scorning his Office. And God saw the untruth in my brother
and me, how wrongly we walked in the Truth: I had traded the book,
transgressing my confessor's commandment, and my brother,
scorning his rule, was zealous about the beast. The Lord deigned to
punish us in this way: devils started afflicting that horse at night
and during the day; she was always in a lather, hard-run, and soon
almost dead. But I was in confusion: for what sin was that devil
embittering our life like this? On Sunday after dinner, during the
private meditations of the Compline, my brother Evfimej was
reciting the Kathisma of the Undefiled, and he cried out in a

loud voice: "Look thou upon me and be merciful unto me!" And   298
dropping the book from his hands, he fell hard against the ground,
struck down by devils. He began shouting and crying out in voices
most vexatious, as the devils had begun afflicting him savagely.
In my house were my other two brothers Kozma and Gerasim,
bigger than Evfimej, but they couldn't hold him. And almost all the
help, near thirty people, held him as they sobbed and wept, crying
out to the Lord: "O Lord, have mercy! We have sinned before thee,
we have angered thy lovingkindness. Forgive us sinners! Have mercy
on this youth, in answer to the prayers of our Holy Fathers!"
But he raged and shouted even worse, and shivered and beat
himself.

But with God's help I was not dismayed by this devilish
commotion. Finishing my Office, anew did I begin to pray with
tears to Christ and the Mother of God, saying, "Queen of Heaven,
all-holy Mother of God! Show me for which of my transgressions
such punishment hath come to me, that having understood I may
repent before thy Son and before thee and commit this sin no
more." And still weeping I sent my spiritual son Simeon to the
church for the breviary and holy water. He was a youth of Evfimej's
sort, about fourteen years old. Simeon and Evfimej lived together
in friendship, rejoicing and sustaining one another through Holy
Writ and their rule, both living staunchly in piety, in fasting and
in prayer. After weeping for his friend, Simeon went to the church
and brought back the book and the holy water. And I began to
recite the prayers of Basil the Great over the frenzied lad, with
Simeon's help: he arranged the censer and candles and carried the
holy water for me; others held the raving boy down. And when
this part of the prayer was reached, "In the name of the Lord
'I charge thee, thou dumb and deaf spirit, come out of this creation
of God and enter no more into him,' but go thou into an empty
place wherein men dwell not, but only God doth descry," the   299
devil wouldn't obey, he wouldn't come out of my brother. And
I again said the same thing the second time around, but still the
devil wouldn't obey and afflicted my brother even worse. Ah, woe
is me! How can I speak of this? It's shameful and I don't dare, but
because of the Elder Epifanij's charge I'll go on.

This is how it was: I took the censer and censed the icons and
the possessed, and then fell hard on a bench, having wept for

many hours. After arising I shouted that same declaration of St. Basil's at the devil: "Come out of this creation of God!" The devil doubled my brother into a hoop, "and rent him sore, and came out," and sat on the window ledge. But my brother "was as one   300 dead." I sprinkled him with holy water. Coming to his senses, he pointed at the devil sitting on the window ledge, but himself said nothing, for his tongue was bound. I sprinkled the window ledge with holy water, and the devil came down to the millstone corner. My brother pointed at him there too, and I sprinkled there with the water too. And from there the devil went onto the stove. And my brother pointed there too. And I was there too with that water. My brother pointed under the stove, but then crossed   301 himself. And I didn't go after the devil, but gave my brother to drink abundantly of the holy water in the name of the Lord. And sighing from the depths of his heart he said unto me, "God save you, Father, for taking me away from the tsarevich of devils and his two princes! My brother Avvakum will bow down to the earth to you for your goodness. Yes, and a 'God save you' to that boy who went to the church for the book and the holy water and gave you a hand in fighting them. He has the likeness of Simeon, my friend. They were leading me along the Sundovik river and beating me, and themselves said, 'You were given over   302 to us because your brother Avvakum traded that book for a horse, and you love her.' So," he said, "I have to talk to my brother, so he'll get that book back and give our cousin money for it." And I said to him, "My light," said I, "I'm your brother Avvakum." And he answered me, "What kind of brother of mine can you be? You're my priest. You took me away from the tsarevich and those princes. But my brother lives over in Lopatišči; he'll bow down to the earth to you." I gave him again of the holy water. And he took the vessel away from me and practically ate it – sweet was that water to him! He drained the water and I rinsed out the vessel and gave him some more, but he didn't drink it.

I spent that whole winter's night stewing over him. I lay down with him just a bit, then went to the church to chant Matins. With me gone, the devils fell upon him again, but easier than before. After returning from church I anointed him with oil, and the devils again came forth, and his mind was made whole. But he was the worse for wear, broken in body by the devils.

He'd look at the stove and shy away in fear. When I went somewhere the devils would start in defiling him. I fought those devils like dogs for about three weeks because of my sin, until I got the book and gave money for it. And I journeyed to my friend, the Abbot Ilarion, and he took out a bit of communion bread for my brother. He lived rightly then, he that's now the Archbishop of Riazan and a torturer of Christians. And I bowed down to the 303 earth before other clergy about my brother, and they pleaded with God for us sinners. And my brother was freed from the devils. Such a sin was transgression of my confessor's commandment! What will come of transgressing the commandment of the Lord? Alas, then only fire and affliction! I don't know how to while away my days! I am swathed in weakness of mind and hypocrisy, I am covered with lies, I am arrayed in hatred of my brother and love of myself, I am perishing in the condemnation of all men; seeming to be something, I am excrement and pus, an accursed man – just plain shit! I stink all over, in body and soul! It would be good for me to live with dogs and hogs in their pens; they stink just like my soul, with an evil-smelling stench. But hogs and hounds stink by their nature, while I stink from my sins like a dead dog cast out into a city street. God save those bishops who covered me up with earth. Though I stink here for myself, working my evil deeds, at least I won't seduce others! So help me, it's good this way!

Yes, and into this dungeon there came to me the lunatic Kiriluško, a musketeer from Moscow and my guard. I cropped his 304 hair and washed him and changed his clothes – there was no end to the fleas. I was locked up with him, the two of us lived together, and the third there with us was Christ and the most immaculate Mother of God. He used to shit and piss on himself, the poor, dear soul, and I would clean him off. He'd ask to eat and drink, but without a blessing he dared not take any. He didn't want to stand during the Office – the devil kept putting him to sleep. And I would whip him with my prayer beads, so he'd start to recite a prayer standing up and make his prostrations after me. And when I finished my Office he'd start raving again. Around me he would rave and drivel, but whenever I went to sit a spell with the Elder in his dungeon, I put him on a bench and without commanding him to get up I blessed him. And while I was sitting with the Elder he'd lie there not getting up, fastened down by God. And lying there

he'd rave. There were icons and books, bread, kvas, and such near
the head of the bench, but with me gone he didn't touch anything.
When I came back he used to get up, and the devil made him do
foul things to vex me. I'd shout, so he would sit down. When I was
fixing our vittles, he'd ask to eat and try to steal some before
dinnertime. But when I said the Lord's Prayer and gave the bless-   305
ing before dinner, he wouldn't eat of that nourishment, he'd
ask for some unblessed. So I stuffed it in his mouth by main force,
and he'd weep and swallow. When I fed him with fish, the devil
in him would rage and howl, and himself say from within him,
"You have taken away my strength!" So after lamenting before   306
the Lord, I would shackle him through fasting and tame him
through Christ. Later on I anointed him with oil, and this eased
him from the devil. He lived with me a month or more. Before his
death he came to his senses. I confessed him and gave him the
Sacrament, and he passed on quickly, the dear soul. And I bought
a coffin and a shroud and directed that he be buried by the church,
and I had a priest recite the forty-day requiem. He lay by me dead   307
for a day, and during the night I arose, and after praying to God,
blessing his body, and kissing him, I again lay down beside him to
sleep. He was my dear, dear comrade! Glory be to God in this!
Now it's him, but tomorrow I too will die.

And there was a lunatic living with me in Moscow – called
Filipp he was – after I journeyed out of Siberia. He was chained
to the wall in a corner of my house, as the devil in him was uncommonly harsh and savage; he would beat and brawl, and the help
couldn't live in peace with him. And sinner that I am, when I came
with the Cross and holy water he became obedient; like a dead man
he fell down before the Cross of Christ and dared do nothing
against me. And through the prayers of the Holy Fathers, the power
of God cast out the devil from him, only his mind still wasn't
quite whole. Fëdor, the fool in Christ, was told to look after him,
he who was strangled by the apostates at Mezen for the sake of
the Christian faith. He recited the Psalter over Filipp and taught
him the Prayer to Jesus. I myself was away from home during the   308
day, and only at night did I minister to Filipp. One time I returned
from Fëdor Rtiščev very heavy at heart, for in his house I had
clamored much with the heretics over the faith and the law. But
at that time a commotion had commenced in my house too. The

Archpriestess and her maid, the widow Fetin'ja, were having high
words; the devil had stirred them up over nothing. And when I
returned, I beat them both and offended them grievously, from a
heavy heart. I sinned before God and before them. Later the devil   309
in Filipp began to rage, and he started breaking his chain in his
frenzy, and shouting past bearing. Terror fell on all the servants,
and the uproar was exceeding great. Wanting to calm him, I went
over to him not having done penance, but it wasn't like before. He
grabbed me and started to beat and flay me and to rip me apart
like a cobweb, every whichway, and himself said, "You've fallen   310
into my hands!" I managed a prayer, but without the works the
words can't heal. The servants couldn't pull him off, but as for me,
I gave myself over to him. I could see that I'd sinned – let him beat
me. But – miraculous is the Lord! – he beat away but nothing hurt.
Afterwards he cast me away from himself, and himself said,
"I'm not afraid of you." So it was bitter for me then. "A devil is
having his way with me," I said. I lay there a bit, listening to my
conscience. Having arisen, I sought out my wife and with tears
began begging forgiveness before her, and myself said, bowing
down to the earth, "I've sinned, Anastasija Markovna, forgive me,
sinner that I am!" And she bowed down to me likewise. Next I
begged forgiveness of Fetin'ja in the same manner. Then I lay
down in the middle of an upper room and commanded everyone
to lash me across my accursed back, five blows each. About twenty
people were there; and my wife and children, everyone, wept and
whipped. And I said, "If anyone does not flog me, he shall have no
part with me in the Kingdom of Heaven." And not wanting it   311
they flogged and wept, and I met each blow with a prayer. And
when all had flogged me, I arose and begged forgiveness before
them. And seeing what needs be, the devil came out of Filipp
again. And I blessed him with the Cross, and he became good-
tempered like before. Later he was made whole through the mercy
of God in Jesus Christ our Lord. To him be the glory!

When I was in Siberia – or still on the way there – and was
living in Tobol'sk, a lunatic called Fëdor was brought to me.
Savage and then some was that devil in him. He had fornicated
with his wife on Easter, heaping curses on the festival all the while.   312
His wife told on him, and right there he fell into a frenzy. I kept
him in my house about two months, and I besought the Deity

much on his behalf. I led him to the church and anointed him with oil, and God had mercy; he became healthy and his mind was made whole. And during the liturgy he started chanting with me from the choir during the Transposition of the Host, and this 313 vexed me. So after beating him in the choir I ordered the sexton to chain him to the wall in the narthex. But he wrenched the ring out of the wall and ran away during the Mass, raging even worse than before. And he went to the senior commander's house; he 314 smashed their chests, put on the Princess' clothes, and drove them out. The Prince was enraged and had him dragged off to prison by many people. But he beat up every one of the poor prisoners there in the prison and smashed the stove. So the Prince ordered him banished to the village, to his wife and children. But he wandered about the villages, up to the most foul mischief. Everyone ran from him. The commanders were enraged and wouldn't turn him over to me. I was forever weeping before the Lord on his account.

Later, a decree came from Moscow ordering me banished from Tobol'sk to the Lena, that great river. And on St. Peter's Day, as I was getting ready to leave in the prame, Fëdor came up to me whole in mind, and before the people he bowed down to my feet there on the prame, and himself said, "God save you, Father, for your grace, that you had mercy on me. It was the third day I'd been running around in the wilderness, and you appeared to me and blessed me with the Cross, and the devils ran away from me. So I came to bow down to you and to ask again for a blessing from you." And looking at him I wept a bit and rejoiced in the greatness of God, for the Lord heeds and succors us all. He brought health to him and happiness to me! And I taught him, and blessing him I let him go to his home, to his wife and children. As for myself, I sailed into exile, entreating Christ our Light, the Son of God, on his behalf, that he might preserve him henceforth from enmity. And when I was journeying back I asked about him and was told, "He passed on about three years after you left, and he'd been living like a good Christian with his wife and children." And that's good for a fact! Let this be to the glory of God!

Forgive me, Elder, together with that other servant of Christ; you have charged me to speak of these things. Although I've already gabbled on and on, still I'll tell you another tale. When I was still a priest, in the same place where the devils afflicted my brother, 315 there was a young widow living in my home. Long ago it was, and here I've gone and forgotten her name! I remember now, she was called Afimja. She'd busy about, and fix our vittles, and do everything right. Just when we were beginning the Office one evening, a devil knocked her to the ground. All lifeless she was, just like stone, it seemed she wasn't breathing; he had stretched her out in the middle of the room, her arms and her legs – she was lying like she was dead. And reciting the "Holy Mother Glorified by All,"   316 I censed with the censer, then laid the Cross on her head, all the while saying the prayers of St. Basil. So her head beneath the Cross was freed, the woman even started talking, but her arms and legs and body were still stiff and stonelike. And I stroked along her arm with the Cross, so that arm was freed, then along the other, and the other was freed too. I stroked her belly, so the woman sat up. But her legs were still stonelike. I didn't dare stroke her thereabouts with the Cross. I thought and thought, then I stroked her legs as well, and the woman was freed entirely. She arose praying to God and bowed down before me. Even so, some snake in the grass – not a devil exactly – was still in her, and it toyed with her like this for a long time. I anointed her with oil and it went away altogether. God granted she was made whole. But two other lunatics, both Vasilijs, were once chained in my house. It's strange to talk about them even – they ate their own dung.

Should I tell you yet another tale, Elder? It now seems somewhat shameful, but here's how it was. In Tobol'sk there was a maid living with me called Anna. She was my spiritual daughter; uncommonly zealous she was about her rule, in church and in private, and she always disdained the seductions of this world. The devil envied her virtue and brought her sorrow on account of her first master Elizar; she grew up in his house after she was brought out of captivity among the Kalmyks. She had guarded her virginity with her purity, and when she was filled with good fruits the devil stole them away. She wanted to leave me and marry her first master, and she started to cry all the time. But the Lord set a devil on her and humbled her, since she no longer heeded me in anything, nor was she mindful of her prostrations. When we'd start to recite the Office, she'd stand in her place with folded hands, and that's how she'd stand straight through. God saw her contrariness and sent a devil to her; once standing there during the office she fell into a frenzy. And I, poor man, I was sorry; I blessed her with the Cross and sprinkled her with holy water, and then the devil left her. And so it happened many a time. But she persisted in her foolishness and stubbornness. And in his kindly cunning God punished her another way: she dozed off during the Office, then fell down on a bench to sleep. And for three days and three nights she slept without waking up. I only censed her now and then as she slept. Then, once and for all, she stopped breathing. She died, I expect.

But on the fourth day she came to her senses. She sat up and wept. She was given to eat, but wouldn't eat. When I had finished the Canonical Office, blessed the help, and released them, I again began to make prostrations in the dark, without a fire. She came to me on the sly and with a prayer, and she fell at my feet. I moved away from her and sat down at a table. And she came close again, up to the table, and weeping she said, "Listen, my lord, to what I was commanded to tell you." I began listening to her. "When I dozed off and fell over during the Office," she said, "two angels came to me, and they took me and led me along a narrow path. And on the left side I heard lamenting and sobbing and pitiful voices. Then they brought me into a bright place, so very beautiful it was, and showed me many beautiful dwellings and mansions. And more beautiful than all the others was one mansion; it shone more than the others, with a beauty beyond words to describe, and it was so very big. They led me into it," she said, "and there were tables standing and spread with linen, and on them were platters with nourishment. At the end of the table a leafy tree was stirring, adorned with many beauties. And I heard the voices of birds in the tree, but now I just can't describe how sweet and nice they were! After keeping me there awhile, they led me back out of the mansion again, and they said, 'Do you know whose mansion this is?' And I answered, 'I don't know, let me go into it.' But they answered, 'This is the mansion of your confessor, Archpriest Avvakum. Heed him and live as he bids you: how to hold your fingers and cross yourself, and how to make prostrations in prayer to God. Oppose him in nothing, so that you may be here with him. But if you don't start heeding him you'll be in that other place, where you heard the weeping. Tell this to your confessor. We leading you aren't devils; look – we have

317

wings and devils don't.' And I looked," said she, "and, Father, there was linen by their ears." And she bowed down to me, begging   318 forgiveness. Afterwards she straightened up in everything.

When I was banished from Tobol'sk I left her there with a spiritual son. She wanted to take the veil, but the devil again had it his way; she married Elizar and had some little ones. And when she heard after eight years that I was coming back, she took leave of her husband and took the veil. But when she was living with her husband, God punished her now and then: a devil afflicted her. And when I arrived in Tobol'sk, she had taken the veil only the month before; and she carried two babes up to me, and placing those tots before me she wept and sobbed, repenting and rebuking herself without shame. And to humble her before men, I shouted at her time and again, and she was forgiven her transgression in repenting before everyone. And when I had troubled her much, I forgave her completely. She entered the church for Mass behind me. And a devil fell upon her during the Transposition of the Host.   319 She started shouting and crying out, barking like a dog, bleating like a goat, and cuckooing like a cuckoo. And I was grieved for her. I left off chanting the Song of the Cherubim, took the Cross from the communion table, and going up into the choir I shouted, "I repudiate thee in the name of the Lord! You have afflicted her enough, devil! God forgives her in this age and that to come!" And the devil came out of her. She rushed up to me and fell before me because of her fault. But blessing her with the Cross, I forgave her from that time forth, and she was made whole in body and soul. And she left for Russia with me. When I was shorn, in that year she suffered with my children at the hands of Metropolitan Pavel in the Patriarch's Court for the sake of the faith and the righteousness of the law. They dragged her around and afflicted her with some to spare. As a nun her name was Agaf'ja.

Father, mothers used to bring their little ones to me in my house when they suffered from rupture. And my own little ones, when they suffered in childhood from rupture, I would say a priestly prayer and anoint all their senses with holy oil, and putting oil on my hand I'd wipe it on the youngster's back and testicles. And by God's mercy the rupture would pass away in childhood. And if affliction belched forth in anyone, I'd do the same, and God would make them whole, because of his love for mankind.

And when I was still a priest, in those first days when I had just turned to my labors in Christ, a devil scared me this way. My wife was grievously ill, and her confessor had come to her. Deep in the night I left our place for the church, to get the book for her confession. And when I came to the church porch, till then a little table had been standing there, but when I came up that table started hopping about in its place, acted on by a devil. But I wasn't frightened, and after praying before the icon I signed the table with my hand, and going over I set it down, and it cut short its capers. When I entered the narthex, there I saw another devil's prank. A corpse was in the narthex, in a coffin on a bench, and acted on by that devil the board on top opened and the shround started to stir, frightening me. But praying to God I signed the corpse with my hand, and everything was as before. When I entered the sanctuary, sure enough the chasubles and dalmatics were flying from place to place, frightening me again. But I prayed and kissed the communion table, and I blessed the vestments with my hand, and drawing close I touched them, and they hung there as always. Then I got the book and left the church. There you have the kind of devilish devices used against us! But enough talk of this. What can't the power of the Cross and holy oil do for the possessed and the sick through God's grace! Yes, and it behooves us to remember this: it's not for our sake, it's not to us but to his own name that the Lord gives the glory. But I, the scum of the earth, what could I do if it weren't for Christ? It is fitting that I weep for myself. Judas was a miracle worker, but for his love of silver he fell to the devil. And the devil himself was in heaven, but for his pride was he cast down. Adam was in paradise, but for his lust was he driven out and condemned to five thousand five hundred years in hell. After this let him who in understanding "thinketh he standeth take heed lest he fall." Hang on to the feet of Christ and pray to the Mother of God and all the saints, and all will be well!

Well, Elder, you've listened to more than enough of my gabbling. In the name of the Lord I command you: write down for the servant of Christ how the Mother of God crumpled that devil in her hands and turned him over to you, and how those ants ate at your private parts, and how that devil set your wood on fire and your cell was burnt but everything in it remained whole, and how you shouted to Heaven, and whatever else you recall, to the glory of Christ and the Mother of God. Heed what I'm saying: if you don't start writing I'll be vexed and no mistake! You loved listening to me, so why be ashamed? Say something, if only a little! The Apostles Paul and Barnabas related before everyone at the council in Jerusalem "what miracles and wonders God had wrought among the Gentiles by them," in Acts, lesson 36; and in lesson 42, "and the name of the Lord Jesus was magnified, and many that believed came, and confessed, and shewed their deeds." Yes, and much of 321 this is found in the Epistles of Paul and in Acts. Tell away, never fear, just keep your conscience clear! Speak, seeking glory not for yourself but for Christ and the Mother of God. Let the servant of Christ rejoice in reading it. When we die, he will read and remember us before God. And we will entreat God on behalf of those who read and listen. They will be our people there at Christ's side, and we theirs, forever and ever. Amen.

Traditional eight-cornered cross sketched by Epifanij (Redaction 3); symbolic lance, reed with sponge, nails, Adam's skull, and initials of "Golgotha was Paradise."

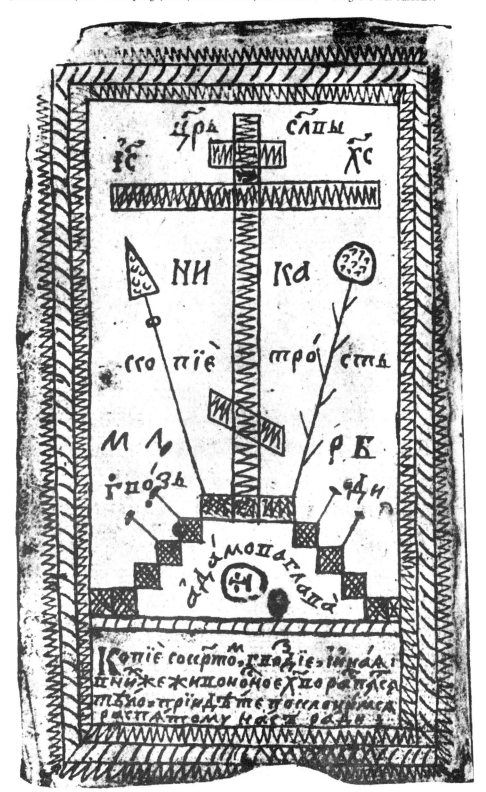

Pall made to the order of Ivan the Terrible (1557)
Satin, colored silks, gold and silver thread

COMMENTARIES AND NOTES

†

Summary depiction of 17th-century Russian eschatology: The Church is a boat sailing on a stormy sea, warring with the forces of evil. This together with the new Jerusalem, Babylon, the Whore of Babylon, foreign heresies and alien faiths, torturers, and heretics (all depicted here) are constantly reiterated images in Old-Believer literature.

ON THE TASKS OF STYLISTICS: OBSERVATIONS REGARDING THE STYLE OF *THE LIFE OF THE ARCHPRIEST AVVAKUM*

V. V. Vinogradov

Every literary work represents an organization of verbal material and is thus subject to investigation by the linguist. He considers it representative of a linguistic type that has developed organically within a specific dialectal environment and is delineated by precise chronological boundaries. From this perspective the linguistic features of a work interest the linguist insofar as they characterize the speech of some social group (i.e., dialect) during a particular historical period; separated from the individual psyche of the author, these features combine with similar linguistic phenomena and establish the stages in the evolution of the language's constituent elements. But this need not exhaust the linguist's interest in literature. After all, a literary work is not only a particular manifestation of collective linguistic activity; it also represents an individual's selection and creative transformation of the linguistic resources of his time, so that particular conceptions and emotions might receive aesthetically effective expression. Here the linguist's task is to find in the selection of words and their organization into syntactic units the psychologically consistent system that unifies an artist's methods, and through it, to discover the ways in which the verbal material is shaped aesthetically. The concept of a commonly shared dialect is replaced by the notion of individual poetic style understood as the aesthetically creative selection, interpretation, and disposition of verbal signs (*simvoly*).[1] The study of individual styles is the fundamental problem of stylistics.

Artists akin in the devices they apply to the available linguistic material comprise what has been called by common assent a literary school. Without exception the general stylistic characteristics of all schools of poetry in every epoch can probably be

117

reduced to a definition of the norms governing the use of verbal signs and their syntactic organization within the boundaries of one dialect or another. From this it would follow that even though the style considered appropriate for each genre by the predominant school in any era defines to some extent the general coloration of the era, that school cannot be recognized as the era's exclusive spokesman regarding its aesthetic norms. It seems to me that the notion of the "style of the era" ought to be relegated to a special area of stylistics, that which studies the aesthetic norms governing everyday speech within dialects. Certainly every speaker of whatever dialect makes aesthetic judgments in selecting one among several possible expressions of a thought. And just as certainly he has at his disposal general norms for making such selections. It seems then that stylistics has two aspects: (1) the stylistics of conversational and written speech in all the diversity of their functions, and in relation to this, their structural types; (2) the stylistics of poetic speech (i.e., the language of literature). The stylistics of everyday speech provides the background against which the uniqueness of poetic creativity is apprehended. Henceforth I will concentrate only on the latter.

Stylistics is confronted by two problems in studying changes in poetic phenomena, considered singly and in combination: individual poetic style and the style of the literary school. Consequently, with regard to poetic language the tasks of historical stylistics are as follows: (1) clarifying the nature and order of changes in poetic style, changes that develop through the utilization and creative transformation by individual artists of the resources from the past and present provided by their language – the standard literary language, the conversational language of the intelligentsia and that of the people – taking into account the complexity of the dialectal aggregates which comprise them. To put it differently, studying individual poetic styles in their historical succession against the background of the general history of the language and the history of linguistic taste; (2) classifying these individual styles into schools through the abstraction of similar characteristics, and indicating the center of gravity in the style of each school; (3) studying how the style of a school disintegrates, how it is transformed into a series of clichés, and how they are reworked in new styles. We must remember, however, that a creative artist is not constrained by the style of any school. Having recourse to many devices for verbal construction, he may in some instances be said to participate simultaneously in several schools. From this it follows that in defining the style of a school it is more expedient to focus on the linguistic proximity of works of art rather than on the linguistic affinities of persons. The style of a school, then, is the totality of shared devices for the selection and aesthetic organization of verbal material within a significant group of literary works chronologically contiguous and authored by various persons. (Such an integral system could only be engendered through the imitation of a "master" by a group of lesser writers.) Any stylistic classification must consider the functional varieties of poetic speech; for example, the language used in the novella, in dramatic dialogues, in the lyric poem are not functionally comparable. Finally, as regards the various kinds of poetic speech, a detailed description of distinctions among the principles governing the selection and disposition of signs, their syntactical combinations, and semantic shifts must obviously be based on the analysis of a large body of material.

In my view a scheme for the stylistic description of any work should include two headings: the verbal sign and composition (or syntax). The former studies the ways in which an artist accomplishes the aesthetic transformation of verbal signs, that is, the devices which govern their use and the distinctions and nuances of meaning created by usage within his aesthetic system: both the nuances surrounding individual signs and the general "type" of semantic transformations characteristic of a writer's oeuvre are equally important questions. Relevant here are the motives for selecting one aggregation or another of related signs, as well as the principal ways in which they coalesce into "nests" on the basis of euphonic, semantic, or other principles. (Here, of course, we are concerned not only with separate words but with fixed expressions, frozen formulas, and quotations.) Only after this is it possible to define the links between the writer's style and the literary traditions which intersect in his work. The second division of stylistics, composition, studies the principles governing the disposition of words: the various types of syntactic organization and the devices for linking and comparing syntactic wholes. We must add that the use in poetic speech of syntactic patterns characteristic of conversational or literary language is complicated and distorted by a variety of factors (euphonic, rhythmic, intonational, melodic) which can either facilitate a general harmony among the constituent elements or emphasize one element as dominant.

On the basis of these observations we can proceed to a description of the style of *The Life of the Archpriest Avvakum*.[2]

Avvakum's *Life* has the form of a guileless oral improvisation, in his words, a "conversation" or "gabbling" (*vjakan'e*); hence, the text contains frequent addresses to listeners, the Elder Epifanij and the "servant of Christ." The narrator also creates the impression of persistently observing the impact his story has on them, and he interrupts it in moments of simulated self-accusation with apologies and pleas for forgiveness directed to them. At one point Avvakum breaks off his tale altogether, pleading with Epifanij to insert into the text his written judgment regarding one of Avvakum's actions (p.75).* The fundamental tone of the work is profoundly personal, the tone of a simple-hearted, trusting narrator whose memories move in a torrent of verbal associations which produce lyrical digressions and a disordered, emotional coordination of narrative segments. And the Archpriest is seemingly too weak to control this spontaneous movement (e.g., "Enough of this, I've wandered a long way," p.76; "Although I've already gabbled on and on, still I'll tell you another tale," p.107). This conversational narration of remarkable events ordered by chronology or similarity (e.g., the episodes concerning persecution by officials or the exorcism of devils) establishes the principal stylistic level and organization of this *skaz*.

At times, however, the *skaz* is supplanted by the solemn sermon; lyrical appeals are addressed to crowds of "true believers" and "Nikonians" standing as it were behind Avvakum's immediate listeners; for example: "Alas! your poor Nikonians! You are perishing from your wicked, unruly ways!" (p.94); "So speak out the name of Christ, you true believers, stand in the middle of Moscow and cross yourself with the Sign of our Savior Jesus Christ, with two fingers ... " (p.100). In alternating the "gabbling" with the solemnly accusatory or persuasive pathos of the preacher Avvakum makes of his *Life* "a book of eternal life." And he begins to illuminate events in his experience with biblical quotations, so that archaic, ecclesiastical stylistic constructions penetrate the conversational element.

---

*Pages indicated in parentheses refer to passages in this volume.

In this connection the narrative *skaz* itself displays a subtle pattern created by two psychologically parallel and mutually conditioning conceptual orders which determine two corresponding stylistic levels. On one plane it is Avvakum's life story, the tale of his "wandering," his "sailing" on the sea of life. But his method of depicting real events from his life is governed by ecclesiastical and biblical literature, within the confines of which his creative intuition revolved. The narration of events is shaped by biblical plots and stylistic formulas, and it is emblazoned with verbal colors drawn from liturgical and hagiographical materials. The "new Gospel" is thus built on the foundations of the old. (Such duality of vision is of course quite general in hagiography.) Before all else, references to biblical stories often occur at the beginnings of episodes and determine to a significant degree their exposition. For example, at the outset of the tale concerning the "loose fish" (*zamotaj*) whom Avvakum saved from his pursuers by hiding him under his wife's sleeping mat, he says, "Like the harlot Rahab of Jericho who hid the agents of Joshua, son of Nun, so I hid him away" (p. 74). Or conversely, the meaning of an event already narrated is then enhanced by the introduction of analogous biblical motifs (e.g., the stories about the solar eclipses, 38–39). Or an entire episode may be compressed into a single sentence and illuminated by solemn similes with biblical referents; for example: "And we baptized him [Avvakum's son Prokopij] on the way, just as Phillip baptized the eunuch long ago" (p. 46). In another instance Eremej Paškov's detachment is destroyed in answer to Avvakum's prayers; Avvakum shapes the exposition by a contrastive comparison between his own behavior and that of Christ in an analogous situation (p. 71). This again casts a certain stylistic reflection on the narrative itself.

More frequent than the use of biblical references in such parallels, however, is the subtle insertion of biblical texts into the speech of characters, the result being the temporary replacement of one set of characters by another. The repentant Evfimej Stefanovič cries out in the words of the Prodigal Son, "Forgive me, my lord, I have sinned before God and before you" (p. 48; cf. Luke 15:21). The same words are used by the cellarer Nikodim after being healed by Avvakum (p. 88). Paškov, tormentor of the Archpriest, speaks in the words of Judas, "I have sinned, accursed man, I have spilled innocent blood" (p. 72; cf. Matt. 27:4). And after a terrible beating by Paškov, Avvakum himself echoes the righteous Job, "Who will set a judge between me and thee?" (cf. Job 9:32; 14:3; 19:7), denouncing himself in the same place for this comparison. Stylistic details from the trial of Christ are apparent in the portrayal of Avvakum's hearing; shortly thereafter Avvakum indicates this biblical reference directly by comparing his enemies to Annas and Caiaphas (93—94). In a series of tales "Pilate" appears as a character, and Avvakum's sons, who in fear denied his faith, are compared with "another close friend," the Apostle Peter (p. 95).

As I noted above, this "book of eternal life" accompanies the biblically conditioned experiences and miracles of Avvakum with religious moralizing, which produces a richer, more colorful stylistic design. The solemn, bookish stylistic level appears in its purest form in formulas of moral exhortation, above all in the brief precepts that conclude numerous episodes; for example: "Thus doth God fashion his people" (p. 48); "Thus it is that God scorneth the scorners, but he giveth grace unto the lowly" (p. 48); and so on. These edifying expostulations can develop into an entire sermon, of which, aside from the exordium, there are two in the holograph of the *Life*: one on the use of the Eucharist in healing, which occurs after Avvakum's first miracle (66—67), and the second in the conclusion of the *Life* proper, before the tales about lunatics. Whether brief or lengthy, these moralistic, exhortative commentaries form a distinct stylistic stratum which is often set off by Avvakum himself; in returning from them to his story he uses variations on the formula *Na pervoe vozvratimsja* ("Let's get back to my story again") to fix his listeners' attention on the interrupted tale.

To summarize: *The Life of the Archpriest Avvakum* is fundamentally a *skaz* ("gabbling"),[3] that is, vividly colored, emotional, conversational speech. At times this narration is merged with elements deriving from ecclesiastical, especially biblical, style, which are found in their purest form in the precepts concluding the narration of particular events. I will discuss these constituent elements of Avvakum's style in terms of the categories I have proposed, the verbal sign and composition.

Most apparent in Avvakum's diction are the ecclesiastical, bookish elements; they are sharply differentiated from their vernacular environment both in outer form and in the principles governing their organization. But the "weaving of words" has no place in

Avvakum's style. Consequently, compound words and constructions involving solemn epithets are rarely encountered in the
Life, contrary to the general inclination toward these devices
observable in the works of other writers of the period. Verbal
signs of this sort consist almost entirely of very familiar ecclesiastical and biblical phrases, that is, groups of words virtually fused
through habitual usage. Habitual usage also determines the nature
of the emotions and mental images evoked by these solemn, bookish
constructions; each is essentially a ready rubric representing a
body of complex perceptions. On this stylistic level events are not
depicted in detail but assigned to a definite type and surrounded
by a nimbus of lofty emotion; actions and scenes are not described,
they are merely named in a solemn manner. For example: *Zavopil
vysokim glasom* 'He cried out in a loud voice' (101–02); the fixity
of this utterance is indicated by similar constructions in *The Deeds
of Digenis Akritas* (*Zavopi glasom veliim veleglasno*), in the *Life*
of the Elder Epifanij (*Zavopel velikim golosom*), and in Revelations
6:9-10 (*Vozopiśa glasom velikim*). Similar observations can be
made about the following expressions: "Sighing from the depths
of his heart" (p.103); "I counted all this as dung" (p. 80); and
"Fear God, who sitteth above the Cherubim and gazeth into the
abyss" (p. 59). Frozen epithets should be considered in this same
category: *tesnyj put'* 'narrow path' (p.109), *glasy umilenny* 'pitiful
voices' (p.109), *serdečnii oči* 'eyes of the heart' (p. 45), and so on.

Also characteristic of Avvakum's style is the frequent use of
familiar quotations from the Scriptures and ecclesiastical texts;
usually they are applied to the events being described without
indication of their source. They may appear as frozen formulas
within larger syntactic constructions or as independent, recurring
statements. For example: "God poured forth the vials of his wrathful fury upon the Russian land" (p. 39; cf. Rev. 16:1); "Let him
that thinketh he standeth take heed lest he fall" (p. 54 and elsewhere; cf. I Cor. 10:12); and "The keepers before the door kept
the prison" (p. 99; cf. Acts 12:6).

The presence of such fixed expressions in Avvakum's style is
scarcely original, but their utilization is. Most remarkable here
is the resuscitation of biblical metaphors, either through development or through linkage to words that contrast with them in
meaning or emotional timbre. Whether linked by contrast or by
similarity to particular aspects of Avvakum's story, these biblical

elements color the *skaz* in a unique manner. For example, Avvakum describes the first time his soul was brought low in ecclesiastical diction: "But I, thrice-accursed healer, I was afflicted myself, burning inwardly with a lecherous fire." Clusters of words then follow, linked by this image of fire: "And it was bitter for me . . . I lit three candles . . . raised my right hand into the flame and held it there until the evil conflagration within me was extinguished" (44–45). Such usage creates a kind of collision between two levels of meaning, the literal and the metaphorical. In the episode immediately following, an introductory biblical citation ("The sorrows of death compassed me . . ."; Psalm 116:3-4) is followed by a series of statements illuminating its factual basis: "They trampled me to death near the church. And I lay dead for more than a half an hour." The flow of these phrases is then broken with a contrasting biblical formula: "And I returned to life with a sign from God."

If this impetuous surge of words emanating from one semantic "nest" reveals Avvakum's talent for verbal association, then his etymological sensitivity (Sprachgefühl) is apparent in his unexpected juxtapositions of words that have diverged in meaning. The result is a pun: *Ja i k obedne ne pošël i obedat' ko knjazju prišël* ("So I didn't go to the service but was served dinner at a prince's instead"; 80–81); cf. *Knigu korm"čiju dal prikaščiku, i on mne mužika kormščika dal; Kak poruga delo Božie i pošël stranoju, tak i Bog k nemu strannym gnevom* [The second and third puns are lost in translation].

Such puns based on etymology return to the verbal sign some portion of its original meaning. But at times the use of words in new meanings leads to word play as well. Word play occurs when a new meaning is indicated by juxtaposing the word with itself in its usual meaning, or when a new meaning is clarified by phrases that refer to matters inaccordant with the word's usual meaning. This device is encountered on both levels of Avvakum's style: "Now there's a death without death for you! Repent you two locked up there, while the devil thinks up something else!" (p. 95). "We buried a man away from death, seeking his repentance before God" (p. 75). "And in return for all this some small boons were sent our way: they hanged two people in my house at Mezen, my spiritual children . . ." (94–95).

The essence of Avvakum's originality in the use of ecclesiastical diction is found not in his word play, however, but in his elimination of the distinct emotional boundary between the solemn ecclesiastical and the vernacular. Relevant here is the accompaniment of ecclesiastical and bookish expressions with vernacular explanations (e.g., "I was voracious [*prial''čen*], that is, I wanted to eat," p. 54 ; "The sun receded unto the east, that is, it went backwards," p. 37). However, this is merely one unremarkable manifestation of a more basic characteristic: in Avvakum's style the two diverse categories of verbal signs intersect, and the homogeneity of conservative verbal constructions governed by associations of contiguity is destroyed. If one accepts N.V. Kruševskij's formulation that "the process of a language's development can be viewed from one perspective as an unending antagonism between a progressive force shaped by associations of similarity and a conservative force shaped by associations of contiguity" (*Očerk nauki o jazyke* [Kazan', 1885] ,116–17),then one must note the extreme predominance in Avvakum's style of semantic combinations evoked by associations of similarity. The conjoining of elements from familiar ecclesiastical formulas and verbal signs from everyday speech is rooted in this strong tendency. Thus, Avvakum's originality here resides not so much in his manner of deploying and linking frozen, indivisible biblical formulas but in the way he splinters them with the vernacular, producing a marked alteration in the emotional and ideational signification of the Church Slavonicisms. Three categories of semantic transformation can be identified.
1. The substitution of a solemn word in a traditional formula with one from the vernacular is frequently observed; a kind of translation results, a shift from the elevated to the unrefined. The semantics of the whole formula are thereby changed, they are resurrected and the formula is imbued with realistic content. For example: "Hang on (*deržis'*) to the feet of Christ" (p.111; cf. "Fall down [*pripadi*] at the feet of Christ"); "They . . . didn't figure out (*ne dogadalis'*) how to seize the crown of victory" (p. 95); "I held to my rule, and up to now I've gotten along little by little" (*tjanus' pomalen'ku*; p. 84); "But looking to heaven I shouted (*kričju*) . . . " (p.59 and passim; cf. the *Life* of Epifanij: "I began to cry out [*načax vopiti*], gazing at Heaven"); "God's an old hand at miracles" (*Bog -- staroj čudotvorec*, p.96); and so on.

2. At times Church Slavonic structures are linked directly to the vernacular, or an abrupt transition from elevated to unrefined phraseology in contiguous syntactic constructions occurs. The Gefühlswerth of both signs, their emotional content and associations, is altered by this juxtaposition: "But Login blazed with the zeal of the fire of holiness, and rebuking Nikon he spat across the threshold into the sanctuary, in Nikon's face" (p. 55). "And that's why Christ our Light scared (*popužal*) me, and said unto me, 'After so great a suffering, dost thou wish to perish? Take heed lest I cut thee asunder!' " (p. 80 .) "As for that interdict of the apostates, I trample it in Christ's name, and that anathema – to put it crudely – I wipe my ass with it! The Holy Fathers of Moscow bless me . . . " (75–76).

3. Verbal signs of biblical origin sometimes prompt verbal associations with everyday vocabulary for Avvakum; the former are thereby provided with a realistic elucidation and deprived of their solemnity: " 'On him a stone shall fall and sweep him away.' Listen to what the prophet says together with the apostle, that a millstone will grind the fool into flour" (redaction 3). [Cf. other examples above illustrating the "resuscitation" of biblical metaphors.]

Central to these three categories are affective dissonances created by the penetration of ecclesiastical phraseology by vernacular elements (usually semantic equivalents of those anticipated) with their concrete, tangible meanings. We must conclude, then, that the vernacular level in the *Life* is shaped by specific norms reflecting this congruency in meaning between the two levels. The great influx of such diction into the genre of the *vita* is the measure of Avvakum's originality, although it is found to a lesser degree in the works of other schismatics. The description of the vernacular level of Avvakum's style must begin with those ecclesiastical images which provide the background for perceiving its verbal signs. The following semantic categories are most characteristic and stable.

1. A traditional ecclesiastical metaphor found much favor among persecuted schismatics during the seventeenth century: they were drowning sailors in a boat in the midst of a stormy sea during a savage winter, and they were poor wanderers on land. The brothers Pleščeev wrote in their "epistle" to their confessor Ivan Neronov:

"For in truth the winter is now savage, and bitter is the drowning . . . Now as regards the Church . . . the waves are ever more: multitudes of zealots for Christ's Church are lying on the bottom of the boat, weeping and suffering." In *A Reflection on a Newly Contrived Means of Self-Slaughter*: "The storm arose, and the wind with the whirlwind did roar . . . and not a little distress was there among the drowning." Avvakum, in his *Book of Conversations*, admits: "But we are still at sea, sailing over the deep, and we do not see our harbor" (cf. "For twenty-two summers I sailed hither and yon"). He describes his general situation in his *Life* (redaction 3) in almost the same words: "That's fine, he's already finished his labors in Christ (*podvig*). But how will we make it to that harbor? We are still sailing upon the deep, the shore can't be seen, we must row zealously" (cf. "With Christ we will sail smoothly to our harbor," ibid.). With regard to dry land the "sailor" is transformed into a "tramp" (*brodjaga*), a "wanderer" (*volokita*). These images neutralize the concrete, realistic meaning of descriptions of the experiences of Avvakum and his spiritual children (who "drag themselves" [*voločatsja*], "drag along" [*taskajutsja*], "wander," and "sail"), making them metaphorical.

Thus, after noting the principal stages of his spiritual journey at the outset of the *Life*, Avvakum tells about one of his own past sins, his repentance, and a vision he then experienced (all of this as motivation for his subsequent suffering and separation from his spiritual children). He describes his boat in the vision as "not adorned with gold but motley colored – red, and white, and blue, and black, and ashen – . . . And I shouted, 'Whose boat is this?' And he sitting in it answered, 'Your boat. Sail in it with your wife and children if you're going to pester the Lord.' And I was seized by trembling . . . 'What sort of voyage will it be?' "(44–45.)When he goes into exile Avvakum recalls this boat: "So then I climbed into my boat again, the one that had been shown to me, of which I have spoken previously" (p. 58; cf. "It was the fourth summer of my voyage from Tobol'sk," p. 64). Two other boats depicted in the *Life* are the "golden boats" of Luka and Lavrentij, who "set [Avvakum and his family] on the path to salvation" (p. 45). Relevant here too are descriptions of storms, as well as the sinking of the Archpriest's boats and his miraculous threefold deliverance from destruction. Thus, this ecclesiastical sign is developed in a series of realistic episodes; at the same time it shapes Avvakum's memories of actual events from his "voyage" and defines the nature of their stylistic reproduction.

General conditions on this dismal voyage are indicated by laconic references in the vernacular to rain and snow: "It was autumn, rain was falling on me, and all night long I lay in the downpour" (p. 60). "Down came the rain and snow, and only a poor little kaftan had been tossed across my shoulders. The water poured down my belly and back . . . " (p. 61 .) Here we can also include the depiction of the Archpriest and his family in their winter quarters: "I was lying naked under birch bark on top of the stove, my wife was right in the stove, and the children wherever. Rain had set in, our clothes were gone, . . . " (p. 70 .) The sun has no place in these stylized landscapes. Therefore, the word "sun" is used in the *Life* only in a metaphorical sense: "he who is the Sun of justice, our Light, and our Hope" (p. 87). And it is only this sun that warms Avvakum: "In a freezing tower . . . God warmed [him] even without clothes!" (p. 61 .) Against the background of these images traditional hagiographical formulas are resuscitated: "Again the devil raised up a storm against me" (p. 46 and passim).

Groups of signs associated with the notion of wandering (*volokita, brodnja*) similarly combine realistic with metaphoric meaning. The time of "wandering" is winter: "For two summers we tramped around (*brodili*) in water, and in the winters we dragged ourselves over portages (*črez voloki voločilisja*)" (p. 63). The same metaphorical pattern, again in the vernacular, extends to descriptions of the ecclesiastical environment in which the Archpriest finds himself: "We saw that winter was on the way – hearts froze and legs began to shake" (p. 52); "the winter of heresy is here (*na dvore*)," (p. 78). In precisely the same manner a realistic description of wanderers stumbling and hurting themselves on the ice in the midst of winter is transformed into an allegorical episode ("The poor Archpriestess tottered and trudged along, and then she'd fall in a heap," etc.; 67–68).

2. The second semantic category has its origins in a traditional metaphor, now dead, that was very popular in hagiographical literature: tormentors are described as beasts ("Those bloodsucking Nikonian beasts"), the antithesis of the people of God. Such imagery is pervasive in Avvakum's writings, and he breaks it down in his *Book of Conversations* by enumerating the beasts

familiar to him: "These people aren't human beings but . . . beasts — wolves, and lynxes, and lions, and bears." The shift of this ecclesiastical metaphor into the vernacular is most strongly felt when Avvakum uses abusive, "beastly" words in similes: concerning the devil, "He throws himself on a man like a mad dog" (*Book of Conversations*); concerning the Nikonians, "God-murdering enemies, mad dogs!" And concerning Nikon: "They debauched the Church together with Nikon, that long-nosed, potbellied, borzoj hound!" As elsewhere in Avvakum's work, the meaning of such "beastly" vernacular in the *Life* is shaped by the hagiographical tradition. The general antithesis noted above is emphasized: "I . . . taught the people of God, and those others I exposed for what they are, the motley beasts!" (85–86.) The bookish formulas, "He bellowed like a savage beast" and "He bellowed at him like a beast" (p. 60 and passim), are utilized directly. The man given to vanity has "beastly" characteristics: "He cavorts like a goat, . . . he rages like a lynx, he craves food like a snake; gazing at the beauty of his neighbor, he neighs like a colt" (p. 78). The depiction of the "enemies of God" conforms to these patterns. Nikon is a "hellhound" (p. 100), a "wolf" (p. 85), and a "fox" (p. 50). "Like dogs" the Nikonians "tore at" Avvakum's beard (p. 86). "Like a bunch of wolf whelps our Russians bounced up howling . . . "(p. 92). "They're wolves for a fact, they don't pity the sheep" (p. 86). "And the bishops started to buck and kick at me like goats" (p. 85). Like mad dogs the enemies of God do not speak but "bark." At one point the metaphor of the hound is realized as it is developed into an entire episode: an official "gnawed the fingers of my hand with his teeth like a dog. And when his throat filled with blood, he loosed my hand from his teeth . . . He was barking away at me." (p. 46.) In this manner ecclesiastical and vernacular signs located in the same semantic plane are interwoven, and both categories are envigorated as a result. And since the actuality of the everyday speech element is the more weighty, Church Slavonicisms break open and take on unusual semantic characteristics.

It is interesting in this context that, aside from Avvakum's habitual usage in vernacular contexts of the traditional formula of self-deprecation ("Who am I? A dead dog!" p. 81, and "I stink from my sins like a dead dog cast out into a city street," p. 104), the few remaining instances of such "beastly" images in the *Life* are found only in comparisons that reverberate with tender emotion. As a result these metaphors are completely transformed. For example, Avvakum describes himself in prison as a "little dog" lying on his "lump of straw" (p. 61).[4] Elsewhere, recalling his former sufferings, he remarks, "In this way I dragged along like a little old beast" (p. 83).

3. The third semantic category is more extensive and its makeup more complex. Analysis reveals new configurations of meanings here, but the general tendency to develop and realize biblical signs on the vernacular plane is preserved. "Satan besought God for our radiant Russia, so he might turn her crimson with the blood of martyrs" (p. 87); this conviction motivates Avvakum's use of verbal signs referring to war, which merge with the rich everyday terminology for fights, tortures, and torments. "And they started to shove me around and beat me – even the patriarchs threw themselves on me. . . . A mighty army for the Antichrist had come together!" (p. 93.) Soon there occurs a shift to the plane of everyday speech: "The troop of musketeers guarded us like brigands." The situation is then reduced to the absurd and its origins explained by reference to the devil: " . . . even went with us to shit. Remember it and you don't know whether to laugh or cry. How Satan had befogged them!" (p. 94.)

Verbal signs referring to the actions (tortures and torments) of the "imps (*šiši*) of the Antichrist," the "destroyers of Christians," are extraordinarily variegated in their associations. Especially vivid examples are the signs "to burn in the fire" and "to build a fire." On the one hand, they arouse in Avvakum's linguistic consciousness the biblical image of "the fiery furnace," the basis for an effective aphorism with contrastive parallelism between its parts: "For him who wants to be crowned, there's no point in going to Persia, Babylon's right here at home."[5] On the other hand, these signs are semantically related to a group of vernacular words referring to the kitchen: "I knew all about his hash-slinging (*strjapan'e*), how few came out of his oven alive" (p. 73). "And in Moscow others of ours were roasted and baked" (p. 99). "The apostates baked him in their fire . . . and like sweet bread was he yielded up to the Holy Trinity" (p. 91). It is interesting to note how this ecclesiastical phrase from the Canticle to the Martyrs ("like sweet bread was he yielded up to the Trinity") is merged here with the vernacular and acquires new brightness from everyday words for culinary activities (*ispeč'*, *žarit'*, *strjapat'*). Perhaps this comparison between righteous men and baked bread is the basis for the miracle involving the fool in Christ Fëdor: "And he, our light, our dear departed, he crawled into the hot oven in the bakery after the bread was taken out, and he sat, his bare backside against its bottom . . . So the monks were in terror . . ." (p. 85.)

Imagery associated with the verbal sign "to hang on the gallows" (e.g., *davit'*, *udavit'* 'crush, strangle') is no less vivid. Such imagery is unique in that it has no specific ecclesiastical source, so that it exists exclusively on the vernacular plane. Most important is the image of grasping, crushing hands, hands into which the soldiers of Christ fall — the hands of the devil, of demons, and of heretics. In this context the colloquial formula "to fall into the hands . . ." acquires special signification: "And here I had fallen into his hands myself" (p. 58). "I was even in the natives' hands" (p. 79). A devil "grabbed me and started to beat and flay me, and to rip me apart like a cobweb, every whichway, and himself said, 'You've fallen into my hands!' " (p. 106.)

Particularly numerous among the designations of the tortures and punishments that accompany the struggle are formulas referring to attacks and beatings. Here the verb form is dominant, the remainder of the formula being the minimum of complements necessary to specify the action: "He . . . beat me and in my vestments dragged me along the ground by my legs" (p. 45); "he attacked, shooting with bows and pistols" (p. 48); "in the middle of the street they beat me with clubs and stomped me" (p. 50); and so on. Usually Avvakum goes beyond a brief reference to the general nature of a particular aggressive act and depicts in the vernacular the sequence of actions that laid him low: "By the church they dragged at my hair and drummed on my sides; they jerked at my chain and spit in my eyes" (p. 54). A description of Paškov's tortures begins with a traditional ecclesiastical formula suggesting martyrdom, "And he bellowed like a savage beast"; it is then illustrated by a series of down-to-earth phrases: "he hit me on one cheek, then on the other, again on top of my head, and knocked me down; grabbing his commander's axe, he hit me three times on the back as I lay there, and stripping me he laid seventy-two blows across that same back with a knout." (p. 60.)

The memory of martyrs "abused" (*obrugannyx*) by the Nikonians evokes for Avvakum the image of "peasants" (*mužiki*): "Shorn and abused like peasants from the village they were" (p. 93). The word "peasant" (*mužik*) in Avvakum's language is rather pejorative, and he uses it freely in scornful recollections of "wizards" and "sorcerers": "She lost heart and . . . sent the baby to a peasant wizard" (p. 70); "And that evening this peasant sorcerer brought out a live ram . . . and started conjuring over it, twisting it this way and that, and he twisted its head off . . . " (p. 71). However, Avvakum also sharpens his depiction of the Nikonians' "general ruin" of his household at Mezen with the help of this same word, by having his persecutors use it: "Pilate questioned him [Luka], 'How do you cross yourself, peasant?' " (p. 95.) (Cf. Avvakum's solemn definition here of Luka's profession, "a tanner by trade.")

The associations of the word "peasant" for Avvakum are to some extent evident in the following negative parallelism: "That devil's (*bes*) no peasant, he's not afraid of a club. He's afraid of the Cross of Christ . . . " (p. 66.) In addition (and despite Avvakum's denial), a significant connection exists here between this image and another semantic grouping based on the verbal sign "devil"; it depends on the obvious homogeneity of their emotional colorations. This needs to be mentioned because descriptions of attacks on Avvakum and his spiritual children by devils frequently degenerate into comedy, owing to the nature of the images evoked by the word "devil." Depictions of struggles with devils are as realistic and down-to-earth in tone and diction as those relating to Avvakum's conflicts with the Nikonians (e.g., "I fought those devils like dogs," p.104), but the tragic atmosphere is radically diminished. The word "devil" is sometimes a synonym for brawler and scandalmonger, for a lover of "playing" (*poigrat'*) in the various meanings of this word (cf. the various meanings of this word in contemporary dialects in the 1922 edition of the Russian Academy of Sciences' *Dictionary of the Russian Language*, vol. 3, p. 107): "Even so, some snake in the grass (*prokuda-taki*) – not exactly a devil – was still in her, and it toyed (*igral*) with her like this for a long time"(p.108). " . . . that table started hopping about in its place, acted on by a devil . . . When I entered the narthex, there I saw another devil's prank (*igra*)." (p. 111.)

Such then are the connections among the semantic groups associated with beatings, humiliations, tortures, and fights.

4. The last category of verbal signs is associated with the metaphor "the people of God" or "the spiritual children" of Avvakum (e.g., "my sweet, good little children [*detuški milen'kie moi*]," p. 89; "dear Afanasij, the good soul [*Afonas'juško milen'koj*] -- he was my spiritual son," p. 91; "praiseworthy little ones [*izrjadnye detki*] they turned out to be," p. 67). Specifically it relates to the simple sentimentalism apparent in Avvakum's diction when he refers to these people. But first we must describe the general principles governing the expression of feeling in Avvakum's style.

Just as one would expect, the group of verbal signs relevant here is extraordinarily small and impoverished (ignoring interjections). Primary are laconic conversational formulas expressing emotion, usually consisting of personal forms of denominative verbs (*Ja pet' oseržus'; o pravile tužu; boitsja; opečalilsja esi;* etc.) or of short-form predicate adjectives (*povinen byvaet; one . . . dobry do menja;* etc.) or more frequently of impersonal constructions (*mne žal'; otradilo emu; mne gor'ko;* etc.). The general tendency here is toward the immediate expression of emotion. One interesting aspect of Avvakum's usage is that these words often do not denote an emotion leading to behavior appropriate to it, but rather the emotion and its behavioral symptoms are presented as if they were parallel external phenomena (e.g., "they were trembling and afraid," p. 74; "I wept and rejoiced," p. 81). Similar to these signs from the vernacular are other expressions for emotion which tend in style toward the ecclesiastical and bookish (e.g., "My spirit was terrified within me," p. 48; "I was seized by trembling," p. 45; etc.). Such abstract expressions are characteristically coupled with designations of actions that illustrate the emotion graphically (e.g., "they were good to me [*učinilis' dobry do menja*]; we forgave one another in the antechambers of the Tsar," p. 46; "Another official . . . raged savagely against me; he rushed into my house, and having beaten me . . . ," p. 45; etc.), or they are clarified through the words of others (e.g., "He was troubled [*učinil''sja pečalen*] over me. 'Why did you abandon your cathedral church?' he says." [p. 50.]). Such illustrations and clarifications are exceptions to the general tendency toward the immediate expression of emotion.

Predominant in the *skaz* are rapidly changing references to the physical symptoms of feelings ("My legs and belly turned blue," p. 63) or hurriedly depicted movements,[6] the emotional basis of which is disclosed in cryptic speeches often involving the introductory formula, "And himself said" (*A sam govorit*): "He bowed nice and low (*nizenko*) to me and himself said, 'God save you!' " (p. 71.) "Ducking behind a pine tree Eremej stopped, his hands folded, and standing there himself said, 'Lord, have mercy!' " (p. 72.) "He started . . . to rip me apart like a cobweb, every whichway, and himself said, 'You've fallen into my hands!' " (p.106.) "Before the people he bowed down to my feet there on the prame, and himself said, 'God save you, Father, for your grace.' " (p.107.)

Considering the great variety of words denoting action, it is remarkable how restricted Avvakum's vocabulary is in depicting displays of feeling among "the people of God"; most intensively used is the verb "to weep" or "lament" (*plakat', plakat'sja*). On the one hand, it is central to a formula for addressing God which is associated with the "path of sorrows" leading to heaven (e.g., "I . . . wept much over my soul before the icon," p. 43; "I wept before the icon of the Lord so that my eyes swelled," p. 45; etc.). On the other hand, the verb "to weep" (*plakat'*) is used consistently to describe the emotions of "spiritual children" in relation to Avvakum and in everyday living; it intensifies the depiction of their poverty and defenselessness, and functions as a synonym for other words denoting suffering ("With me gone my wife and children sat on the ground by the fire, my daughter with her mother -- both were weeping"; p. 83 and passim). Avvakum endows all his spiritual children with the gift of tears, and only once is the verb "to weep" used in relation to an "enemy of God" – Paškov, and this just before he repeats Judas' speech.

This sentimental tone so characteristic of Avvakum's tales about his spiritual children is intensified by other devices, the most important being his extensive use of diminutives, a significant feature of what he refers to as his "simple speech" (*prostoreŏie*). Large groups of diminutives do not appear early in the *Life*; the first examples are isolated and discretion is evident in their use in relating tragic or difficult moments. For example, the traditional affectionate formula for addressing a priest, "My lord and (little) father" (*Gosudar' naš batjuŝko*), is used for the first time by

Avvakum's persecutors; this provokes the Archpriest's sarcastic response, "Will wonders never cease! Yesterday I was a son of a whore, and now, Father!" (p.48.) But as the narrative moves from scenes of personal persecution involving various "officials" (*načal'-niki*) to the description of the approaching "winter" of heresy, diminutives appear in great numbers and in various functions. Very important here are words denoting objects either belonging to Avvakum or somehow related to his activities; as in old Russian petitions the diminutives suggest these objects are trivial and of little value in order to elicit sympathy: " . . . seizing me they raced away . . . to my poor home (*dvoriško*)" (p. 50). "He gave me two miserable old nags (*kljački*) for the little ones and for our pitiful belongings (*ruxliško*)" (p. 67). "Down came the rain and snow, and only a poor little kaftan (*kaftaniško*) had been tossed across by shoulders" (p. 61). This subjective tone becomes even more concentrated and sentimental in diminutives denoting objects that either ease Avvakum's sufferings in some way or that figure in his religious ideas and activities: "They . . . gave me a little pile of straw (*solomki*)" (p. 61). "He led me . . . to the bench and sat me down, and put a spoon in my hands and a tiny loaf (*xlebca nemnoško*) and gave me a dab of cabbage soup (*štec*) to sip . . . " (p. 54). "Sometimes they sent a little piece of meat (*mjasca*), sometimes a small round loaf (*kolobok*), sometimes a bit of flour (*mučki*) and oats (*ovseca*), as much as could be scraped together, a quarter pood and maybe a pound or two more, sometimes she saved up a good half pood (*polpudika*) and sent it over" (64–65). At times this tenderness extends to virtually all the nouns in an utterance, creating its general "luminescence"; for example, "Spread out a bit of cloth (*platočik*) on a small box (*korobočku*) . . . and light a little candle (*svečku*) and put a dab of water (*vodicy*) in a little bowl (*sosudce*). Ladle out some with a little spoon (*ložečku*) . . . " (66–67.)

Interesting here as well is the use of diminutives in the first half of similes to create an emotional aura around the subject of the sentence. This stylistic device is encountered most frequently in connection with Avvakum and his spiritual children (e.g., "Like a little dog [*sobačka*] I lay on my lump of straw [*solomke*]," p. 61 .) Of course this emotional aura is generally characteristic of Avvakum's depiction of his spiritual children; he refers to them with tender diminutive forms of their names (e.g., Afonas'juško,

Terent'juško) and describes them with corresponding epithets, the most frequent being *milyj, milen'kij* 'sweet':[7] "The good souls *(milen'kie)* were glad to see us, . . . dear Terentij *(Terent'juško)* and his comrades . . . " (p. 76); "looking at us they wept, the dear souls *(milen'kie)*," (p. 76); and many other examples. Exclamatory intonation makes the emotional weight of this epithet even more apparent: "My dear, sweet friend *(milen'koj moj)*! He fears God, the little orphan *(sirotin'ka)* in Christ." (p. 87.) "My sweet, good little children *(Detuški milen'kie moi)*! You suffered for Christ!" (p.89.)

Frequently Avvakum heightens the emotional intensity even further by using, most often as secondary predicates, the vernacular epithets *bednyj* 'poor' and *gor'kij* 'bitter'; they are made more palpable by the virtual absence of other epithets in the swiftly moving narration: "the poor souls, they *(one bednye)* both ate and trembled" (p. 60); "They were somewhat eased, the poor souls *(Im bednym legče stalo)*" (p. 67); "The poor Archpriestess tottered and trudged along, . . . the poor dear *(bednaja)* started in on me" (p. 68); and so on. Such epithets are occasionally attached to the Nikonians, but with ironic, sarcastic intent: "Alas, you poor Nikonians!" (p. 94.) And in the third redaction of the *Life*: "Twenty musketeers, a lieutenant, and a captain stood over us without let-up. They protected us, did us favors, at night sat there with fires, even took us outside to shit. Have mercy on them, O Christ! Those people were just plain, good musketeers, and you won't have other children of their sort! They suffered there, what with all that fussing over us, and if some small privation came along, they were obliging in every way, the dear souls *(milen'kie)*. Those pitiful sufferers *(gorjuny)* would guzzle till they were drunk, and they swore blasphemous filth, but still they are as good as the martyrs."

The final epithet here, *gorjun* 'miserable wretch,' its diminutive form *goremyka*, and the vernacular poetic appellations *svet* 'light,' *kormilec* 'benefactor,' and *nadežda* 'hope' are also important in this general context: "I wept and blessed him, the miserable soul *(gorjun)*," (p. 86); "and it's good enough for us – to suffer for the sake of Christ our Light *(svet)*!" (p. 87.) These techniques for creating an emotional aureole about others are applied to the Archpriest himself. In recalling the past he occasionally gazes upon himself as on a pitiful stranger and speaks in the third person:

"All alone, this poor, miseried old Archpriest (*bednoj goremyka protopop*) made a dogsled . . . " (p. 63); "You loved, Archpriest, of the famed to be friend; love then to endure, poor wretch (*goremyka*), to the end!" (p. 65.) There are also a few instances of such self-description in expressions of personal grief: "As for me, poor man (*bednomu*), it was bitter, but nothing could be done" (p. 93).

Such statements stand out vividly against a contrasting background of epithets expressing self-deprecation. Owing to their unusual emotional environments, however, these epithets lose their traditional character; for example: "He didn't pass his radiant life (*podvig*) in story-telling, not like me, accursed man" (*okajannoj*, p.91). At times such self-condemnation becomes genuinely vulgar: "There's a good man for you! – another shit-faced Pharisee. . . " (p. 60). In contrast, the Archpriest is addressed by his spiritual children, whether stalwart allies or repentant sinners, with an abundance of tender expressions of the sort described above.

Such then are the categories of verbal signs found in Avvakum's *Life*; the nature of their stylistic utilization depends in large measure on matters which I will treat under the heading of composition, or syntax.

This compositional analysis is facilitated if the *skaz* is not isolated from declamatory, pathetic narration; rather I will classify the various syntactic types in terms of their general semantic functions. Then the principles governing the interweaving of the two stylistic levels will be defined automatically. Three general headings are useful here: (1) the predominant simple syntactic patterns, their stylistic motivations, and their distribution; (2) the devices for conjoining and juxtaposing syntactic wholes; and (3) their organization through sound and rhythm.

Simple syntactic patterns are most common in Avvakum's *Life*; their organization is conditioned by their conformity to the primitive, folkish form of his *skaz*, which is based on the swift communication of actions seemingly perceived in their objective, uncomplicated immediacy. Episodes succeed one another rapidly, and within each, only the protagonist's actions and the minimum of accessory information are related; neither the physical appearance of other characters flitting in and out of the narrative nor the conventional descriptions of setting attract our attention. Consequently, short independent sentences consisting of a verbal core surrounded by two or three complements predominate; such sentences are sometimes joined together, forming fused sentences with multiple predicates: "I lit three candles and stuck them to the lectern, and raised my right hand into the flame and held it there . . . After dismissing the young woman, laying away my vestments, and praying awhile, I went to my home deeply grieved." (p. 45.) "By the church they dragged at my hair and drummed on my sides; they jerked at my chain and spit in my eyes" (p. 54).

Several other syntactic features are related to this emphasis on action. For instance, the accumulation of synonymous expressions ("weaving of words") is not present in Avvakum's style, and this characteristic distinguishes him to a greater or lesser degree from other writers of the period. Only a few formulas consisting of pairs of synonyms denoting actions are to be found here: *lajala, da ukorjala* ("She yapped and scolded," p. 61); *branju, da laju* ("I blast[ed] and bark[ed]," p. 54 ; cf. *branju . . . i ukorjaju*, p. 58); *plakala i rydala* ("She wept and sobbed," p.110); *propoveduja i uča slovu Božiju* ("preaching and teaching the Word of God," p. 43); *blagodejstvovali i celili* ("They performed good deeds and healed," p.68 ; cf. *isceleli i ispravilisja*, p. 68). In addition, the verb *žalovat'* 'to show favor, to confer a boon' is always accompanied by another verb which specifies the action, in the manner of old Russian petitions: *požalovala-poslala* ("She showed us her favor – she sent . . . ," p. 70; cf. *žaluete-podčivaete* ["You've favored me with your lovingkindness," p.76]; *požaloval – ko mne prislal desjat' rublev* ["He showed his favor and sent me ten rubles," p. 84]; *požaloval-pomolil''sja* [" . . . that he might favor us and pray . . . " p. 68). Usually the second half of each formula clarifies the first while moving the exposition forward.

Another characteristic of folkish conversational syntax frequently encountered in the *Life* and tending to emphasize action is the use of one-membered, personal sentences, i.e., sentences lacking an expressed grammatical subject where the originator of the action is known. Most important here is the use of the third-person singular form of a verb as predicate. This technique is particularly striking when Avvakum depicts the actions of persecutors, especially of Nikon and Paškov, whose images are apparently so permanently etched in his mind that they do not require verbal expression. Thus, certain kinds of behavior are associated with specific actors, and their explicit verbal identification becomes superfluous. Such sentence structure depends in part on the fact that Avvakum is most often concerned with only two contrasting kinds of behavior – his own and that of his enemies. "At this time, after me, [they] seized (*vzjali*) Login, Archpriest of Murom" (p.55). "[He] was killing (*pomoril*) everyone with hunger; [he] wouldn't let anyone leave (*nikudy ne opuskal*) to get a living" (p.64). "[I] didn't dare (*ne smeju*) go near his place – [he] was no end riled (*bolno serdit*) at me. Secretly [I] sent them (*poslal*) some holy water . . . " (p. 67.) In accordance with this basic compositional feature of the *skaz*, the predicate is usually emphasized by being placed in sentence-initial position. When logical stress places a modifier in initial position, the predicate frequently follows immediately, thereby preventing the disintegration of a single complex perception (e.g., *Ves' vozmutili grad* "They stirred up the whole town," p. 56).

The swiftly moving, systematic narrative is interrupted at times by emotional interjections expressing Avvakum's attitude toward the depicted event, both initially and as a memory (e.g., "Ah – it was bitter for my soul then, and it's not sweet even now," p.71). This device is most important in moments of high pathos, when exclamatory interjections, prayerlike exclamations, and apostrophes momentarily interrupt the narration like abrupt verbal gestures. Most frequent are exclamations expressing grief or amazement: *Ax, gore!* ("Ah, what misery!" p. 50 and passim). *Uvy grešnoj duše!* ("Alas for my sinful soul!" p. 64). *Čudno! Čudno!* ("It's a miracle! a miracle!" p. 73). How important expressions of amazement can be in relation to meaning is apparent in the following example, the tale about Avvakum's miraculous replenishment while he was in prison. From the very outset everything prepares the way for this tone. In his normal usage, the word *polatka*, usually 'cell,' appears without an attribute, but here it is termed *těmnuju* 'dark': "They tossed me in chains into a dark cell . . . " (p. 54). This darkness and the consequent indistinctness of visual perceptions are emphasized immediately: "Locked there in darkness I bowed down in my chains, maybe to the east, maybe to the west. . . . After Vespers there stood before me, whether an angel or whether a man I didn't know and to this day I still don't know, but only that he said a prayer in the darkness." The unexpectedness of this miraculous materialization is intensified by the playful statement immediately preceding: "No one came to me, only the mice and the cockroaches." Avvakum concludes this tale in one of his favorite ways, with a statement rather stylized in its casual laconicism: *Da i ne stalo ego* ("And he was gone"). But then the same statement is unexpectedly repeated with the intonation of amazement: "The doors didn't open, but he was gone!" An explanation is then provided for the entire mysterious episode: "It's amazing if it was a man, but what about an angel? Then there's nothing to be amazed about – there are no barriers to him anywhere."

Frequent as well are brief invocatory exclamations consisting of traditional formulas which are used to herald the appearance of heroes on the scene or to conclude tales about them: *Slava Bogu o sëm!* ("Glory be to God in this!" p. 105 and passim). *Spasi ego, Gospodi!* ("Save him, O Lord!" p. 55).

In most cases the exclamatory outburst makes the nature of a particular emotion immediately obvious. But sometimes the exclamatory tone is linked to an antecedant or subsequent interrogative tone, and the emotional vibration of the combination is more complex. As is natural in narrative *skaz*, interrogative sentences are less numerous here than exclamations; most important is the question, *Da čto mnogo govorit'?* 'But why go on and on?' by means of which transitions from one theme to another are effected. For example: "But why go on and on? Just spit on their doings . . . ." (p. 76.) "But why go on and on? If there were no champions, there would be no crowns." (p. 99.) These questions are perceived against a background provided by a group of formulas expressing omission which are lexically homogeneous with them but different in tone: *Mnogo o tom govorit'!* 'Plenty could be said about that!,' *Da polno tovo govorit'!* 'But enough talk about this!' and so on. Their frequent use creates the impression of deliberate suppression of both verbal color and details, thereby intensifying the effect of the material actually narrated.

Apart from these formulas of transition, there is another type of rhetorical question found in Avvakum's *Life*; it aims to induce in the listener an admission of the inevitable, unalterable nature of the events described. Such questions are used to intensify the most tragic episodes; for example: "But what could be done if Christ and the most immaculate Mother of God deigned it so?" (p. 63). "But what's to be done? Let those broken hearts (*gor'kie*) suffer for the sake of Christ." (p. 65.) "But what do you expect? They're wolves for a fact, . . . " (p. 86.)

Thus the development of the *skaz* within the boundaries of individual episodes is made more complex by abrupt shifts in tone between contiguous sentences whose laconicism further emphasizes the tonal difference; this dissonance is either resolved or intensified in the episode's conclusion. Four types of episodic conclusions are found in the *Life*. The most numerous are cadenced, invocatory, exclamatory formulas: "Thus doth God fashion his people!" (p. 48.) "Thus it is that God scorneth the scorners, but he giveth grace unto the lowly" (p. 48). "Christ is strong enough to have mercy and save us all!" (p. 95.) In certain instances the conclusion consists of a question designed to evoke a sympathetic response: "See then, my listener, didn't Eremej suffer for our sake, and even more for the sake of Christ and his Truth?" (p. 73.) "And was it for me, accursed man, to forget the abundance of God's benefactions?" (p. 81 .) In one instance an episodic conclusion has the form of a profound precept aphoristically expressed (gnomic parallelism): "Neither famine of bread nor thirst for water destroys man; but a great famine it is for man to live, not praying to God" (p. 83). The fourth type is the solemn, repentant conclusion (e.g., the tale concerning Avvakum's violation of the commandment of his confessor [p. 104] or the episode involving two widows [60–61]).

Such is the basic level of composition in Avvakum's *Life*. It is further diversified by inserted dialogues and by oratory which alternates the insistent tone of the agitator with solemn recitations of prayers and ecclesiastical texts.

At times this work also displays a clear tendency toward more complex syntactic constructions and toward their systematic disposition in series, the constituent members of which are related to one another through comparison or contrast. In their simplest form such constructions are quite brief: "Christ carried me through, and the most immaculate Mother of God led me." Cf. here the contrast (negative parallel) following immediately: "I fear no one, only Christ do I fear," and the comparison: " . . . when the womenfolk are pleasant, then everything will be pleasant in Christ" (all on p. 79).

In accord with the general and fundamental contrast between the devil (and his children) and God (and his children), descriptions of the actions of the two groups appearing in organized syntactic groupings are arranged in parallel, with semantic contrast occurring either in all their parts or in their concluding statements; for

example: "I saw how the devil had hardened her heart; I fell
down before the Lord, . . . And the Lord, our most merciful
God, softened the soil of her heart." (p. 70.) "He was sailing in
the prames with both weapons and men, but I heard . . . that
they were trembling and afraid . . . . But I . . . gathered together
the old and the sick and the wounded, those of no use there, . . .
we climbed in a boat . . . and journeyed wherever God might
direct, fearing nothing." (p. 74 .) "The official . . . loosed my
hand from his teeth, and leaving me he went to his home. But I,
thanking God . . . I went to Vespers." (p. 46.)

When Avvakum is not concerned with such contrasts, episodes
from his experience are sometimes depicted in syntactical groupings
arranged in what might be called steps, intensifying both the
meaning and emotional impact of the narration. Occasionally this
structure is emphasized by a refrain which concludes each of the
constituent parts. For example: "After resting . . . I abandoned
wife and children and with two others headed along the Volga
toward Moscow. I escaped to Kostroma – and sure enough, there
they'd driven out the Archpriest Daniil too. Ah, what misery!
The devil badgers a man to death! (*Vezde ot d'javola žit'ja net!*)
I trudged to Moscow and presented myself to Stefan, the Tsar's
confessor, and he was troubled over me. 'Why did you abandon
your cathedral church?' he says. Again more misery for me. The
Tsar came to his confessor . . . to be blessed and saw me there –
again more heartache. 'Why did you abandon your town?' he
says . . . Still more misery." (p. 50.) A similar structure can be
seen in the tale concerning a devil in church (p. 111), reminiscent
of certain pages in Gogol's "Vij," with origins, of course, in folk
poetry. An effective combination of the devices of contrastive
parallelism and the "ascending staircase" is found in the narration
of Avvakum's trial (92–93).

The methods described above for organizing the composition
of the *Life* in the *skaz* manner yield to another principle when
descriptions are introduced or the depiction of events is slowed
by remarks about the conditions or environment in which they
occur (retardation). However, descriptions in Avvakum's *Life*
are isolated and fulfill peripheral tasks. For example, magnificent
landscapes in Siberia are twice described (59, 77), in both cases
to intensify the human action by contrasting with it. Avvakum's
descriptions are always enumerations of things observed, the

attributes of which function as predicates evoking a visual image: "The mountains [were] high, the forests dense, the cliffs of stone, standing like a wall – you'd crick your neck looking up! . . . Geese and ducklings with red plumage, black ravens, and grey jackdaws also live there." (p. 59 .) On two occasions such predicates in similar constructions evoke not only visual images but as purely emotional epithets they depict feelings of profound distress: "The river [was] shallow, the rafts heavy, the guards merciless, the cudgels big, the clubs knotty, the knouts cutting, the tortures savage – fire and the rack! – people [were] starving, . . . " (p. 64). "The land [was] barbarous, the natives hostile . . . " (67–68).

The simple logic governing combination of and contrast between syntactic groupings is occasionally complicated by certain rhythmical features; words are arranged in such a way that harmonies are created between the morphemes concluding two segments of a sentence. A couplet results – a device very popular among schismatic and other seventeenth-century Russian writers. *Otstat' ot lošadej ne smeem,/ A za lošadmi itti ne pospeem* ("We dared not leave the horses at length; keeping up with them was outside our strength"; p. 68); *Evo iscelil,/ A menja vozveselil* ("He brought health to him and happiness to me"; p.107); *Ašče by ne byli borcy,/ Ne by dany byša vency* ("If there were no champions, there would be no crowns," p. 99 ; cf. *I načal skakat', i pljasat', i besov prezyvat'; Agrofena, bednaja moja goremyka, ešče togda byla nevelika; čto nyne arxiepiskop rezanskoj, mučitel' stal xristijanskoj; zaxotela ot menja ot"iti i za pervova xozjaina zamuž pojti*).

In other instances, in prayers and in *akathistoi* which Avvakum addresses to himself, a more complex rhythmical ordering occurs, producing what we would call a free verse which divides into stanzas (the last line of each having a dactylic ending) and displays a variety of poetic devices. The following prayer, reminiscent of the Psalms, is an example:

Послушай мене, Боже!	Hear me, O God!
Послушай мене, Царю небесный– Свет!	Hear me, O King of Heaven, our Light!
Послушай меня!	Hear me!
Да не возвратится вспять ни един от них,	Let not one of them return here again,
И гроб им там устроиши всем!	And prepare thou a grave for them all in that place!

Приложи им зла,	Bring evil down upon them,
Господи, приложи,	O Lord, bring it,
И погибель им наведи,	And lead them to destruction,
Да не збудется пророчество	That the prophecy of the devil
дьявольское!	shall not come to pass!

In the same manner, having fastened on the hagiographical common-place "blessed things," the cellarer Nikodim recites before Avvakum a rhythmically organized speech utilizing the devices of anaphora and epanodos, in which each successive syntactical unit represents a segment, as it were, of the one preceding: "Blessed is this cloister, for such are the dungeons it possesses!/ Blessed is this dungeon, for such are the sufferers it possesses!/ And blessed are the fetters!" (p. 88.)

In summary, Avvakum's *Life* can be viewed as an ingenuous, swift-moving *skaz* sometimes diversified by exclamatory and interrogative interjections and by solemn recitations of biblical texts that occasionally become sermons; it is sometimes embellished as well with puns, humorous folk sayings, and couplets, or is occasionally transformed by the measured rhythms of solemn divine worship.

A general conclusion can be drawn from the preceding stylistic analysis: before historical research can be undertaken, the style of the individual writer must be studied in isolation, outside any tradition, as a unique system of aesthetically organized linguistic devices. Lacking this inclusive description of the constituent elements of a writer's style, together with their functions, one cannot make penetrating observations about his links with past literary traditions. Such description and classification are immanent and static in nature, and they must be guided by the principle that an individual style is the product of the mind of an individual writer, thereby avoiding the inclusion of norms alien to him. The dynamics of individual style are also taken into account in such a study. Works of a single writer appearing at various times are not considered together but rather in their chronological succession. Each work must be viewed, in Croce's phrase, as "an expressive organism of completed thought," as a unique system of stylistic interrelationships; but it cannot be isolated completely from the others, for they are all products of a single poetic consciousness in its organic development. A more complete understanding of the constituent elements of the style of a particular literary work is possible if the investigator draws on other works to discover all their potential significance and meaning for the writer under study.

On the basis of this thorough study, individual works can be organized into cycles, the style of each cycle being described as the system of devices common to all works included in it. Changes in a writer's style over time are then represented either as the replacement of one system by another or as the partial transformation of a single system, the nucleus of which remains constant. This is what I call the functional immanent method of stylistic analysis, a method familiar to linguists. Baudouin de Courtenay, Ščerba, de Saussure, Sechehaye, and more recently Meillet and others have developed and validated similar methods for dialectology. The application of this method in stylistics is essential because the majority of Russian efforts at stylistic analysis (especially recent ones, e.g., the works of B.M. Éjxenbaum and V.M. Žirmunskij) are methodologically unsatisfactory owing to their confusion of the two levels of analysis, the functional immanent and the historical.

The results of studies utilizing this method will be more inclusive and thorough when they deal with contemporary literature. The reason is obvious: the general norms governing word usage and syntax in a familiar dialect are immediately accessible to us. These norms provide the background against which what is individual and creative in an artist can be assessed. Reconstructing the interrelationships among linguistic elements and understanding their functions in the style of a writer from the distant past presuppose a knowledge of these general norms during that historical period. Such knowledge can be acquired only through extensive study of texts from that period. Of course a certain leveling-off of subtle nuances in the meanings of words is inevitable in such an undertaking.

No matter how productive functional immanent studies of individual styles may be in resolving general linguistic problems, they cannot carry out all the tasks of stylistics. A writer's work is important not only as a closed microcosm with its own system of interrelationships but also as one link among many in the chain of changing artistic styles. The position of a given writer's work within the intersecting lines of traditions is established by comparing it stylistically with earlier works in the same or different genres by other writers; then his subsequent influence on literature and on the language of the literate population can be assessed. Here it is important to describe how the aesthetic integrity of works is fragmented (as Gončarov put it, "the conversion of a fortune into kopecks"), the resultant "pieces" finding various degrees of application in the works of other artists or in the language of everyday life. These investigations will clarify the movement of stylistically determined aggregations of "aesthetic objects" in terms of schools.

In such studies one cannot avoid a certain degree of schematism in comparing the relevant facts: stylistic devices lose the uniqueness they possess in individual works, since the process of comparing similar phenomena (different to the degree that the minds which produced them were different) involves abstraction of the more general features. However, this problem can be minimized by a clear understanding of the historical perspective and by preliminary functional immanent analyses, where works of individual writers are described as integral systems of stylistic phenomena in which specific elements possess a defined sphere of meaning and function in definable ways in the conception of the whole. Then one can avoid the danger of failing to see during the process of comparison fundamental similarities beyond the nonessential or of linking functionally diverse phenomena because of their external similarity.

Silver cross, 17th-century

FURTHER REMARKS ON *THE LIFE*
OF THE ARCHPRIEST AVVAKUM

by Kenneth N. Brostrom

Near the middle of his *Life* Avvakum pauses, apparently in a state of anxious uncertainty. Having related how he and his family once saved the life of a scoundrel by lying, he turns to his confessor Epifanij and requests his judgment on their action (p. 75).* Epifanij answers by recording in Avvakum's manuscript, in his own hand, his approval and blessing. The Archpriest's consternation is belied, however, not only by the deliberate ostentatiousness of this public confession but by Epifanij's response itself: it is squeezed (especially the final line) into the space provided him by Avvakum (see first five lines of script in photo, p. 148). That is, the Archpriest left a place in the manuscript for Epifanij's judgment and then wrote, "Good enough, Elder, God save you for your charity!" — this *prior* to Epifanij's actual response. It is possible Epifanij had already indicated what his response would be, or at least his attitude toward this event; or perhaps the Archpriest was confident the Elder would never deliberately discredit him. In either case, the spontaneity of this exchange is specious. It was important to Avvakum to demonstrate his undeviating commitment to the truth, and to do so he engaged in deception.

We might simply ignore this brief charade were it not for the obvious fact that Avvakum aims here to enhance his own image. And even a single instance of guile makes us cautious in analyzing Avvakum's self-portrait as it is created during the course of his autobiography. But how far are we to go? Are we to assume that the Archpriest's narrative should be read with distrust in all comparable instances — for example, that we ought not accept at face value his descriptions of miracles, especially those that

*Pages indicated in parentheses refer to passages in this volume.

follow upon the mutilation of his fellow prisoners at Pustozersk? Here one might argue that Avvakum was a clever strategist who resorted after his final imprisonment to the hagiographical tradition of the miraculous in order to enhance their public images by this ancient sign of heaven's approval — and his own by association. Robinson supports this interpretation by showing how Avvakum seems to have retreated in time from his early, unambiguous affirmations of these miracles: when bitter doctrinal strife arose between him and Deacon Fëdor, the Archpriest claimed that his opponent had again lost the power of speech, that his severed hand, with which he had claimed to write his epistles, had withered, and that in shame Fëdor had asked that it be buried in the earth (Robinson, p. 287). However, the notion that Avvakum's record of these miracles is guileful and false, that it reflects the strategic needs of the moment only, rests finally upon the assumption that he was capable of genuine cynicism, that he was at best a desperate partisan for whom the end, the triumph of the Old Belief, justified forbidden means (lying about the works of God). Such a position is very different from exposing the petty deception noted above. There is, after all, something childishly naive about that game with Epifanij — Avvakum didn't leave enough space! Much of the argument below implicitly rejects any such under-standing of Avvakum's character. When we consider the fact that the other prisoners at Pustozersk also reported these miracles, it seems sensible to assume that, however we might now interpret these strange events, Avvakum almost certainly perceived a miracu-lous element in them.[1]

Our certainty here is increased by another undeniable fact: Avvakum believed in the possibility and reality of miracles precisely of the sort he described. To doubt their possibility would have threatened the very foundations of the faith for which he spent years in exile and in prison, for which he endured monumental suffering, lost everything he loved in this world, and met death in the fire. This unquestioning belief in miracles is characteristic of Avvakum's medieval mind, and it provides a rough measure of the psychic gulf that exists between him and us.[2] Yet an effort must be made to bridge this gulf if we are to understand Avvakum's *Life* in any depth. This task has many pitfalls, for what may seem to be true of his mind and personality may not be so in fact. We have already seen how apparent ingenuousness and spontaneity may not be that at all. It is possible, if rather improbable, that Avvakum's style was itself a product of a calculated effort to construct a particular public image. Yet, despite such imponderables, there is much we can say with a high degree of certainty about Avvakum's mind and world view. The first part of my argument attempts to do precisely that; the second part applies my general observations to Avvakum's autobiography, in the conviction that this undertaking will illuminate its structure and meaning.

If we bear in mind the medieval qualities of Avvakum's vision, we are less likely to interpret the thematic implications of his dyadic style in a facile manner. All too often it has been viewed in the critical literature as a product of a distinct cleavage between this world and the next, wherein Avvakum's unreflecting commitment is, in one way or another, to the former. Certainly his acute sensitivity to others and to the world around him, his down-to-earth language, his pugnacious attitudes and behavior, his earthly visions of heavenly things, his class origin and historically determined association with "antifeudal, democratic social forces"[3] all support this view. Vinogradov demonstrates in detail, however, the frequent, forceful merger in Avvakum's style of the bookish and the vernacular, as well as of the hagiographical and the quotidian, and he implies they are undifferentiated thematically. Avvakum's revolutionary style is in fact thematically holistic in its demolition of the dualism inherent in traditional ecclesiastical literature, where the Truth is inseparable from the archaic language in which it is expressed and partially detached thereby from contemporary life. It is true that Avvakum defended literally to the death the letter and gesture of the old ritual. But this is not to say that Truth itself depends on style. Men do, in this sense: they must cling to the unchanging, sanctified old ritual in divine worship because it is God's will, because it is the divinely established means to communion with him (see Introduction, p. 17). Avvakum's thematically holistic, dyadic style outside worship reflects not dogmatics but the very foundation of his world view: that God is immediate, he and his Truth are indeed omnipresent in this world and the next — different but inextricable dimensions of his one creation. Evidence of the presence of heavenly power in earthly things is encountered everywhere in the *Life*: signs in the heavens and elsewhere, heaven-sent punishments and admonitions, healings, miracles, and visions. Avvakum is representative of the unadorned medieval mind; Aquinas' empirical proofs of God's existence would have seemed frivolous and perhaps blasphemous to him, for whom life in this world was quite simply "a book in which the hand of God hath writ." Thus, we may perceive a stylistic dissonance only, not a tension between the here and the hereafter, in, for example, Avvakum's swift transitions from traditional ecclesiastical formulas of self-deprecation to plebian expressions of self-hatred.[4]

The erosion of European man's awareness of a spiritual realm of perfect goodness is a relatively recent historical phenomenon; it is likely that the interpretive error of exaggerating the breach in Avvakum's *Life* between that realm and this world originates here. Dmitrij Čiževskij bluntly summarizes the discontinuity that exists between Avvakum's simple certainties and the mind-boggling complexity of our own metaphysical uncertainty in saying, "His attacks are the outcome of his point of view that all questions are already solved and that he has the right answers."[5]   These "right answers" proceed directly from Avvakum's conviction that the will of God is not only knowable but known. It is declared in Holy Writ, the writings of the Holy Fathers, and the traditions of ancient Russian Orthodoxy. The path to salvation is thus well-marked but hard and steep: understanding God's will, a man need only live by and for it, come what may: "One of the Holy Fathers hath said it well, that one path lies before us all."[6]

Avvakum's courageous, combative self-assurance, in many ways so admirable, was nevertheless largely the product of arrogance and presumption; he never doubted that in matters concerning the faith he spoke as it were *ex cathedra*, infallibly, by God's authority. One of his more unattractive traits was thus the vindictive rancor he displayed in denouncing Old Believers who dared disagree with his authoritarian interpretations of his one law, the sanctified traditions and texts of old Russian Orthodoxy. He opens the *Life* quite characteristically in proclaiming that through their innovations the Nikonians have sullied and separated themselves from the known Truth of the universe; and he clinches his proof with one telling example: they have eliminated the epithet "the true" (*istinnyj*) from the Creed. Like many of his contemporaries, Avvakum is a study in fanaticism, where extreme individualism and egomania are so often inseparable from willing enslavement to some supreme authority.[7]

While recognizing and applauding Avvakum's monumental spiritual energy, we cannot ignore the primitive aspects of his religiosity. Indeed, it is sometimes difficult to distinguish the religious practices of Avvakum and his contemporaries from the magical conjurations of paganism. And if their bloody debates over ritual were not without theological substance, they still ignored Christ's own rebellion against religious formalism in the name of more pressing spiritual matters (see, for example, Mark 2:23—28 and Luke 18:9—14). Genuine piety, when coupled with a slavish devotion to ritual, is ever threatened by a mechanistic heresy, the degeneration of religion into a quid-pro-quo relationship between man and God: man acts in a clearly prescribed manner and God responds, predictably, appropriately and promptly. Clearly this is nothing but conjuration, and Avvakum practiced it to the point of heresy. A good example in the *Life* involves Eremej Paškov's military expedition into Mongolia. In an effort to discredit a devil's prophecy of victory and rich spoils, Avvakum calls upon God to send destruction down on the Russian force (years afterward, in writing the *Life*, he condemned this prayer for its un-Christlike malice). Later, compassion moves him to pray for his friend Eremej's deliverance. And so it comes to pass: all are destroyed save Eremej. Thus, in responding mechanically to Avvakum's wicked prayer, God becomes his accomplice in evil, seemingly the helpless victim of theurgical cause and effect.

This implication, accidental but still heretical, reflects the lack of talent for systematic thought which produced the long-recognized doctrinal inconsistencies in Avvakum's works. [8] Two brief examples are offered here. In contradiction to the foregoing, Avvakum emphasizes elsewhere the powerlessness of his prayers when evil is ascendant within him, or when repentance and faith are lacking. Similarly, in the Introduction to the *Life* he associates astrology with those who are "perishing" outside the true faith, then uses it himself in identifying the astral signs of God's wrath against Russia. We may say, then, that self-assurance, simplicity, and logical inconsistency are characteristic of Avvakum's thought.

If Avvakum's dyadic style is harmonious with his sense of the immediacy of God's Truth in both this world and the next, it does not follow that the traditional medieval tension between them is not everywhere evident in the *Life*. The assertion made above, that they are different aspects of God's one creation, minimizes not their differences but the distance between them. The immediacy of God's Truth does not make a monist of Avvakum, however, just as his insistence on life temporal and life eternal does not rest upon a full-fledged Manichaean dualism. Avvakum affirms a mitigated dualism, perhaps what J. H. Billington had in mind in speaking of his "semi-Manichean view of the world."[9] Important as this thematic tension is to the structure of the *Life* and to our discussion below, there is another, very different tension, often evident in Avvakum's inconsistencies, which generates much of this work's energy and rich complexity: a tension between event and meaning. Avvakum always understands the meaning of events and almost always fathoms human actions; yet his various understandings may be incompatible. For example, two implicit questions dominate his understanding of contemporary history: Does the tumult in the Church herald its demise and the reign of the Antichrist, or can the old, pure Orthodoxy of the Third Rome be restored, ushering in the Millenium? As Zenkovsky has shown,[10] such uncertainties tormented all Old Believers after the Ecumenical Council of 1666–67, which ratified most of Nikon's reforms and anathematized both the old ritual and its leaders. Avvakum asserts or implies either one or the other of these historical hypotheses at various junctures, despite their simultaneous incompatibility. The reign of the Antichrist implies passive struggle, that is, patient, saintly suffering in the promise of a future reward; restoration of the Third Rome implies the converse, active struggle. As history undergoes such transformations in Avvakum's vision, so too does his depicted personality: at times he embodies saintly endurance, at others the spirit of the battle-scarred veteran ready for another skirmish. Not consistent understanding but the ready answer dominates Avvakum's metaphysic. Such answers, conventional verities drawn from Holy Writ or tradition, tend to be partially discrete in Avvakum's usage and therefore potentially contradictory. Each in isolation is an absolute statement of God's will and plan for the lives of men. Thus, the Archpriest chastises himself profanely for questioning the justice (i.e., the reasonable meaning) of his terrible beating by Paškov (60–61); unlike the sometimes rebellious Job, he possesses the full statement of God's will and way, and he comforts himself by recalling one part of it (Heb. 12:5–8).

Certainly this tension between event and meaning was not apparent to Avvakum, as it is to us who are discomfited by non sequiturs and contradictions in declarations of God's unambiguous will. The reasons for asserting that this tension accounts for much of the *Life*'s richness and vitality will become evident below. Here it is important to understand that this tension is exacerbated by the *Life*'s didactic function: Avvakum must have all the answers, he must explain to Old Believers why they are winning when they seem to be losing in their struggle with the forces of darkness. Explanation of the ways of God to man is the *sine qua non* of Holy Writ, and Avvakum makes this the task of his *Life*: he dares to call it "a book of eternal life."[11] Its aim is to continue the declarations of God's will found in the writings of the Holy Fathers by teaching men how to take responsibility for the salvation of their souls in the present moment. This elevation of autobiography into Holy Writ helps explain the authoritarian self-confidence evident in Avvakum's erratic interpretations of events and human actions. It also suggests why he was unwilling to discuss with his allies confused or obscure passages in the old Slavonic texts: they and tradition provided him with an unshakable buttress, an ever-ready, absolute point of reference in his cosmic struggle and in his teaching. The psychological need for such support is understandable when we remember Avvakum considered himself a beseiged general in the final apocalyptic battles of the ancient war between heaven and hell.

In sum then, Avvakum aims to show through sermonizing, appeals to authority, and above all else, through the events of his own experience the immediacy and specificity of God's Truth in this world. Thus are the quotidian and the divine inextricable in his mind. And if the tangible presence of that Truth seems at times uncertain, if his suffering and losses (and by extension, those of his followers) seem beyond measure, Avvakum still trusts that all things are ultimately in God's hands and conform to his will.[12] So he concludes his confession of faith in the Introduction to the *Life* with a declaration of God's foreknowledge of all things, and his subsequent narrative is peppered with seemingly automatic references to that will ("What could be done if Christ and the most immaculate Mother of God deigned it so?"). Such unquestioning acceptance of the conditions of his life, like his acceptance of the old ritual, sometimes leads Avvakum to a radical anti-intellectualism, where mindless submission becomes the virtue of self-effacement: "Just you suffer for the conformation of the fingers and don't reason over much. And I'm ready to die with you for this in Christ." [13] Yet Avvakum's obscurantism is fundamentally optimistic: We know all we need to know and live by it, so God is with us. Who then can finally stand against us?

These general prefatory remarks and the detailed commentary below will show why critical discussions which concentrate on Avvakum's vigorous narration of events ("harbinger of the novel," and so on) and his verbal style must inevitably distort both the aesthetic essence of this work and the kind of complex unity present in it. In fact, a narrow emphasis on Avvakum's uniquely personal manner makes it possible to deny the presence of any genuine unity in the *Life*, as the assessments of both Issatschenko (see Preface) and Vinogradov in his later years [14] have shown. N. S. Demkova has taken a broader view in rejecting the compositional amorphousness implied by all commentaries, however approving, which fail to go substantially beyond regarding the *Life* as a "conversation" or an "ingenuous improvisation." Her analysis isolates two types of narrative, one being factually oriented and chronicle-like, the other the more discursive narrative of "the complete novella," which she finds characteristic of key episodes in "the moral development of the hero." [15] Although this understanding differs from my own, it is an important emendation to analyses that assume the *Life*'s narrative structure is of secondary interest, viewing it as primarily chronological and biographical or as a simple adaptation of the traditional *vita*'s linkage of discrete, didactic episodes through the figure of the protagonist. My approach to this question shares Demkova's interest in the depiction of the protagonist; but it is based on the problematical premise that certain assumptions can be made regarding the personality of the author which greatly enhance our understanding of the *Life*. To cite a simple example, I suspect that Avvakum's references to both a vengeful, wrathful God and a loving, merciful God have more to do with aspects of his own nature than they do with uncertainty about Old and New Testament theology, although these traditional references are not irrelevant. This approach often illuminates textual detail, and it ultimately clarifies the manner in which the *Life*, in style, theme, and structure, exists in a dialectical tension with the religious literary tradition.

Vinogradov's careful description of the fusion of prototypal biblical events and events in Avvakum's own experience directs our attention to an important feature of the *Life*'s tendentiousness: the movement between and the frequent merger of the universal and the particular. This characteristic medieval duality of vision places apostasy in the Russian Church in the context of the ancient struggle between heaven and hell both conceptually and structurally. For example, after the initial doctrinal blows directed against his enemies, Avvakum moves in his Introduction to a confession of faith which is, in effect, a cosmic *Prologemenon* to his autobiography. His first conflicts with the forces of evil continue this universal vision in their essential lack of causal dependence on time and place. A specific historical context begins to shape Avvakum's cosmic struggle only after his first contacts with Tsar Aleksej Mixajlovič, Stefan Vonifat'ev, and other leading religious and political figures. This merger of the universal with unique historical circumstances continues to the final pages of the *Life* proper; thereafter, the causal dependence on time and place is severed in the supplementary tales about lunatics. Not one of them deals directly with the Nikonian heresies and apostasy in the Church.

It is useful to digress here briefly to illustrate the notion of "dialectical tension" introduced above. Critics who associate these final tales with the traditional device of concluding a *vita* with a group of miracle stories are partially correct. Miraculous healings occur, and they imbue the healer with the odor of sanctity. Yet the extremes of self-vilification here muddy the image of the saint. The simple, traditional purpose of such tales becomes more complex, for now we encounter a saint trailing disclaimers, a saintly sinner or a sinning saint. Thus, Avvakum used a traditional hagiographical vehicle with unitary subject matter (here, delimited by the ancient ecclesiastical literary formula, struggle with devils) to summarize his self-understanding as a man of God and a "Holy

Father" to his followers. Essentially metaphorical, this self-depiction is organized around traditional religious motifs which clash with one another when sharing a single human referent (the details will be discussed elsewhere). Tension is created between event and meaning, and we perceive one way in which the *Life* comes into a dialectical relationship with tradition.

The metaphorical quality of these final tales is perhaps an inevitable product of Avvakum's correlation of the universal and the particular; and a metaphorical (sometimes allegorical) impulse is often evident in the *Life*. It is a critical commonplace to consider this impulse a natural product of medieval religiosity, for it has always been a mode congenial to writers committed to *realiora* beyond present *realia*. Certain remarks by D. S. Lixačëv concerning medieval "abstraction" in general apply to Avvakum here in particular: "Abstraction is engendered by attempts to glimpse in everything temporal and perishable, in the phenomena of nature and human life and in historical events, symbols and signs of the eternal, the supernatural, the spiritual, the divine." [16] This habit of simplifying and generalizing fluid phenomena by relating them through metaphor to a set of static conceptions is consistent with Avvakum's hagiographically inspired use of biblical analogues for his own experiences on the one hand, and his distillation of their essential, eternal truth through quotation of Holy Writ on the other. His sensitivity to the presence of God's hand in the affairs of men together with his irrepressible tendentiousness should have alerted us more than they have to the pervasive, patterned nature of representational phenomena in the *Life*. Recognition of them would certainly prevent any critic from placing exclusive emphasis on the narrative line and its style.

Of course, it would be false to suggest that recognition of certain metaphorical patterns is not common in the critical literature. Vinogradov devotes more productive effort to examining them than most (e.g., those relating to boats, vagabondage, winter, beasts, and so on). Early on in his argument he remarks that Avvakum's "method of depicting real events from his life is governed by ecclesiastical and biblical literature, within the confines of which his creative intuition revolved" (p. 121). I believe this cryptic observation to be correct, and it undergirds my effort to extend our knowledge of this dimension of the *Life*. This remark implies, and Vinogradov's analysis shows, that these meta-phorical patterns are premeditated only in part, and that habitual, conditioned perceptions figure prominently here as well. Indeed, the tension between event and meaning largely depends upon inconsistencies in automatic responses to experience.[17] Conse-quently, I do not wish to dismiss outright the extensive literature which affirms the ingenuous oral qualities of Avvakum's prose style. But my commentary will show that more deliberation is evident here than is often assumed.

There is one characteristic shared by all Avvakum's metaphors which is not indicated by Lixačëv's description of the transcen-dental impulse behind medieval abstraction; those "attempts to glimpse" (*popytki uvidet'*) the Eternal in the evanescent suggest the post-Romantic elusiveness of the ineffable rather than its medieval immediacy. Avvakum's metaphors and symbols lack the allusiveness and indeterminacy so often characteristic of these tropes in modern non-Realistic literature. They function within a closed system and their referents are specific and immediately comprehensible. (The same historical considerations undergird my conviction that Avvakum's imagery, renowned for its "con-creteness," is only superficially "Realistic"; with its primary transcendent dimension it is alien to the vision and methods of modern Realism.)[18] The conceptions that generate this imagery are not truths about life for Avvakum, they constitute life itself. An apt analogue for such "transcendental phenomenalism" is found in the Orthodox theology of the icon: "Icons . . . [are] a kind of window through which the inhabitants of the celestial world [look] down into ours and on which the true features of the heavenly archetypes [are] imprinted two-dimensionally. The countenance of Christ, of the Blessed Virgin, or of a saint on the icons [is] therefore a true epiphany, a self-made imprint of the celestial archetypes." [19] These remarks clarify the role of icons in the Orthodox conception of the liturgy as a progress toward the Eucharist, during which the manifest heavenly con-gregation embraces the earthly congregation within the church, and they momentarily become one. Steeped in such thought, Avvakum quite naturally discovered that life everywhere presents itself imprinted with God's Truth.

Nothing was more transparently true for him than the ancient belief that life in this world is torn by "the struggle between two fundamental principles" (*bor'ba dvux načal*),[20] between Good and Evil, God and the devil, Christ and Antichrist. Virtually every critic has affirmed the importance of this theme in the *Life*, for it is the supreme criterion used by Avvakum to select his narrative materials; as he puts it, "I will tell about the high points of my hardships" (*Stanu skazyvat' verxi svoim bedam*).[21]   From this perspective, narrative momentum is generated by " the complex and constantly repeating intersection of the lines of 'Good' and 'Evil' "[22]   in episode after episode, these experiences always existing "within the general context of the eternal conflict between good and evil."[23] Recognition of Avvakum's great and protracted sufferings cannot conceal the fact that his unrelenting pursuit of this conventional medieval theme amounts to monomania; its ubiquity registers the impact of his bellicose nature on his depiction of the nature of things. Struggle is the dynamic principle to which all Avvakum's metaphors can ultimately be related, and it generally determines the depiction of character and event as well.

The terms of the struggle are specific: the battle, at once personal and cosmic, is joined between those who know, love, and live by the will of God and those who would subvert it, between *Us* (the Children of God) and *Them* (the Children of Satan). This simple polarization of an inevitably fluid and complex human reality conceals the particular fissure between event and meaning noted above: Can the Third Rome be restored, or has the reign of the Antichrist begun? Here the pellucid will of God turns opaque, and the aim of the struggle is consequently unclear: Is it national ecclesiastical restoration or individual endurance to the death?

Avvakum's ambivalence over the eschatological questions that tormented his age is related, for us, to a timeless philosophical problem, the conflict between predestination and free will. Whenever Avvakum refers to the Antichrist, or proclaims God's fore-knowledge, or announces the helplessness of men (especially his own) before the will of God, he affirms the predestined course of events in Russia. Yet he devoted his ample energies at Pustozersk to changing the hearts of his Tsar and countrymen through the written word, he frequently refers to the behavior of others in the past and present, condemning or praising them for their continuing or changing religious commitments,[24] and he views his own life as it moves toward a martyr's death and crown as an unremitting series of tests in which success or failure depends on his spiritual tenacity and strength of will.[25] "Christ calls us to come freely," says Avvakum (p. 99), as it is each man's duty to assume responsibility for the state of his own soul.

A striking instance of this contradiction is encountered in Avvakum's description of the mutilation and miraculous healings of his comrades at Pustozersk. These episodes near the end of the *Life* proper are offered as compelling proof that God approves the Old Belief; they exhort Russians either to persevere or to rehabilitate both the Church and their own souls. Yet these champions of the old ritual, including Avvakum, are also hapless prisoners, apparently powerless to halt the legions of the Antichrist. That Avvakum was oblivious to the contradictory implications of this appeal is aesthetically unimportant; such inadvertant vacillation over the meaning of events and the ability of good men to alter them enriches this very human self-portrait of a powerful personality in crisis – the worst crisis his imagination could conjure.

Avvakum's preoccupation with spiritual endurance, whether his own or that of others, proceeds directly from an ancient Christian understanding of the nature of the struggle. Traditionally the forces of evil are aggressive and violent, while goodness, though ultimately stronger, is passive and patient. "The meek shall inherit the earth," not by the sword but through their good example and works. (The kenotic ideal is compatible, of course, not only with historical fatalism but with freedom.) Passivity permeates Avvakum's depiction of his own behavior when the forces of evil assault him: he yields himself up to beatings and floggings by officials, Paškov, and patriarchs, he bears the inhuman conditions of his imprisonments without a murmur, he awaits Paškov's executioners while admonishing his family, "For whether we live, we live unto the Lord, and whether we die, we die unto the Lord."[26] In this we see a typical medieval relation, essentially metaphorical, often established between action and a celestial archetype: the kenotic Christ awaited his executioners in the Garden of Gethsemene, he yielded himself up to their floggings, and "he was obedient, even unto death." Only rarely is Avvakum actively aggressive, and then he is usually justified by another aspect of Christ's nature, Christ "of the terrible eye," Judge of the world. Early in the *Life* he drives a group of *skomoroxi* (minstrels and entertainers) and their dancing bears away from his village, as Christ drove the money-changers from the Temple in Jerusalem (p. 46). Similarly, he beats Ivan Struna and a lunatic for disorderly behavior in churches (56, 107). Departing once from the archetype, a vexed and depressed Avvakum beats his wife and her maid for squabbling with one another. As penance for this aggressive, evil deed he compels them and all his household to flog him. Being good people, they comply reluctantly and unaggressively, with weeping and wailing (p. 106).

Avvakum's general adherence to the tradition of passive struggle does not produce a portrait of a meek and humble servant of God. To the contrary, he seems a man strongly inclined to violence who has imposed a stern behavioral code upon such impulses. The delight he takes in the story of Login's expectorating in Nikon's face (p. 55), his desire to do the same (p.100), and above all his raging diatribes against his enemies tell the real story. These eruptions of hatred and spleen create another instance of that dialectical tension between the *Life* and tradition noted above. They exist in an unstable equilibrium with all the traditionally edifying examples of self-mastery; they suggest a conflict between what the protagonist is and the ideal self he would like to be – a point to which I will return. The result is a more complex, vivid depiction of a human personality than traditional literary canons, strictly observed, would allow.[27]

Passivity in battle would be the tactic of men *non compos mentis* were special reinforcements not available to them. But then, ready access to heavenly power is consequent upon fruition of that sublime spiritual state which undergirds this rock-ribbed passivity. The immediacy of such access for the right people is evident in Avvakum's ministrations to those possessed by devils. Confession combined with a series of sanctified ritualistic gestures place physician and patient in harmony with God's will, removing all barriers between them and God's healing power: "I sprinkled them with tears and holy water and anointed them with oil, chanting supplications in Christ's name, and the power of God cast out the devils from these men . . . Except by these Mysteries I am unable to heal." (p. 66 .) Thus Avvakum is more an agent than a healer: "They were made whole, not because of my merit – no way in the world! – but because of their faith" (p. 66). Similarly, Avvakum often views his enemies not as ill-intentioned scoundrels but as pawns in the powerful hands of the devil. Such examples illustrate the concrete nature of Avvakum's perception of "the struggle between two fundamental principles" in his own experience.

These principles are related to the traditional Kingdoms of Light and Darkness – although again, extreme Manichaean dualism is not descriptive of Avvakum's world view. More satisfactory terms are the realms of the spiritual and the physical; they allude more fully to the antithetical characteristics associated in the *Life* with the cosmic forces joined in battle. Equally important, the simple polar opposition between these terms helps us to specify inconsistencies between event and meaning that contribute to the mitigation of Avvakum's dualistic vision. Although he consciously conceives of existence as a finite struggle in which the Good will ultimately triumph, he gaze tends in fact to fasten on particular phenomena from the vantage point provided by one pole or the other. Thus, a single reality (events, environments, persons, images) may be illuminated with God's beneficence or darkened by the devil. To use a now familiar example, events may signal the approaching defeat or victory of the enemies of the Old Belief. Or referring to an image discussed in detail below, water may symbolize the forces of destruction or serve as a catalyst in spiritual rebirth. At any moment, then, life in this physical world may inspire hope and confidence or a despairing desire to abandon it once and for all. In either case we observe Avvakum's automatic recourse to two traditional visions: of God as maker of all things visible and invisible, and of this world as the kingdom of the flesh and the devil. In general, then, these terms specify the two principal referents in Avvakum's metaphorical system.

Storms and stasis – Satan's storms raised up against Avvakum and the Russian Church and the stasis of the Elect's staunch passivity – are immediate products of Avvakum's medieval understanding of the patterned contrasts between these two realms. Storms involve change, often violent and dangerous; as metaphor they are related to life in this world, limited in time and space and characterized by flux, struggle, suffering, and death. The realm of the spiritual is outside time, free of the limitation of space, filled with joy and peace, forever unchanging. "I am here briefly, while I am there eternally."[28] This commitment to the changeless Truth of a timeless reality is evident everywhere in the *Life*, from Avvakum's opening attacks on the Nikonians for falling away from this Truth to his refusal "to move the eternal boundaries established before our time"(p. 100). Equally evident is his knowledge of what it means to live and struggle and suffer "briefly" in this world, amidst the fluctuations of fortune. A distilled metaphorical expression of Avvakum's metaphysic is found in his famous vision of the three boats.[29]

The boats of Luka and Lavrentij, Avvakum's deceased spiritual children, are of gold, and they sail with stately grace (*strojno*) down the Volga. Gold is the color of Paradise (the background of the icon "window into heaven" is most often of this color), so both the appearance and measured movement of these boats are symbolic of the glorious, undivided stasis of eternal life. Avvakum's boat, however, is "motley colored" (*ne zlatom ukrašen, no raznymi pestrotami*), and it races toward him out of the Volga as if it wants "to swallow [him] whole." The appearance of this vessel and its rapid, aggressive movement are representative of the vicissitudes, the reversals of fortune and perils of life in the realm of the physical. As Vinogradov observes (126–128), this boat metaphor is linked to the storms, the rain and snow, and the winter ("of heresy") that later lay the Archpriest low during his voyage. Beyond flux, danger, and death, the boat's particolored appearance implies a lack of wholeness, not only in life on earth but in the boat's intended passenger: division and incompleteness are inevitable consequences of living between God and the devil. Well might Avvakum feel trepidation before this vision, for the helmsman summons him not only to hazards but to a transformation of his life. If he can make of it a *podvig*, a prolonged, titanic labor in Christ, he will figuratively transform his vessel's motliness into monochromatic gold, an emblem of his hard-won wholeness.

In a consistent manner, then, Avvakum uses the notion of motliness to describe the defiled Greek Orthodox Church ("Orthodoxy has become motley in color . . . with you," p. 92) and his enemies ("the motley beasts!" p. 86).

Unlike those degraded ecclesiastics, however, his boat is exceedingly beautiful, like those of Luka and Lavrentij. Such beauty is the product of right living, which can mean, in Avvakum's mitigated, contradictory dualism, either labor and struggle in this world in service to the historical mission of the True Church,[30] or imitation of the martyrs, whose final victory followed upon their exit from this world. In either case, the ready hand of God ever holds forth the possibility of sanctified experience, that is, experience suffused with spiritual beauty. Just as the Orthodox liturgy moves toward the communion of heaven and earth in the Eucharist, so right living can lead to momentary mergers of immediate experience with the eternal. Here merger and not transcendence seems the more satisfactory term, since Avvakum creates the impression not of moving beyond the realm of the physical to the spiritual, but of obliterating temporarily the boundary between them. For example, his visions follow upon a "loss" of eyesight only (his eyes swell shut from weeping [p. 45], he is in a light sleep [p. 80], he has spent three days in the darkness of a prison cell [p. 54]). And there are times when one of the onerous inevitabilities of life in this world, physical pain, is temporarily alleviated for Avvakum as his right actions effect this merger. The miraculous healings of the mutilated martyrs at Pustozersk are an extension of this pattern.

Such visions and miracles often signal God's approval of the Old Believers. It follows that these events are never experienced by those firmly ensconced in the enemy camp. Other distinctions between *We* and *They* are similarly clear-cut, all of them deriving from either an affirmative or an antagonistic relation to the will of God. Whereas life in harmony with that will requires a fundamental allegiance to the realm of the spirit while laboring in this life, the "enemies of God" are completely immersed in the physical alone. They are thus "animals," that is, beings who have so sullied their souls that they have become in effect soulless. Vinogradov discusses the manner in which Avvakum transforms sinners and his personal enemies into animals (128–129), particularly aggressive carnivores such as dogs and wolves. Indeed, the Archpriest's first act of aggression against the forces of evil is to drive out a group of *skomoroxi*, who are not mentioned at all, but only their bears. The venerable medieval tradition of metaphorical animal imagery also attaches to the death of a cow at the beginning of Avvakum's career a meaning beyond what Robinson, for instance, sees here, a "realistic," homey adaptation of a hagiographical tradition wherein the death of a parent or relative prompts the hero to take his first steps on the path to a holy life.[31] The eternal death of an animal awaits all who turn away from the will of God; this conviction governs Avvakum's use of animal imagery and motivates his lengthy struggle to win eternal life.

Beasts are one category in a complex of related images, often metaphorical, which derive from the spiritual consequences of immersion in the realm of the physical: "Just look at that mug, accursed Nikonian, look at the belly — fat you are for a fact! How can you hope to squeeze through the Heavenly Gates? For they are narrow, and narrow and grievous is the path leading to life."[32] This image of the fat belly, recurrent elsewhere in Avvakum's works, is not typical for the *Life*, but it isolates the referential common denominator in all such imagery, that is, hedonistic satisfaction of physical desires. Certain categories of images examined by Vinogradov are related thematically in this way; for example, carnivore imagery, kitchen imagery, and the image of grasping, clutching hands are all used in connection with Paškov (polar bear, p. 74 ; oven and "hash-slinging" [*strjapan'e*], p. 73 ; hands, p. 58). Important here too is unrestrained or aberrant sexual appetite. One minor character commits incest with his daughter (p. 56), and an official kidnaps and rapes the daughter of a poor widow (p. 45). Paškov tries to force two elderly widows to marry Cossacks while they are en route to a nunnery to take the veil (p. 59). Another man fornicates with his wife on Easter, cursing the festival, and falls into a frenzy (p.106), while a pure young virgin suffers from the same affliction after desire causes her to marry(108–10). Denunciation of the lustful excesses of others, particularly of priests and their women, brings violent retribution down on the wrathful Archpriest's head (p. 50). And he experiences great spiritual anguish over his own lustful response to a dissolute young woman's confession early in his career (43–45).

In the last example Avvakum utilizes a hagiographical common-place wherein a future saint's temptation is sexual in nature. Sexual excess has of course always been a hallmark of a sinful world in the Christian tradition. Beyond this general traditional context, the Apocalypse provided another specific source for such imagery. When Avvakum's wife urges him to "unmask the whoredom of heresy" (p. 79), and when he refers several times to "the whore of Rome," we encounter other expressions of the eschatological preoccupations of this era, where the "great whore" astride a great "beast" was associated with the reign of Antichrist:

. . . there I saw a woman mounted on a scarlet beast which was covered with blasphemous names and had seven heads and ten horns. The woman was clothed in purple and scarlet and bedizened with gold and jewels and pearls. In her hand she held a gold cup, full of obscenities and the foulness of her fornication, and written on her forehead was a name: "Mystery, Babylon the Great, the mother of whores and of every obscenity on earth." The woman, I saw, was drunk with the blood of God's people and with the blood of those who had borne their testimony to Jesus. (Rev. 17:3–6)

Here and in the following chapter of this visionary narrative we encounter the intersection of images of ungoverned sensuality and beasts, together with motley colors,[33] profanation, and aggression against the Children of God. Avvakum consistently associates all of these with his enemies, who in serving Satan become part of the dark forces in this world which make struggle inevitable for the True Believer.

The stark contrast between the carnivores and those exhausted by labor, fasting, and suffering is generated by Avvakum's strong tendency toward "iconic" depiction, where characters embody the fixed, unadulterated essences of good or evil. The segregation of characters into types is of course a fixture in medieval Russian literature, as it is likely to be in any literature which not only reflects but above all seeks to propagate a particular world view. Characters (and more broadly, images) in the *Life* are for the most part inseparable from the doctrines and beliefs of Orthodoxy, which also provides a set of rigorous ideal standards against which thought and behavior may be judged. This is what Lixačëv calls the medieval method of generalization, accomplished by subsuming everything in life through deduction to a normative ideal.[34] Certainly this statement defines the general dynamics of the imagery and of characterization in Avvakum's *Life*. But there are exceptions which create here, to a lesser degree than elsewhere, a tension between event and meaning.

Although Avvakum consistently ascribes good behavior to the believer's staunch, untiring commitment to the right kind of faith, he is fundamentally ambivalent about the origins of evil. Often he follows an Orthodox tradition in attributing the wickedness of his enemies to the devil's inspiration, a notion grounded in the belief that men are essentially good, made in the image of God, and that sin represents a diminution of this godly essence: "The devil is wicked to me, but all men are good to me" (p. 80). But he frequently discovers in wickedness man's weakness, his capacity for corruption and iniquity. Here too he finds archetypal justification, in Annas and Caiaphas (p. 93), in St. Peter (p. 95), in Adam, Judas, and Satan himself (p. 111). This inconsistency is again a product of Avvakum's automatic responses to experience. Thus, Nikon is a wolf and a fox, the evil genius of the schism; but he is also moved by the devil (indeed, he is depicted here as qualitatively different from other men, as Satan's special agent in the world, the spiritual antithesis of a saint).

Avvakum's awareness of human weaknesses and of man's potential for evil can obviously provide a causal explanation of evil much closer to verifiable experience than indictment of the devil. (Lord Chesterton quite reasonably wondered why Christians abandon so eagerly the doctrine of Original Sin, since it is the only one which can be proved.) Such explanations of sinful behavior occur rather frequently in the *Life*, without reference to the devil, biblical analogues, or other archetypal identification. To cite one brief example, Avvakum himself once failed to maintain his daily rule owing to "feebleness and terrible hunger" (p. 83). Despite Avvakum's categorical patterns of thought, he produces in such instances a simple psychological explanation of behavior which again brings his *Life* into a dialectical relationship with tradition: we recognize here in primitive form a method of characterization primarily associated with later literary movements.[35]

Often interesting in this context is the behavior of Avvakum's opponents, who are by definition, at the moment of collision, in the camp of the devil. For example: Avvakum's denunciations culminating in a "short little epistle" are the apparent cause of the terrible flogging he receives from Paškov. Earlier he is abused by Vasilij Petrovič Šeremetev (p. 46) and later exiled from Moscow (p. 85) for words and actions similarly provocative. We recall here his close brush with death in Jur'evec-on-the-Volga; after an initial nod to the devil and a formulaic reference to punishment for his own sins, Avvakum specifies the immediate cause of his difficulties, his fulminations against the fornication of "the priests and their females" (p. 50). Such examples multiplied simply give substance to a general impression created by the *Life*, that it is often Avvakum himself, not the devil, who "raises up storms" by provoking his enemies to violent reprisals. His stereotyped depiction of his own physical passivity under attack does little to conceal the mutual rancor evident in these collisions. "Almighty lively it was" (*Zelo bylo mjatežno*) says Avvakum of the Mass during which he was unfrocked and thunderous anathemas were exchanged by victors and victims alike. In such cryptic remarks the prototypal is momentarily overwhelmed by a vivid impression of the elemental impulses inevitably present in mutual hatred and malignant vindictiveness.

These few examples indicate that psychological "analysis" of characters is far from a deliberate or consistent method in the *Life*, and that Avvakum is mistakenly called a "master psychologist" by several critics. It is nevertheless interesting, and significant historically, that this faltering movement away from the prototypal and toward a realistic appraisal of motivation on rare occasions complicates the judgment of behavior, so that a character's unambiguous assignment to the camp of friend or enemy becomes impossible. For instance, Avvakum says of Kozma, a deacon and scribe, "I don't know of what spirit that man is," owing to his contradictory actions in public and private (p. 86). Is he of God or of the devil? Far more important, however, is the depiction of Paškov. Although Avvakum initially identifies him with the enemy ("He burned and tortured and flogged people all the time . . . And from Moscow he had orders from Nikon to afflict me"; p. 58), in time the distinct outline of this black silhouette is effaced. When Paškov loses himself in an orgy of gratuitous cruelty, the lamenting Archpriest attributes it to mental derangement, not to the inspiration of the devil ("I don't know why he went off his head like that!" p. 64). After this passage, references to Paškov's brutality and vindictiveness are partially offset by his decent and even good actions (deference shown the Archpriest, and repentance). This together with Avvakum's recognition of his own provocations leads to an uncertain retreat from final judgment that goes beyond a formulaic abstention from condemnation: "Ten years he tormented me, or I him — I don't know. God will sort it out on Judgment Day." (p. 74.)

More important than the wicked acts of the wicked are the wicked acts of the good. That the Children of God should from time to time slip off the "narrow and grievous path" is not altogether surprising either in relation to the literary (and biblical) tradition or to Avvakum's understanding of the good life as willed obedience to the will of God (thus his continuing interest in the biographies of people from his past). Perhaps no writer in medieval Russia understood better than he how difficult such obedience can be. This understanding combined with medieval self-deprecation must have dictated his use of a traditional pattern for depicting repentance and conversion to the Old Belief: not his own efforts but potent divine intervention (miracles or punishments) almost always effects the change in the sinner's stubborn heart. On the other hand, reprehensible actions by good people are always rooted in human weakness and are given a psychological causal explanation. Pëtr Beketov defends the blackguard Ivan Struna out of misplaced pity and finds a bitter death (p. 58); Paškov's daughter-in-law Evdokija Kirilovna appeals to a peasant sorcerer out of fear for her sick child's life (p. 70); Ivan Neronov, Avvakum's former confessor and mentor, accepts the reforms after long imprisonment and much physical suffering (52–54); and so on. Avvakum is loath to associate any of his allies past or present directly with the devil unless, like Matvej Lomkov, they have fallen away completely: "He was good before, but now the devil's swallowed him whole" (p. 56). Unlike the enemy, the spawn of hell, these sinners are never eager students "instructed" by the devil; rather, the Evil One tricks Avvakum's sons, just as the spirit of the Antichrist "deceives"

Neronov. And if the devil "hardens the soil" of Evdokija Kirilovna's heart after weakness has set her on the wrong path, that soil is swiftly "softened" again.

The failures of good people are all attributable in one way or another to the hold this world has on all men. Avvakum understood in an elemental way the obstinate vitality of the flesh, and there are moments in the *Life* when he grieves deeply over his own bodily needs. In Siberia, for example, when starvation compels him to eat unclean flesh and carrion, he laments, " 'Who will give my head water and a fountain of tears that I might weep for my poor soul,' which I wickedly sullied with worldly pleasures?" (p. 64). We recognize here and in Avvakum's great admiration for the asceticism of the holy fool Fëdor that radical dualism which lay behind the protracted mortifications of the flesh in service to the spirit practiced by countless generations of anchorites, a tradition reaffirmed by Avvakum's contemporaries Kapiton and the Forest Elders. But here, more than anywhere else, it is experience that forces a compromise between a normative ideal and psychological realities. Avvakum had learned a bitter truth, that prolonged physical suffering does not liberate man from his flesh but rather binds him to it: "There was a time that I broke down in my rule from feebleness and terrible hunger. Hardly any [of it] was left, ... So I dragged along like a little old beast, grieving about my rule but not able to hold to it." (p.83 .) This knowledge is another element in Avvakum's mitigated dualism, and it explains, for example, his pragmatic approval of ascetic Fëdor's plea that he be permitted to abandon traditional dress in order to hide in Moscow after escaping torture in prison, where they had been "forcing [him] toward that new Sacrament of the Antichrist" (p. 89). The decision is justified by Fëdor's eventual martyrdom, the ultimate test of loyalty to the Old Belief. Similarly, Avvakum never condemns worldly wealth or power in his followers as long as first allegiance, as he understands it, is given to the spirit. So he loves and elevates Boyarina Morozova and her sister (p. 84). Recognizing the weakness of the flesh, he will compromise to preserve that allegiance. But there can be no mitigating circumstances in the long run. The normative ideal is the final measure, and a man must be willing to "bear all things" when it becomes necessary, finding strength to subdue his weakness, as Avvakum managed to do in Siberia, and was doing in his frozen pit at Pustozersk.

I must re-emphasize that Avvakum's understanding of behavior contains merely the germs of rational causal thinking, rather frequent but isolated instances where experience and a rudimentary psychological knowledge provide an explanation for behavior and (more rarely) influence moral judgment. While complicating and enriching a scheme of character depiction in which one or two motives are assigned automatically, such thinking does not move Avvakum very far away from the medieval "vertical" apprehension of experience, where meaning is measured by absolute moral categories proceeding from the Higher and the Lower, and toward a more modern "horizontal" frame of reference, the terminus of which is causal determinism. The tension between the realms of the physical and the spiritual is thus completely ascendent over any contrary tendency. Before discussing other specific metaphors governed by this dichotomy, it is appropriate to examine briefly the nature of narrative time in the *Life*, in order to see more clearly how flux and change (implying, for us, cause leading to effect) are related to the eternal and unchanging.

As Lixačëv has argued, characters in medieval literature transcend time to some degree through typological segregation, because their association with eternal archetypes partially extricates them from the circumstantial moment.[36] Despite the obvious presence of such types in the *Life*, Lixačëv has perceived in it an important innovation, a "subjective," "egocentric" structuring of narrative time that anticipates phenomena in modern literature by departing from the objective temporal movement, seemingly independent of the narrator's psyche, which was traditional (Ibid., 254–55): "Avvakum sees his past from the present,... [and] the 'egocentrism of the present' is the characteristic feature of Avvakum's autobiographical writing. He expresses his present attitudes toward the past now, he forgives or curses his former tormentors and blesses his former fellow sufferers now, he recalls what has happened to them after a particular event or in the present time ... To a certain extent, the past is the present for him." (Ibid., p. 306.)

In the course of his argument (Ibid., 303–06), Lixačëv develops an analogy between time structure in the *Life* and the "egocentricity" of visual perspective, which appeared in Russian painting during Avvakum's lifetime. Each episode from the past is apprehended subjectively from the writer's perspective in the present, at the moment of writing; not the external, real succession of events but their "inner," psychological succession dominates his narrative. Real chronology is often fragmented, as Avvakum moves through time from event to associated event. And when adjacent episodes are not so displaced, the temporal relationship between them is almost always approximated subjectively by general adverbial expressions, not specified by reference to dates or historical events (e.g., "after a little while," "after this," "next," "then," "at that time," "another time," "another year," and so on).

Lixačëv's argument is perceptive and interesting, yet it obscures the relationship between the temporal and the eternal in the *Life.* In restricting his discussion for the most part to the "horizontal" dimension of Avvakum's narration, where the relation of present moment to past event is of primary interest, Lixačëv discovers an apprehension of experience that greatly resembles the subjective relativism frequently encountered in modern literature (310–11). From this perspective it is reasonable to say that, for Avvakum, the "indeterminacy of time, its flux, and flow, and agonizing prolongation" are most important (p. 304). But such observations must be greatly modified once the "vertical" dimension of Avvakum's vision is taken into account. As Lixačëv himself observes, "The present judges the past in Avvakum's *Life*" (p. 306), and it is the process of judgment that shapes almost every episode according to the fixed, antithetical characteristics of the physical and the spiritual. If this application of what, in the author's view, are absolute moral measures of meaning can still be viewed as subjective, it certainly does not produce a vision of life dominated by flux and change alone: the circumstantial moment, the specific and evanescent, always bears the imprint of the divine.

This process of imprinting results in a high degree of thematic repetitiveness, a recognized characteristic of medieval literature. It is this, I think, that explains Avvakum's recourse to expressions such as "Why go on and on?" and "Much could be said about that"; rather than attempting through a zero description to express amazement at life's complexity and variety, as several critics have suggested, Avvakum is trying here to make a long story short. His "listeners" know only too well truths constantly reiterated by experience. That Avvakum provides more specific information about life in Russia than was traditional is important, but it should not lure us into the error of perceiving in his *Life* something resembling the inclusive vision often encountered in Realism. Avvakum has very little in common with Roman Jakobson's little boy ("a typical Realist") who wondered, in solving an arithmetical problem involving a bird flying from its cage to a forest, what color the cage was.[37]

The rigid structuring of experience through this process of imprinting would seem to have more in common with the flat, two-dimensional surface of the icon than it does with visual perspective. Yet Lixačev's observations are certainly germane to the question of time-structure in the *Life*. A more precise definition of the relationship between the narrational present and narrative past will perhaps clarify the situation here. In visual perspective the foreground and background are distinct, yet they are bound together by the sense of continuous, unbroken space between them. We see here a simple analogue for a phenomenon frequently associated with memory used as a literary device in the modern period. Audience and writer share an assumption of change or development of personality over time, so that present and past are distinct, yet organically connected. A dual perspective on particular experiences often results, a dialectical process whereby a single personality provides two significantly conflicting perceptions of single events. It is as if events were refracted simultaneously through two similar lenses, one having characteristics systematically derived from those of the other (a classic example is Turgenev's *First Love*). It is precisely this that is lacking in Avvakum's *Life*. We encounter here not two perspectives but one, not two lenses but one. The present does not grow out of the past so much as it repeats it. Avvakum's use in narration of iterative verb forms makes this clear. Equally important, the use of the present and perfective future tenses and, above all, the potency of Avvakum's voice abridge the temporal distance between narrational present and narrative past, virtually precluding the depiction of growth and maturation. There is no deliberate, or significant, development of the man, only of his struggle. His personality in the past mirrors his personality in the present.[38] In this way the "perspective" inherent in autobiographical first-person narration

174 The Life of the Archpriest Avvakum

is flattened as Avvakum persistently resorts to repetitious iconic representation.

Avvakum's inclination toward metaphorical expression figures importantly in this archetypal structuring of experience. Analysis of specific metaphors and metaphoric imagery not yet introduced into argument again reveals Avvakum's tendency to view phenomena, often inconsistently, from the two vantage points established by the realms of the spiritual and the physical (see above, 162—63). For example, we have argued the oscillations in Avvakum's personality between bellicose warrior and passive martyr are conditoned by his optimistic and pessimistic assessments of the possibilities for a restoration — that is, whether he views this world as primarily in the hands of God or of the devil. Similarly opposed are his two widely discussed descriptions of Siberian landscapes (59, 76—78). The first follows upon Paškov's decision to drive the Archpriest into the mountains to live with the beasts of the forest. Perhaps Demkova exaggerates the ominous quality of this passage in arguing it expresses the physical powerlessness and insignificance of man in the face of nature's might (157—58). The ominous quality itself is real, however, for Avvakum suggests that death awaits him in the impenetrable forests and deep ravines of those great mountains. Yet a dissonant, almost lyrical tone is created here by his enumeration of the multitudes of birds and beasts that populate those forests — all of them beyond the reach of a starving man ("You'll lay your eyes on them but never your hands!"). This lyrical tone dominates the second passage, which occurs during Avvakum's description of the journey out of Siberia. Here intimations of danger and death disappear altogether, as Avvakum enumerates even more insistently the varieties of beauteous life found around Lake Baikal, a magnificent part of God's world. The partial contrast between these passages depends upon the two vantage points from which Avvakum views life in this world: the physical world may be hostile and inhabited by (some) dangerous beasts, or it may be beneficent and beautiful, populated by the creatures of God's creation. So Avvakum transforms his enemies into ravening beasts while eulogizing the "good little black hen" that fed his children during the return to Russia ("Every little beast and bird lives to the glory of him, who is our most immaculate Lord, and for the sake of man as well"; 68—70).

Particularly interesting in this regard is the stark contrast between the landscapes described in these two passages. The second compares the area around Lake Baikal to a medieval walled city "made by God"; the impression of a fitting, planned orderliness here is opposed to the primeaval wildness of nature in the first passage. Thus, similar physical environments bear antithetical imprints of the spiritual and the physical. The swiftness that sometimes marks Avvakum's movement from one vantage point to the other can be seen in the didactic contrast he establishes between the second, "pure" landscape and mankind. There he summarizes the sinful inclinations of men by striking parallels between them and various beasts, this immediately after his exaltation of the creatures that swell the riches of God's creation.

Analysis of other imagery involving material things yields analogous results. Water, for example, is an agent of both death and rebirth. The metaphor of the abyss, the "deep" (*pučina*) on which the boats of True Believers sail, apparently establishes the link between water and the forces of destruction. So Avvakum is almost drowned three times, he is caught in a great storm on Lake Baikal, and he is forced to haul barges along frigid cataracts in Siberia until his "legs and belly turned blue" (p. 63). Water as a purifying sacramental, an agent of new or renewed spiritual life (holy water), is even more traditional, and Avvakum is never without it in his struggle with evil. Here "to be athirst" has a primary spiritual referent, a state of weakness and weariness which can be alleviated by the water of the spirit only. For instance, in one essentially allegorical episode Avvakum finds himself alone, exhausted and athirst, in the midst of a vast, hostile — and metaphorical — winter landscape in Siberia. After a humble prayer in which the thirsting Archpriest compares himself to a "dead dog" (i.e., a man of moribund spirit), a miracle opens the ice of the lake on which he stands. Replenished and strengthened by the fresh water, he hurries on "across the ice, where I had to go, to my children." (p. 81.) We understand children here as the "spiritual children" whose salvation always justifies continuing the struggle in which the Archpriest is frequently wearied and spiritually athirst. Significantly, this edifying allegory follows Avvakum's description of that comfortable period in Moscow after his Siberian exile when he backslid and "was just about stung by that stinger, the spirit of the Antichrist" (p. 80). It generalizes the notion of spiritual thirst and specifies the means for quenching it. Then, lest the point be missed, Avvakum explains his allegory in the next passage: "And it was often that way with me, at other times during my wanderings." And after describing his past efforts to fulfill faithfully his daily ritualistic obligations, he adds: "For as the hungering body desireth to eat and the thirsting body to drink, so doth the soul desire spiritual sustenance, my Father Epifanij. Neither famine of bread nor thirst for water destroys a man; but a great famine it is for a man to live, not praying to God."

We conclude from this solemn formulation that Avvakum was not only aware of the dualistic connotations of water, but he could use them to aesthetic ends (here, a contrastive parallelism). Elsewhere he is cast into a prame after his terrible flogging by Paškov, and he spends the night there, lying in water and under a frigid autumn downpour (59–60). In an often cited passage Avvakum rebels against God in prayer by questioning the justice of this cruel punishment. Then in wrathful self-judgment he wonders that the prame did not sink beneath him, and he remembers he began to die. But the water threatening to draw the life from his body splashes in his mouth instead, and reviving he repents his sin. The next day the Archpriest continues to suffer from the freezing rain and snow, but he comforts himself with a statement by St. Paul explaining why the righteous must suffer (Heb. 12:5–8).

The instance of contrastive parallelism cited above indicates the duality characteristic of water is associated with food as well, especially with bread. In fact, that solemn utterance culminates a section of the *Life* (80–83) organized by the metaphor of dining, which figures so prominently in the Orthodox liturgy and in Orthodox thought about the Kingdom of Heaven.[39] The section begins with an etymological pun discussed by Vinogradov (p.124): "So I didn't go to the service, but was served dinner at a prince's instead" (*Ja i k obedne ne pošël, i obedat' ko knjazju prišël*). Shortly thereafter, in the passage clarifying the allegory of the miracle on the ice, Avvakum refers to his daily devotions as dining (*Tak i obedaju* 'That's how I supped'; p. 81), this preceding the edifying peroration cited above. Similarly, Avvakum's terrible hunger in prison and his miraculous replenishment by an angel (p. 54) can be read allegorically: on the third day, his physical vision dulled by constant darkness (see above), he is spiritually resurrected and given strength to endure the ordeals that follow immediately. The merger here of bread as sustenance for both body and spirit is indicated by the meager quantity given the Archpriest: food in quantity is consumed, not by the Elect, but by men with great bellies. And in the Introduction to the third redaction of his *Life*, Avvakum juxtaposes spiritual and physical sustenance, the former coming from God and the latter, from women in their kitchens: "May God grant that you receive of the moisture of the earth and the dew of heaven over and above your need, and may he increase in your home all beauty and grace. Eat the old of the old and spew out the old that comes with the new — there will be plenty of everything and more left over. The Lord give you bread and meat and fish; from the women [who prepare them] let these blessed breads be eaten!" [40]

Fire is used once in a similar metaphorical manner, again to didactic and aesthetic ends. In recalling the young woman's confession of various sexual sins, Avvakum compares his lustful response to a "lecherous fire" (*ognem bludnym*, p.45). But "Fire" (*ogn'*) is also one of the consequent names for God enumerated in the opening lines of the *Life*; and Avvakum places his right hand (cf. the right hand of God, at which the Elect shall stand on Judgment Day) in the flames of three candles, symbolizing the Trinity, to extinguish "the evil conflagration within." This evil blaze of the flesh is consonant with Avvakum's definition of hell as "fire and affliction" (*ogon' da muka*; p.104); but fire, like water, is also an agent of purification in Orthodox thought and Russian tradition.

The duality of sanctified and unsanctified water, bread, and fire is traditional, of course; its origin is located, at least in part, in the blessing and sanctification of earthly substances (water and oil, the elements in the Eucharist), in the ancient Christian practice of speaking about spiritual matters in terms of physical things, and ultimately in the conviction that the life of men on earth is ever in need of purification. Indeed, the goal of Avvakum's struggle is to achieve an analogous sanctification of his own life and the lives of his followers. My analysis here attempts to show, however, that these images *tend* to bifurcate in Avvakum's usage, each of them producing two partially discrete images with antithetical, sometimes irreconcilable connotations. Perhaps the image of darkness, inseparable from its antipode light, provides the best illustration of this movement.

Like motliness, light is a stable image in the *Life*. Avvakum cites it as one of the four "connatural and true" names for God, he uses it frequently as a venerative epithet in referring to Christ and good men, he associates it with the Truth and the True Way to God that traditionally passes through the darkness in which men become lost: "If we say we have fellowship with him while we walk in the darkness, we lie and do not live according to the Truth; but if we walk in the light, as he is in the light, we have fellowship with one another . . . " (I John 1:6–7). The ultimate referent here in tradition is the uncreated divine light of God "emanating," for example, from the background of icons, which are shadowless and independent of the sun's created light. The consistent connotations of this image in the *Life* are not surprising, considering its antiquity and ubiquity in the Judeo-Christian tradition. But darkness is more complex; it may symbolize either the forces of Satan and/or spiritual failure only, or the necessary context of life in this world within which men search for and find the light. Although Avvakum's ambivalence here is related conceptually to the old theological questions regarding the necessity of evil, it would be fruitless to seek any consistent response to this problem in the *Life*. The automatic response, not systematic thought, is at issue here. Thus, devils are of the powers of darkness, and Avvakum treats them as such. Yet the very devils that oppose him, that must be exorcised, are very often identified as agents of God's punishment as well. Quite simply, they serve both heaven and hell.

Darkness as an emblem of evil and spiritual failure concludes Avvakum's most encompassing summary of human frailties. In a famous passage discussed above, he compares man in his weaknesses to various beasts, and then adds: " . . . he doesn't pray to God; he puts off repentance to his old age and then disappears. I don't know where he goes, whether into the light or into the darkness." (p. 78.) Consistent with this perception are the heavenly signs of "God's wrath against men" described by Avvakum: the sun is eclipsed when nations chosen by God (Russia and Israel) give themselves over to evil, while its motion is stayed and the light of day extended when they fight the good fight (38–39). Avvakum is forced to abandon his family and flee the town of Jur'evec at night to escape an angry mob (p. 50), and he later has a similar experience in Tobol'sk (p. 56). His first arrest occurs at night (p. 54), and it is nighttime as he utters his wicked prayer for the destruction of Eremej Paškov's troop (p. 71). Two of the assaults upon the Archpriest by officials occur at night (45–46, 48), and there is always a dark cell awaiting him in the prisons of his enemies. In the final supplementary tale (p. 111) Avvakum goes to his church "deep in the night" to fetch the missal for his wife's confession, as she is deathly ill, and in the darkened house of God he is repeatedly frightened by a devil. Similarly, in these same concluding tales, Avvakum beats his wife and her maid unjustly at night (105–06), and he fails, because of his own sin, to exorcise the devils from his brother Evfimej during the night in which the latter was struck down. And so on.

Evfimej is one among several peripheral figures in the *Life* who are thus scourged at night; and to be scourged by God is always a summons to repentance for Avvakum. For example, two of the Archpriest's tormentors, the third official Evfimej Stefanovič (sic) (p. 48) and the Cellarer of the Pafnut'ev Monastery Nikodim (p. 88), are afflicted at night and repent before the Archpriest. Here we perceive darkness as the necessary context within which the light is to be found. And so the pure but rebellious maid Anna comes to repent before the Archpriest (who is praying in darkness) and to tell him of a vision in which she was led by angels along "a narrow path" past hell to a "bright place" (*svetloe mesto*), where she was shown the heavenly mansion awaiting her confessor (p. 109). This use of darkness is typical for depictions of Avvakum's own spiritual failures. The hour seems to him like midnight (p. 45) as he returns home in despair after responding with lust to the wanton young woman's confession, but in his repentance he is rewarded with a vision in which light and color predominate. Similarly, his rebellious judgment of God's injustice after his terrible flogging occurs at night (p. 60), but his repentance is followed by relief from pain. And a beating Avvakum receives from a lunatic causes him to repent his own nocturnal beating of wife and maidservant, to seek their forgiveness, and to find a penance in being whipped by his entire household, some twenty people.

Anna's vision of paradise indicates the link existing in Avvakum's thinking between spiritual perceptions and light; visions typically occur in darkness. This helps us to understand how the prison cell, often a pit dug into the earth and covered over, is manipulated by Avvakum into a metaphor expressing the True Believer's lot in this life: moments of illumination are experienced in that darkness, which, with the surrounding earth, represents the hold this world and the flesh have on the spirit. The metaphor is enhanced by the word "dungeon" (*temnica*) with its connotation of darkness (*tëmnyj, temnota*). And the Archpriest emphasizes the obvious analogy that can be struck between those pits and the grave by repeating the phrase, "sitting there [locked up], buried in the earth" (*sidet' v zemle zakopan*). [41]

The light at the heart of this darkness transforms the grave from an emblem of defeat into a promise of victory. Retention of this light and escape from that darkness motivate all Avvakum's labors in Christ, including his endless nocturnal prayers and obeisances (he began to pray *every night* after that critical youthful experience, witnessing the death of a cow, a beast). Transfiguration of motley Russian life and lives to the luminous gold of paradise is the goal of those labors. And if the powers of darkness cannot be driven from the Church, then those walking in the uncreated divine light will find its source beyond the darkness of the grave: "Don't grieve about this accursed life, but rejoice and be glad in the righteousness we have in the Lord, for they [i.e., martyrs for the Old Belief] have passed from evil into the good and from darkness into the life of light." [42] Spiritually transfigured lives are beautiful according to the medieval Russian measure, the extent to which present *realia* embody the beauty of the celestial: men are "beautiful" insofar as they have regained the image of God first given to them at creation. [43] Such beauty has no essential physical embodiment, despite Avvakum's awareness of things; rather, physical qualities are figurative expressions of the spirit suffused with the beauteous light emanating from the throne of God: "Behold, thou art fair, my lovely one, behold thou art fair, my beloved. Thine eyes burn as the flame of fire, thy teeth are white more than milk; thy countenance is more than the rays of the sun, and thou shinest ever in beauty, as the day in its strength.' (Laud of the Church)" (p. 99.)

Allegory: *Purity as a Maiden Most Beautiful.* She is surrounded by symbols of life and light, has direct access to heaven, and masters the beasts and devils inhabiting this world. The sinner Adam (mankind), afflicted with death, languishes beneath the earth.

These notions are helpful in approaching the problem of Avvakum's self-depiction. Certainly he considered the lives of the old saints and martyrs to be beautiful, and he longed to create that same beauty in his own life. Yet he hesitated to claim this achievement for himself in the *Life*; as we remarked above, he is a "saint trailing disclaimers." Of all Avvakum's contradictions, his belligerence and tenderness, arrogance and humility, his hatred and love, the most important is his sinful saintliness. In his inability to define once and for all who he is we find the most significant product of the tension between event and meaning. However inadvertant this tension may have been, it contributes more than any other single factor to the discordant humanity of Avvakum's self-portrait.

This conflict is recognized in the critical literature. For example, Čiževskij asserts the Archpriest is inconsistent in viewing himself as both sinner and prophet, and perhaps as a saint (374–75). Stokes is inconsistent himself in arguing Avvakum made an apparent claim to sainthood in writing his *Life* (p. 231), later stating that the work does not glorify its author but rather demonstrates the validity of resistance to the reforms: God will support even an admitted sinner if the cause is right (236–37). Demkova argues that the idea of sainthood grows progressively stronger from the first redaction to the last (p. 35). These arguments illustrate the attention critics have given to the problem of the relationship between Avvakum's autobiography and the genre of the *vita*. Before all else, it must be said that the word *žitie* 'life' in Avvakum's usage is broad enough to encompass the lives of saints and sinners alike, just as it is, with certain reservations, in contemporary standard Russian. We must exercise here the kind of semantic caution V. E. Gusev displays in stating that the word *prostorečie* in Avvakum's usage is not so much our contemporary stylistic category ("substandard speech") as it is an approximate synonym for "native language" (see Avvakum's famous statement on *prostorečie*, p. 208), in contrast to *krasnorečie* (i.e., language and style heavily influenced by foreign, especially Greek models).   We are misled if we consider *vita* in its specific literary referent, "life of a saint," a completely adequate translation for the title of Avvakum's autobiography.

The word *žitie* for Avvakum means "life-story," conjoined with the related notion of "life-style." Consequently, it can be comfortably linked with adjectives as diverse as *gnusnoe* 'vile,' *svetloe* 'bright, of light,' *roskošnoe* 'luxurious,' *dobrodetel'noe* 'virtuous,' *okajannoe* 'accursed,' *slaboe* 'weak,' *rastlennoe, grexotvoritel'noe* 'rotten and sin-laden,' and so on.[45] In speaking about life as existence either here or yonder and without particular reference to time, Avvakum tends to use the word *život*. Thus, he saves the life of a scoundrel, bringing him "from death to life" (*ot smerti k životu*, p. 74); but he also refers to his autobiography as "a book of eternal life" (*kniga života večnago*) and speaks of "the path leading to life" (*život*) (Ibid., 54, 139). These two words are not sharply differentiated in meaning for Avvakum, however, and he often uses them synonymously. For example, in his "First Conversation" he refers in a matter of a few lines to life in this world as *okajannoe žitie* 'accursed life' and as *život* ("We don't know how long our life [*život naš*] will stretch out" — clearly implying a temporal dimension), while life in paradise is called "the life of light" (*žitie svetloe*; cf. examples above using *život*; Ibid.,126–27). The issue of importance in the present context is that the word *žitie* did not possess a narrowly delineated ecclesiastical or literary referent for Avvakum; it thus presented no semantic impediments to his undertaking, describing his own spiritual victories and failures. It is likely the general Christian tradition of self-deprecation and humility contributed as much to Avvakum's defensive explanations of the reasons that impelled him to write his *Life* as the conventions of a genre.

This is not to say that *žitie* as a genre, as opposed to the word, placed no constraints on the Archpriest. Being profoundly committed to ecclesiastical traditions, he almost certainly had no desire to *challenge* a particular tradition in his *Life*. Indeed, recognizing the singularity of autobiography, he defends his own primarily by appeals to the Christian heritage. Nevertheless, his genre was traditionally reserved for the authentic deeds of saints and martyrs, and this, together with the tradition of humility, made certain adjustments desirable. Occasional vehement admissions of sinfulness set a self-deprecatory distance between the Archpriest and those saints. And among the several reasons that have been suggested in the critical literature for his use of the vernacular might we not include a humble desire to differentiate himself from the great saints of the past, whose *Lives* were written in the language of the Church? In using the vernacular Avvakum not only communicated more effectively with his often unlettered audience, but he identified himself more closely with them. Unlike a saint, he was not a man completely apart. From this perspective, his style may be viewed as more appropriate, a lesser violation of "etiquette" (to use Lixačëv's term), than deliberate use of the traditional high style.

Whether humility, real or feigned, figured so prominently in these matters is difficult to determine, especially as the author's voice is so often congested with pride. Without trying to establish the actual mix of vanity and humility we can say that Avvakum departs not at all in his self-depiction from the patterns of thought we have been examining. He views himself in the same inconsistent manner he views all experience, from the vantage points provided by the realms of the physical and the spiritual. The result again is repetitious iconic representation, the "fixing" of a complex psychological reality by its association with archetypal images that transcend a particular time and place. Insofar as Avvakum participates in the life of the spirit, he reiterates, like all saints, the life and behavior of Christ. Insofar as he is enmeshed in this world, he is a depraved sinner whose only access to hope lies in reiterating the Parable of the Prodigal Son (Luke 15:11–32). It is in this context that I find Robinson's generic description of the *Life* as a "confession-sermon" (*ispoved'-propoved'*) most useful.[46] (Although references to other biblical figures are relevant to these patterns, their individual importance is slight.)

Christ and the Prodigal signify antithetical responses to the will of God. Whereas Christ for Avvakum is a monolithic figure, unwavering in his perfect obedience, the Prodigal is lacking in wholeness and a failure owing to his hedonistic immersion in the life of this world. Christ is of gold as it were, while the Prodigal is motley and beastlike (his failure – in great [spiritual] hunger, feeding swine and envying them their food – had special appeal for the Archpriest).[47]

The logical inconsistency between these two self-images results once again from Avvakum's automatic recourse to traditional concepts and archetypal patterns in specifying the meaning of actions and events. We may view these images as generally discrete, for they reflect that segmentation of experience fostered by the "vertical orientation" toward existence discussed above (p. 171), where moral evaluation of persons and disjunct events has a structural function analogous to that of rational causation or general logical or conceptual consistency in the literature of the modern era. (Recall the glorification and denigration of Prince Igor' in separate portions of the *Slovo o polku Igoreve*.) Yet it would be wrong to suggest that these images are completely isolated from one another: after the Archpriest beats his wife and her maid unjustly, he makes confession in the words of the Prodigal, "I sinned before God and before them" (p.106), and he repents by bowing to the earth before the offended women, echoing once again those words, "I've sinned, ... forgive me" (p.106). Then, like Christ before the Last Supper (Luke 22:12), he retreats with his entire household to an "upper room" (*gornica*), where he humbles himself. But unlike Christ, who washed the feet of his disciples (Mark 13:4–16), the prodigal Avvakum demands and gets what he apparently deserves, a thorough scourging. The tension between these two images is maintained when Avvakum's household initially resists his command, as the Apostle Peter resisted Christ's humble ministrations. The Archpriest repeats virtually verbatim Christ's admonition to Peter in saying that any who refuse to whip "shall have no part with me in the Kingdom of Heaven" (cf. Mark 13:8).

The collision of these self-images recalls the dualism of water in the episode of Avvakum's rebellion against God (p. 60), but it is significant beyond the aesthetically pleasing dissonance it creates. Ultimately the logical contradiction between them is of secondary importance. If the image of the author threatens to bifurcate like water and fire, it never does so in fact, because the Archpriest's virile, strident voice unites these opposites, just as it collapses the temporal distance between present and past. We understand this contradiction finally as a product of Avvakum's psychological complexity and inadvertant uncertainty about his own historical significance. We are concerned, then, with the familiar problem of identity, a distinctly modern theme arising by accident, as it were, in the alien milieu of medieval Russian literature.

Generally Avvakum seizes upon one archetype or the other to specify his moral identity in any particular episode: he knows at any given moment, *usually* with certainty, who he is, saint or sinner. For example, in the first supplementary tale (101–04) Avvakum sins and fails to exorcise his brother's devils. He is thus a prodigal, and after cursing himself he adds, alluding to the archetype: "It would be good for me to live with dogs and hogs in their pens; they stink like my soul, with an evil-smelling stench. But hogs and hounds stink by their nature, while I stink from my sins like a dead dog cast out into a city street." Yet in the tale following immediately, he imitates the Good Shepherd in caring for, teaching, and healing the lunatic Kiriluško. Nevertheless, the dissonances emanating from his penitential scourging (above) indicate why categorical separation of these self-images is not quite justified. What is more, the *Life* shares with traditional representatives of its genre a single pedagogical task, to show men how to live. Yet each evocation of the Prodigal represents a departure from the normative ideal of the saintly life: while teaching by negative example, it proves the fallibility of the teacher. We may conclude, then, that as the first glimmerings of rational psychological motivation are found in the *Life*, so too do we encounter here the seeds of a protagonist's *conscious* uncertainty about his identity. Perhaps the most interesting but problematical example is Avvakum's plea for Epifanij's judgment of his lie (p. 75). Despite the deception practiced here (see 147–49), the moral dilemma described may have been real to the Archpriest, and his response to it reflects the uncertainty we encounter elsewhere: although Avvakum finds in Rahab of Jericho a positive biblical analogue for his action, he still cannot decide whether it was saintly or sinful, whether he mimicked Christ or the Prodigal. In strictly formal terms, then, there is a degree of similarity between Avvakum's self-depiction and that, say, of Dostoevskij's Underground Man, who identifies himself at various times with the incommensurable images of Napoleon and insects. A clear measure of the gulf between them, however, is the contrast between the Underground Man's tormented awareness of his uncertain identity and Avvakum's rare and scarcely perceptible nods of acknowledgement. But then, the Underground Man has no foundation in faith on which to erect an identity, something Avvakum has to surfeit.

Thus Avvakum moves erratically between a sense of Christlike potency and mission and a penitent awareness of his sinful frailty before the will of God. As the Christ, God's Son, he interprets the Truth for men; as the Prodigal he bows down before the Father, acknowledging betrayal of his sonship. It is chiefly repentance that links the two images, for it enables prodigal Avvakum to begin anew the imitation of Christ, and to renew through prayers, visions, and wonders his intercourse with the divine. If repentance works for this one sinner, it will work for all Russian sinners. And Avvakum's *Life* is finally this, an urgent summons to national repentance.

Avvakum's abrupt movements between logically discontinuous archetypes can be seen, oddly enough, in a passage dealing with Paškov. The Archpriest recalls how Eremej Paškov once announced to his father that the latter's difficulties were God's punishment for Avvakum's flogging. After first attempting to murder his son, Paškov repents, using the words of Judas: "I have sinned, accursed man, I have spilled innocent blood." Eremej responds by bowing before his father and repeating the Prodigal's confession, momentarily illuminating this harsh man with the ultimate divine archetype. And forgetting Judas, Avvakum applauds Eremej's filial piety because it accords with God's will. Yet in the next few lines Paškov is once again planning to torture Avvakum to death. (72–73.)

Unlike the children of darkness, Avvakum is never led astray by the devil, [48] for his departures from the Father's will, like the Prodigal's, are always his own doing. And like the Prodigal he can be overwhelmed by recognition of his own weakness and wickedness. It is primarily passages expressing spiritual frailty and contrition, and not specific references to the Prodigal himself, that reflect this archetypal pattern. It is clear nevertheless that this great and familiar parable of repentance was firmly embedded in the Archpriest's consciousness. The Prodigal's confession, "I have sinned against heaven and before thee," is the only remark by a biblical figure repeated at intervals in the *Life* (48, 73, 88, 106); and Avvakum compares himself at some length to the Prodigal swineherd in the Introduction to his *Book of Conversations* (see note 47). There are two passages of violent self-vilification in the *Life*, the first occasioned by the Archpriest's rebellion against his heavenly Father after Paškov's flogging (60—61), the second by his rebellion against his confessor (i.e., his so-called spiritual father [*duxovnyj otec*],101—04). He refers in the latter to the Prodigal's beasts in their pens (see above), and he strikes a parallel between the binding commandments of his spiritual father and of his Father God; in the former Avvakum's repentance culminates in a biblical passage that provides him with an unambiguous sign of his continuing sonship. To such specific references we may add his frequent expressions of self-deprecation (e.g., "I, a sinner, . . . " "But I, accursed man, . . . "), often in hagiographical formulas which we cannot safely assume to be devoid of genuine content, and his admissions of his inability without help to shape and save his own life amidst the dangers and temptations of this world (his three near-drownings, his temptation by the debauched young woman, and so on). Both sinfulness and powerlessness are proclaimed when the Prodigal casts himself upon his father's mercy.

The image of the Prodigal's father is obviously commensurable with the image of Christ, especially with Christ the Good Shepherd, so we might well anticipate that Avvakum would view himself not only as the Prodigal but as the Prodigal's loving, forgiving father. (Samson Virin, a character in Puškin's famous story "The Stationmaster," views himself in precisely the same way, as the Good Shepherd and as the Prodigal's father.) Shortly before the villainous official Evfimej Stefanovič falls down before Avvakum and repeats the Prodigal's confession, the Archpriest remarks sarcastically to Evfimej's wife, "Yesterday I was a son of a whore, and now, Father!" (p. 48). And later, after he heals the withered right arm and leg of Paškov's grandson (i.e., the side of the body associated with election to the Kingdom of Heaven), Paškov bows low before the Archpriest and says, "You act like a real father, you don't remember our wickedness" (70—71). Yet this same father is swiftly transformed into the Prodigal in his animal pen. In the next episode Avvakum maliciously calls down destruction on Eremej and his troop: "This bad shepherd destroyed his sheep, from bitterness he forgot what is said in the Gospel . . . There in my little pen (*xlevina*) I shouted out in lamentation to the Lord . . . " But the Good Shepherd returns when Eremej, lost in Mongolian territory (the one surviving sheep), is blessed by Avvakum in a vision and shown "the road, in what direction to journey" (71—74). Similarly, in the next episode this same good shepherd gathers the old, the sick, and the wounded, together with two scoundrels, and brings them all from Siberia back home, to Russia (p. 74). Helping others to find and remain on the "true path home" is of course the principal didactic task of the *Life*.

Such certainty about the significance of his life is the rule for Avvakum, not his moments of indecision. After all, he had the Truth in hand, and thus the criteria necessary to adjudge himself saint (or sinner) in any particular experience. And even an occasional saint will perceive those occasions against the normative life of Christ, just as icons of saints are conceptually inseparable from icons and the archetype of Christ. [49] The impact of the traditional hagiographical imitation of Christ on Avvakum's autobiography is apparent, and such parallels are often noted in the critical literature. For example, Avvakum's experiences before and during the Ecumenical Council of 1666–67 resemble in certain particulars Christ's experiences in Jerusalem prior to his crucifixion. Both leaders return to the holy city of their national religions, both are initially received warmly but soon find themselves in confrontation with the leadership of the religious establishment. As old conflicts are reignited and the masses are swayed by Christ and Avvakum, their destruction becomes the goal of plots hatched by church leaders. Both are arrested, reviled, and beaten, both refuse to compromise their principles and are condemned. And there are moments in the *Life* when Avvakum clearly anticipates his own Golgotha.

As saints are inseparable from the image of Christ, Avvakum is not inconsistent in also viewing himself as one of the disciples who were exhorted by Christ before the Last Supper (in the prophetic, apocalyptic thirteenth chapter of Mark). There the disciples are warned: "But take heed to yourselves; for they will deliver you up to councils; and you will be beaten in synagogues; and you will stand before governors and kings for my sake, to bear testimony before them. . . . And when they bring you to deliver you up, do not be anxious beforehand what you are to say; but what is given to you in that hour, say it, for it is not you who speak, but the Holy Spirit." (13:9, 11.) And recalling his own hearing before the patriarchs, Avvakum proclaims, "God opened my sinful lips and Christ put them to shame!" [50]

Pursuing the parallels between the Archpriest and Christ, we recall the similarity between Avvakum's physically aggressive actions and Christ's attack upon the "den of thieves" in the Temple. Likewise, Paškov's recitation of Judas' confession, "I have sinned, accursed man, I have spilled innocent blood," surrounds Avvakum with the aureole of Christ. The healing of the cellarer Nikodim echoes Christ's healing of a leper (Mark 1:43–45) in that the cellarer and the leper noise about their miraculous recoveries and crowds of people descend upon the two miracle workers. Beyond such specific references, Avvakum often reflects in word and deed more general Christlike characteristics. We have mentioned, for example, his theological self-assurance, his physical passivity under attack, and his premonitions of martyrdom. Most important, perhaps, is his devotion to suffering for the Truth. One senses that Gethsemane was never far from Avvakum's mind, for the duty of accepting undeserved suffering lay heavy upon him. This above all provokes the outburst of self-hatred we encounter after he recalls his rebellious response to Paškov's flogging: unlike Christ he momentarily demands justice, that his and not God's will be done. Inevitable suffering is not rightly considered a cross to be borne, for it is not chosen; and so, during his return from Siberia, a doubtful and hesitant Avvakum resolves upon his wife's exhortations to take up his own cross once again, and to "unmask the Nikonian heresy with boldness," despite the dangers (78–79).

The fixed essences characteristic of these archetypes suggest that "psychologist" Avvakum was only marginally more perceptive in depicting himself than he was in describing others. Certainly his narration offers us abundant material for psychological analysis; but this is not to say that the Archpriest is interested, even remotely, in the complexities of his own psyche. And when his eventful wanderings end in the prison pit at Pustozersk, his attention turns not inward but outward, to the suffering of others. The physical and spiritual miseries of that incarceration must have seemed rather humdrum to the militant Archpriest, offering him no new "high points" in his life of hardship. The bestial mutilations of his fellow prisoners and the executions of his followers elsewhere were far more compelling from his dramatic, apocalyptic perspective on events. And it is to events, not psychological states, that narrator Avvakum is drawn first of all. Unlike many first-person narrators in the modern era, Avvakum is not talking to himself about himself; he is teaching God's children about final things, and his rich, charismatic personality emerges willy-nilly in the process, almost by accident. [51]

Some remarks on the narrative structure of the *Life* will clarify the general framework within which Avvakum's system of metaphors is realized. The improvisatory qualities of Avvakum's narration are obvious. But it is an error to overemphasize its capricious spontaneity and consequent tendency toward structural formlessness. Signs of unrestrained impulse are here, but it would be well to remember that artistic improvisation implies a freedom limited by conventions, by the materials at hand, in one way or another by the general artistic "context" in which it occurs. For example, fragmentary, episodic narrative is common in the *žitie*, so its presence in the *Life* almost certainly is not a product of free association. This segmentation seems to proceed, as I noted earlier, from a "vertical" orientation toward experience which subjects generally discrete episodes to an appraisal primarily moral in nature, not analytic; the aim is to illustrate eternal truths that inform man's life with meaning rather than to discover a human truth or explore a human condition with all its temporal, environmental, and psychological variables. Consequently, causal connections between adjacent episodes are usually weak and often nonexistent.[52] But this by no means eliminates the possibility of linkages of a purely thematic nature between or among episodes. With specific regard to the *Life*, there is in it a tension between biographical chronology and thematic associations involving repetitive metaphors, the symbolic number three, and the principle of test and reward. In addition, traditional elements in the structure of the *žitie* impinge on biographical chronology, producing a degree of generic organization. This tension between linear chronology and principles that tend to restructure it is created by Avvakum's calculated efforts to highlight the meaning of particular experiences. Such techniques are thus consistent with his use of biblical analogues or edifying aphorisms and commentaries. The meanings specified do not reflect an encompassing consistency of vision, as we have seen. We are moved, however, not by this but by Avvakum's impassioned conviction that intimations of victory are everywhere evident in a chronology of suffering and eventual defeat, relieved only by brief respite and scattered earthly rewards. So far was Avvakum from imagining the possibility of genuine defeat that he virtually challenged Tsar Aleksej Mixajlovič in his "Fifth Petition" to execute him and to bury his body in a ditch or in excrement, or to burn it or sink it in water. Christ will not forget his scattered bones any more than those of martyrs who perished so in the past; and on the Last Day he will certainly raise them up again. [53]

Demkova's detailed comparison of the various redactions of the *Life* has shown that there was a relative shift over time in Avvakum's emphasis, from narration of events to edifying explication of their meaning. [54] Thus, the tension described above eventually produced a qualitative change in Avvakum's autobiography. Since its general chronological movement is apparent, my principal aim here is to examine the ways in which the intensification of meaning produces a more structured narration than the categorical phrase "ingenuous improvisation" might suggest.

In general the repetitive metaphors examined above, generated by the principle of struggle, provide significant thematic links between episodes. For example, in the opening segment of the *Life*, Avvakum implies the struggle between the flesh and the spirit by remarking that his father was a drunkard, while his mother was God-fearing and given to fasting and praying. He immediately associates his own life with that struggle in describing his youthful spiritual awakening, which occurred in darkness one night after the "beastly" death of a neighbor's cow. Then, after summarizing briefly his marriage and career in holy orders, the Archpriest gives substance to this theme by recalling his onetime sexual temptation, profound remorse, and purification by fire. Carnal desire, a leitmotif associated with the hedonistic children of Satan, and repentance are thus catalysts for Avvakum's vision of the boats examined above in detail; all its constituent elements are representational, contrasting the realms of the physical and the spiritual and affirming struggle to remain true to God's known will as the principle of right living. Here too is the pattern established wherein Avvakum's physical sight is inhibited as his spiritual senses (here, "eyes of the heart" [*serdečnii oči*]) become more acute, apparently in response to his need for spiritual sustenance (later [spiritual] bread and water).

The replenished Archpriest now confronts the first assaults (the "storms") launched against him by the devil's beastly henchmen, beginning this narrative with a quotation from Psalm 114 (116 in the English Bible): "The sorrows of death compassed me, and the afflictions of hell gat hold upon me; I found trouble and sorrow." The first official continues the theme of sexual transgression, while the next "barks" and "gnawed the fingers of my hand like a dog"; in the following episode Avvakum drives out "two great bears." Similarly, the metaphors of wandering, near-drowning (water in its perilous form), and winter (the spiritual death of the "winter of heresy") soon make their first appearances. This, together with the numerous individual examples examined previously, is sufficient to indicate how Avvakum's narration is partially organized by a persistent movement toward metaphors that fix the essential meaning of particular episodes and relate them to one another.

A preoccupation with symbolic numbers was characteristic of the apocalyptic mentality of Avvakum's era. The number three, associated with the Holy Trinity and with Christ's resurrection on the third day, usually connotes purification, death and rebirth, and spiritual victory to the Archpriest; it occurs within episodes and sometimes establishes a bond between them (those occurring in triads). The symbolic value of this number makes of it an image analogous to others examined above; the importance Avvakum attaches to it is perhaps indicated by his lengthy citation of Athanasius the Great's commentary on the doctrine of the Trinity in his own confession of faith (40–42), which is followed immediately by a summary affirmation of the Incarnation, Passion, and Resurrection on the third day. In these same introductory pages Avvakum also dwells at length on threefold, as opposed to fourfold, laudation, and on the three trinities that comprise the nine orders of the heavenly host. And he remarks that the company of Simeon, Archbishop of Siberia, wept "for about three hours" during an ominous solar eclipse in 1654. Here three has no obvious symbolic value, and its use may be the result once again of Avvakum's automatic recourse to the familiar and traditional. Several other occurrences of this number probably reflect remembered biographical fact. Such instances are ignored in the discussion below.

First let us note the use of the number three within particular episodes. Owing to his lust for the young woman come to confess, Avvakum is "thrice-accursed," and he burns his right hand in the flame of three candles to cleanse himself of the lecherous fire within. His repentance is rewarded with the vision of the three boats. During the third day of his first imprisonment he miraculously receives food, he assumes from an angel. While in Tobol'sk on his journey to the èast, Avvakum and the Archbishop leave the body of the disgraced Pëtr Beketov in the street for three days, all the while praying for his soul before finally burying him "with honor" (p. 58). Immediately thereafter Avvakum reports Neronov's prophecy of the "three pestilences that come of schism in the Church." The Archpriest is camped three versts away from Paškov when the latter's executioners bear him away to the flogging that Paškov initiates with three blows to his head, a violent violation of blessing with the sign of the Cross, followed by three blows with his symbolic commander's axe (čexan) on Avvakum's back. Later Paškov tries and fails three times to shoot his righteous son Eremej (p. 72) after the latter had condemned him for flogging Avvakum unjustly. Near the end of the *Life* proper Avvakum describes the mutilation of his comrades at Pustozersk, who fortuitously are three in number; Lazar's mouth is healed three days after his tongue was cut out, and after two years have passed, at the beginning of the third, his tongue is regenerated in a space of three days. In the supplementary tales a lunatic named Fëdor wanders in delirium through the forests until, on the third day, Avvakum appears to him in a vision and exorcises his devils (p.107). And the rebellious virgin Anna falls into a trance for three days and nights, then "dies" and experiences her vision of Avvakum's heavenly mansion (p.107).

The association of the number three with spiritual victory is particularly evident in triadal linkage of episodes. After Avvakum's vision of the three boats he is nearly drowned three times, the third miraculous escape being narrated in greatest detail (59, 63). A similar triad involves assaults upon the Archpriest by three different local officials early in his career; after twice bearing such affliction, in the third episode Avvakum emerges triumphant

(45–48). Although the real chronological relationship among these three episodes is not clear, the third is set off from the others by events which probably intervened in fact; we see here that tension between simple autobiographical sequence and thematic association noted above. (Similarly, real sequence is observed in the near-drownings but reduced in importance owing to the emphasis on three such events achieved by juxtaposing the latter two.)

In both triads temporary victory is succeeded by renewed struggle and suffering. Avvakum often utilizes a principle for establishing a loose association among episodes which may be designated by the traditional notion of test and reward; spiritual reward follows upon successful suffering, and it inevitably passes into renewed testing, this until the final heavenly reward is won. It is perhaps significant here that Avvakum views his life as broadly tripartite: his early experiences; his Siberian exile and return; and his renewed conflicts, second exile, and present imprisonment, in which he awaits that final victory, whether it be ecclesiastical restoration or the eternal reward of the martyr.

Two tests through suffering followed by some spiritual victory as a reward is a discernible if not rigorously consistent pattern in the *Life* up to Avvakum's return from Siberia. His habitual recourse to traditional ideas led, probably inevitably, to understanding this early period as a time of testing comparable to that experienced by many saints as they began their spiritual vocation. Although the notion of the test is encountered throughout the *Life*, it dominates the first parts (Avvakum refers there to his pre-exile years as an *iskus* 'prolonged test'); his spiritual success there prepared him to enter upon his national ministry and leadership of the Old Belief. Triadal organization is obviously harmonious in its connotations with this general understanding of the earlier portions of his autobiography. Insofar as this triadal organization is realized, it affects the narration of purely personal experiences only; references to events from the early history of the schism sometimes interrupt this narration but exist as it were on a different level of significance, as if Avvakum wished at this point to avoid identifying himself (still not fully tested) with the destiny of the Orthodox Church, which was itself entering a time of terrible testing. As with the innocent Job, so too had "Satan besought God for our radiant Russia, so he might turn her crimson with the blood of martyrs" (p. 87). It is only after his Siberian agonies that Avvakum is deemed worthy of being addressed by Christ himself, who warns him in a dream during the return journey to "beware, lest thou be sundered from me" (p. 80 ; cf. Matt. 24:51). And so Avvakum soon abandons his comfortable moderation and embraces in earnest his vocation as the leading defender of the one true Church of Christ.

More specifically, after the victorious episode involving the third official, Avvakum remembers how he was trampled by a mob in Jur'evec-on-the-Volga and then the disapproving reception he was given by the Tsar and Vonifat'ev in Moscow, where he fled ("Still more misery"; p. 50). After summarizing Nikon's elevation to the patriarchate and his initial reforms and repressions, Avvakum then describes his own arrest and miraculous replenishment after spending three days in a dark prison cell (the third personal experience in this series). Avvakum next recalls the beating he was given by a group of churchmen the following morning, and, after detailing the miracles surrounding Archpriest Login's stiff resistance to Nikon, he notes how he was publicly humiliated on St. Nikita's day and very nearly sheared. But his transfer to Tobol'sk culminates in a victory over the forces of evil when he whips Ivan Struna for rioting in church. However, Struna's friends and supporters threaten the Archpriest with death, and for almost a month he must go into hiding. After describing the death of Pëtr Beketov and referring to Neronov's prophecies, Avvakum tells of his transfer into the troop of Paškov and of his first near-drowning. The third episode in this series is his terrible flogging by Paškov, his rebellion against God, repentance, and deliverance from pain. Similarly, his imprisonment in the frigid Bratskij fortress and sufferings on the Xilok river culminate in his third near-drowning and miraculous rescue. Likewise, his sufferings near Lake Irgen and along the Nerča river and a description of the ways in which he and his family struggled against starvation are succeeded by a victory achieved in exorcising two madwomen, Paškov's favorite houseservants. The next, essentially allegorical episode depicts Avvakum and his wife struggling across the ice of a winter landscape, a symbol of the inescapable conditions of their life on earth; it is followed by the description of the little black hen "crushed . . . because of our sins." A clear victory then ensues, when Avvakum heals Paškov's grandson. The last episodes preceding the return to Russia concern the disastrous Mongolian expedition; this narrative is tripartite, but spiritual victories occur in both the second and third parts.

It might be objected that a variety of affirmations are encountered here in episodes I have associated with the test, and not with spiritual victory. But for Avvakum endurance alone is a victory, even when no obvious reward is forthcoming; reward will come eventually, so he never despairs. A more serious objection to the above analysis is that the boundaries between episodes are not in every case as precise as I have implied. My aim here, however, is not to prove the existence of a carefully elaborated structure but to demonstrate there exists in these personal experiences a kind of tripartite rhythm, not necessarily deliberate, in which memories of tests are linked irresistibly to memories of spiritual rewards. Significant in this context is the verb *vosstat'* 'to arise'; its connection with the notions of renewal and spiritual rebirth makes its frequency in Avvakum's narration another measure of his commitment to the inevitability of victory, no matter how deep the suffering; after Good Friday there must be an Easter.

The principal corollary of tests leading to rewards is that sin culminates in punishment. Initially this would seem to confront Avvakum with a serious problem, despite the number of persons in his experience struck down for transgression by devils and death: the greatest sinners of his age remain generally untouched, while True Believers suffer unremittingly. But we have seen there are no real theological problems for Avvakum, and we will add here that these two principles are inseparably linked in the closed system of his thought: unpunished evil is the single necessary condition for testing the righteous: "To this end doth God suffer the visitation of offenses, so there might be an Elect, so they might be burned, might be purified, so those tested by tribulation might be made manifest among you" (p. 87). If the ultimate reward of those tested and found true is inevitable, so too is the final punishment of the wicked.

Lixačev has observed, "The nearer we get to the end [of the *Life*], the freer the narration becomes. [Avvakum] recollects discrete episodes and arranges them not chronologically but, more accurately, thematically." [55] It would be even more accurate to say that Avvakum departs sharply from a fairly strict adherence to the chronology of his own experience only as he leaves Siberia. The explanation is to be found once again in his understanding of that early period: having successfully endured testing, he is now prepared to enter upon his ministry, just as Christ left the wilderness and the tests he underwent there to fulfill his destiny. Even though the early portions of the *Life* are obviously didactic, it is only now that we encounter an extended sermon involving a chronologically free utilization of illustrative personal experiences combined with edifying commentary. And tripartite association of episodes disappears. So, after Epifanij's interjected approval of Avvakum's righteous lie (p. 75), the latter launches into a vehement rejection of the anathema and interdict laid upon him by the Nikonians — heretics whose ecclesiastical prohibitions are invalid and thus irrelevant to his post-Siberian ministry. He follows these violent fulminations by a cursory summary of the return journey as far as Baikal, which provides the basis for an edifying excursus on God's bounty and man's beastly ingratitude, concluding with the formula, "Forgive me, I have sinned worse than all men." The formula is by no means automatic, for it provides a transition to the familiar passage wherein Avvakum, standing at the threshold of his destiny, is overcome by fear and doubts about his calling and is strengthened in his resolve by his battered but unbreakable wife.

In this way the image of Christ emerging from the wilderness is sullied by human weakness. But Avvakum's admission of spiritual frailty is not an exercise in humility alone; he introduces here the subject of the sermon that follows: the need to remember enduring courage when the true faith is threatened by a complacency bred of sloth and cowardice. So Avvakum next remembers how he and his wife confronted imminent death at the hands of Siberian tribes with a courage grounded in unflagging trust in the benevolent will of God. This break in real chronology is followed by Avvakum's memory of the honors he received upon his return to Moscow; their rejection is explained by the warning he received from Christ in Tobol'sk during the return journey (another temporal retrogression). Complacency and lack of courage come of immersion in the things of this world, and so the Archpriest observes, "I counted all this as dung and I gain Christ, being mindful of death, even as all this doth vanish away." But he returns insistently to his own weakness, not only in Moscow but earlier in Siberia, by elaborating the metaphor of spiritual hunger and thirst (see discussion above, 175–77), which stands at the heart of his sermon (79–84). The sermon is developed through illustrative Siberian experiences whose chronological relationship to one another is undefined, and it culminates in the tale about Paškov, whose spiritual hunger (he neglects his rule) is rewarded by hunger in physical fact: a great flood washes away fields of newly planted grain (*xleb*). Avvakum summarizes this sermon on the need to remember vigilence, courage, and endurance: "But I have chatted enough about this; let's get back to my story. It is needful for us to remember and not to forget all these things, nor should we be negligent in godly concerns; and we simply must not barter them for the seductions of this vain age."

Avvakum's resolve to practice the virtues here preached leads quite logically to the renewed conflicts, second exile, and imprisonment that follow. In this third and last portion of the *Life* proper we observe first of all a broadening of vision. The narrative ceases to focus so exclusively upon Avvakum's own experience and on the people directly associated with it. The "high points of [his] hardships" are here, but with increasing frequency he turns away from them to describe the righteous suffering and martyrdom of others. This probably reflects Avvakum's predilection for active struggle and crisis, which end for him when he is immobilized by imprisonment. But this more inclusive narrative also depicts general warfare between the Children of God and Satan, not isolated skirmishes involving one lonely warrior. As the violence and viciousness of the wicked are intensified, so too is the hagiographical nimbus of sanctity surrounding the right-hearted. Avvakum's self-depiction also becomes monumental in nature, as he emphasizes almost exclusively his aspiration to the example of Christ; consequently, his associations with Christ are most frequent here. And the typological segregation of Russians into two camps reaches its extremity in the peroration (99–100): the True Believers will be martyred and crowned with victory, while the reformers are associated with Satan and the Antichrist, with Babylon (Babylon, the great whore of the Apocalypse), and with Islam (the Turkish contagion in the Greek Church).

As I stated previously, the supplementary tales resemble the traditional group of miracle stories at the conclusion of a *vita*;

a series of episodes depicting miraculous healings, free in chronology and repetitious in content, imbue the protagonist with the odor of sanctity. Yet the image of the saintly healer is sullied in this instance by passages of self-vilification, and Avvakum becomes what I called earlier "a saint trailing disclaimers." We have seen that such dissonance is characteristic, and it motivates my description of these final tales as a metaphorical summary of Avvakum's understanding of himself as a servant of God and spiritual father to his followers. If such tales serve an analogous purpose in tradition, the result in the *Life* is not the affirmation of a spiritual monolith but a fragmentary sketch of a committed, flawed, living human being.

The fact that Avvakum still lives makes a great deal of difference, of course: his continuing struggle with the evil within and without dominates these tales. In a sense Avvakum prepares us for a return to the former in the final lines of the *Life* proper: "I am a sinful man, a whoremonger and a plunderer . . . " The tale following strips these lines of their formulaic quality by giving them a specific experiential referent; it culminates in the Prodigal's animal pens as the Archpriest curses his wretched, sinful nature and consequent failure to exorcise his brother Evfimej. The metaphorical level of meaning in the tale is apparent from the outset: both men are punished for neglecting spiritual obligations because of their preoccupation with a horse (i.e., a beast). Their specific sins of omission involve what Avvakum understands to be the fundamental demands made on the man who would be saved: daily spiritual discipline (Evfimej abandons his rule), affirmation of the doctrines of ancient Orthodoxy (Avvakum trades a book containing these truths for a beast, the horse), and obedience to the known will of God (Avvakum compares his failure to fulfill his confessor Vonifat'ev's will to this greater failure in obedience). So "for about three weeks" the Archpriest is unable to exorcise his "brother," a genuine blood relationship that here acquires rich metaphorical meaning.

Although the devils that descend on Evfimej come from God, they are obviously associated with the beasts of Satan in Avvakum's mind ("I fought those devils like dogs"). The antiquity of this motif, struggle with devils, renders these final tales timeless; they place the entirety of Avvakum's previously described experience in the context of the ancient struggle between heaven and hell. As I noted above, none of them deals directly with schism in the Church.

The heaviest emphasis in these tales is on the protagonist's role as teacher and healer. Whereas Avvakum's attitude toward *jurodstvo* 'foolishness in Christ' is traditionally approving, he views most psychic derangement, especially sudden derangement, as a visible manifestation of a soul disordered by evil. Healing implies not only purgation but conversion of the lunatic from "wrong-headedness" to the right patterns of thought and behavior. In this Avvakum summarizes one of the major goals of his *Life* and life's work, while showing himself to be at the same time an instrument of God's healing grace.

Previous analysis will suggest ways in which the metaphorical level of other individual tales may be understood. Although the complement of these tales varies from redaction to redaction, Avvakum always concludes them with an experience illustrating his human helplessness while experiencing victories that depend on God's benevolent strength. This is an episodic counterpart to the declaration of humility at the end of the *Life* proper.

In the foregoing discussion, numerous references have been made to the literary tradition and Avvakum's relation to it. An effort has been made to include only those aspects of the tradition which are frequently mentioned and widely accepted in the critical literature. To define in detail the relation of Avvakum's *Life* to the tradition of the Russian *vita* is a problem far beyond the limits of the present study. It would depend in any case on a historical morphological study of the Russian genre as it treats the martyr, ascetic, and warrior; to my knowledge such a study does not exist.[56]   Yet some of the most striking features of the *Life* have obvious literary historical significance, and they have generated a great deal of critical commentary. Much of it in the Soviet Union has emphasized the ways in which this work reflects tendencies toward modern literature (specifically Realism) generated above all else by the growing secularization and "democratization" of Russian culture during the seventeenth century.[57] My argument has stressed the traditional religiosity of Avvakum's world view. While I recognize the complex mixture of old and new in the literature of this period, I remain dubious about any claim that he participated directly in such "progressive" historical developments.

Yet Avvakum appeals to numbers of contemporary readers who find little if anything to interest them in medieval Russian literature. This fact provides a center of gravity for the following tentative and by no means inclusive or systematic historical speculations regarding this work.

I have already suggested that Avvakum's pursuit of traditional hagiographical goals brought his *Life* into a dialectical tension with that tradition. For example, if we ignore his fiery Russian nationalism,[58] then it was probably the didactic function of hagiography that motivated more than anything else his use of the vernacular. Yet this created a conflict with the traditional style that Avvakum himself recognized. Or again, as Stokes has pointed out, "The medieval hagiographer . . . did not aim to demonstrate the sanctity of his subject. This had been made known by God and communicated to the world by the Church through its canonization of the saint. The hagiographer's task was didactic; to make use of the established fact for the propagation of Christianity; to teach people the reality of Christ's presence in the world and of the never-ending struggle between good and evil; to show them that a virtuous life and heroic exploits for the faith are rewarded by eternal bliss." [59] Avvakum's goals were precisely those of his literary forebears, but he lacked their most basic "material," a recognized saint. Nevertheless, being by nature averse to innovation (despite his many innovations), he turned to the nearest existing literary form, the *vita*, when he resolved to teach through the example of his own experience. But the use of this form to any recognizable degree brought with it the saintly archetype, and whatever uncertainty Avvakum felt about God's judgment of his career was certain to be exacerbated by the inevitable tension between *žitie* as personal experience and *žitie* as saintly *vita*. We recognize this tension on the first page of the holograph of this redaction (photograph in Robinson, p. 141): there, written in Epifanij's own hand, is his "charge" that Avvakum write his *Life*, "so that the works of God shall not pass into oblivion." Reference by the writer to some external motivation for writing a *vita* was an established tradition (Robinson, p. 45); here Avvakum takes that tradition a step further to justify an undertaking in which he recognized something fundamentally inappropriate from a traditional point of view. This and other efforts at self-justification should qualify our acceptance of the links described by Zenkovsky between the *Life* and examples of quasi-autobiography earlier in the Russian literary tradition.[60] The formal links identified in this important article are undeniable. But Avvakum obviously felt himself to be writing within the larger tradition where genuine autobiography had no established place. Recognizing this helps us to explain more fully the dissonances we have examined in Avvakum's depicted personality.

Psychological and moral volatility were not unknown in the Russian *vita* before Avvakum. They are typical, for example, of the highly embellished style ("the weaving of words") which appeared in this genre in the late fourteenth and early fifteenth centuries and became part of the tradition. But as Lixačëv has argued at length, the treatment of character here is still fundamentally categorical; characters are good, evil, or evil-become-good, and never an unresolved, dissonant mixture of the two.[61] What is more, the volatile emotions encountered in this style are severed from any understanding of personality as an integral whole; extreme emotions are thus deemed worthy of description without reference to the personality that experiences them. If this tradition may have influenced the discontinuous categorization and volatility of Avvakum's depicted personality, it is of no help in explaining this single, complex personality's capacity both to unite and to maintain a continuing, unresolved tension between these extremes. For it is precisely Avvakum's rich personality and his monumental suffering that rivet our attention. His participation in the seventeenth century's extension of the *vita* into the realm of contemporary life and the fact that his use of the vernacular was a radical break with the normative assignment of styles to genres are unlikely to arouse in us anything more than academic interest. But we respond more immediately to this: that Avvakum expressed more fully than his contemporaries the new, still tentative recognition in literature that men exist beyond absolute categories, that they combine in themselves both good and evil.[62] And we who have long since grown accustomed to the diverse rhythms, intonations, and styles of countless first-person narrators, we can understand and respond directly to the enormous emotional range of Avvakum's voice, the immediacy and force of which affirm the validity and significance of individual experience.

It would be absurd, of course, to transform the Archpriest into our contemporary. He was very far from understanding the life of the individual as we do, just as he had no conception of literary movements, or of contemporaneity, or of the artist's self-affirmation through innovation and originality. His greatest artistic achievements were by-products of his pursuit of goals by no means literary, and much that we value in his work would be incomprehensible to him. Still, I believe it useful and interesting to view the *Life* against a modern background, which I do very briefly in conclusion.

Avvakum's pungent style and his immersion in the life of his era create together a singular dissonance in the religious spirit transmitted by his *Life*. If his rigidity, anti-intellectualism, and superstitions are unimpressive, he also abandons the solemn abstractions of traditional hagiographical religiosity. He communicates a faith grounded not only in the books but in experience, an almost physical sense of fiery commitment, unshakable in the kind of tragic, unjust, brutal circumstances that have often shattered belief in our own time. Only once (after the flogging by Paškov) does his faith seem to falter, but the ready answer quickly supplants nascent doubt. Avvakum's faith is a closed system in which doubt does not and cannot exist, especially when logical inconsistencies are never recognized. Here Avvakum carries to an extreme the charismatic, emotional qualities that are so important in distinguishing Russian Orthodoxy from Western scholasticism in the Middle Ages.

But we also recognize here that gulf which separates Avvakum as a traditional hero, who moves in a universe charged with meaning, from the so-called modern hero, who often lives in doubt and anxiety. Avvakum's unquestioned conviction that he understands life has the same axiomatic quality that we encounter, for example, in Tolstoj's Cossacks (*The Cossacks*), a work that explores the conflict between traditional and modern perceptions of existence. The Cossacks live spontaneously in the present moment, with an almost nonexistent awareness of past and future. The protagonist Olenin longs to be a Cossack, but with his modern consciousness he is profoundly aware of his *individual* past and future, his *individual* life-story, whereas the Cossacks view themselves as reiterating a culturally transmitted, prototypal Cossack life-story, where the future like the past is "known." Avvakum's repetitious use of the word *podvig* 'heroic deed' to describe his life and those of other True Believers, and his world view in general, are similarly patterned. His faith makes life predictable; its gifts are prophecy and power. On the other hand, as Irving Howe has remarked in his brilliant introduction to the anthology, *The Idea of the Modern in Literature and the Arts:*

The modern hero has lost the belief in a collective destiny. Hence, the hero finds it hard to be certain that he possesses — or that anyone can possess — the kind of powers that might transform human existence.

Men no longer feel themselves bound in a sacred and often enough, in a temporal kinship. Hence, the hero finds it hard to believe in himself as a *chosen* figure acting on behalf of a divine commandment or national will . . . One likes to feel, . . . that in certain kinds of ancient or traditional heroes there was a union of value and power, a sense of the good and the capacity to act it out. [63]

In continuing defeat traditional hero Avvakum discovered unending sources of strength. After his final imprisonment he began to write in the conviction that the written word, in Christ, could change the world. The desired change did not occur, but the Archpriest always believed heroism in the traditional sense to be a genuine possibility, and his *Life* is in large measure a record of such heroism and a manual for potential heroes. His conviction that power was his through a life lived in harmony with God's will never wavered. In his fifth and last petition to Tsar Aleksej Mixajlovič, written from prison at Pustozersk (1669), Avvakum belligerently tells of a vision in which his weakened body grew to encompass "heaven and earth, and all creation," while his powerful addressee "rules in freedom only the Russian land."[64] And Demkova has shown how those elements in the *Life* which detract from Avvakum's saintly image are largely suppressed in its final redaction, while its traditional hagiographical features are enhanced (35, 93–101). Anthony Stokes has described eloquently Avvakum's continuing faith in the face of overwhelming failure: "The story that he made the sign of the cross in the old manner as the flames rose about him may be untrue, but it represents the truth" (p. 235).

We may wish to view Avvakum as a man whose delusions gave us a literary masterpiece while leading him through a futile, terrible life to a pointless, barbaric death. We may also feel an uneasy admiration for his fierce commitment to ideals far more important to him than personal comfort, safety, or happiness; in this he is akin to the greatest champions of the human spirit — and to some of its more dangerous fanatics. Above all we recognize in him an authentic human voice, freed from the solemn facelessness of the church style and vividly expressive of those extremes of sentiment — the tears and the tyranny — which seem often to mark the Russian spirit. This voice is human too, from our perspective, because we recognize in it a modern complexity, a lack of consistency that may at times be understood as repressed uncertainty or as a tension between the ideal and the all too real. If Avvakum aspired to sainthood, we view him as a man, limited to be sure, but with a powerful, charismatic personality which was fortuitously preserved for future generations in his *Life*, written by himself.

†

Annotations on *The Life of the Archpriest Avvakum*

The information included in these annotations is drawn from a variety of sources, but above all from the copious, valuable notes contained in A. N. Robinson's edition of the *Life*.

1.   The honorific rank of archpriest (*protopop*) was the highest open to the married "white" (as opposed to the monastic "black") clergy; an archpriest was often considered equal in rank to a bishop by common Russians. His duties might include serving as rector of the principal church in a city, as supervisor of the clergy in a small district, and as vicar to a bishop. The name Avvakum is the Russian form of Habakkuk.

2.   Avvakum uses the Old Russian term for confessor, "spiritual father" (*duxovnyj otec*), and it figures significantly in his traditional understanding of the sonship of believers and the fatherhood of God. Consequently, this "charge," standing at the beginning of the holograph of the second redaction of the *Life* and written in Epifanij's own hand (see photograph in Robinson, p. 141), is intended to justify an autobiographical undertaking which otherwise would violate the medieval literary norm of authorial self-deprecation and humility. Choice of a confessor was a private matter for each believer; earlier Ivan Neronov, sometimes called the "father of the Russian reformation," and the notable Stefan Vonifat'ev, the Tsar's confessor and Neronov's close associate, had both served Avvakum in this capacity (see annotations 56, 57).
        Avvakum utilized Epifanij's charge in the first two redactions of his *Life*; it is separated from the holograph of the third redaction, appearing at the very end of that volume, after the second part of Epifanij's *Life*. A new, more solemn charge by Epifanij now introduces the *Life*; it is preceded by the following salutation by Avvakum (and then a lengthy quotation from St. Dorotheus on love): "To you, the succorers of the Church, I offer here my *Life* from my youth to the age of fifty-five years. For Father Dorotheus described his life to his disciples, exhorting them to long-suffering (Sermon 4, sheet 49); and in like manner, prevailing upon you to love Christ Jesus our Lord, I will tell you of those things done by me, a good-for-nothing servant of God, in the name of the Father, of the Son, and of the Holy Spirit. Thanks

207

be to God forever.

Here is a book of eternal life for you, my beloved child; remember me in your prayers and don't forget Epifanij. I did the writing, but he helped with his prayers. In all things the Lord will bless you and your wife, Marija Pimenovna, and your children, and daughters-in-law, and grandchildren, and kin, and acquaintances, and friends, both men and women, and all who love you. And let him blessing you be blessed and him cursing you be accursed. May God grant that you receive of the moisture of the earth and the dew of heaven over and above your need, and may he increase in your home all beauty and grace. Eat the old of the old and spew out the old that comes with the new — there will be plenty of everything and more left over. The Lord give you bread and meat and fish; from the women [who prepare them] let these blessed breads be eaten!"

Dorotheus was a sixth-century Syrian monk, the Archimandrite of the Monastery of Majume; his *Instructions* containing certain autobiographical materials were published in Moscow in 1652, while Avvakum was living there.

The volume containing the holograph of the third redaction of the *Life* also includes, as a separate item, Avvakum's famous defense of vernacular Russian: "This is written by the sinful hand of the Archpriest Avvakum, according to the exhortation and blessing of his confessor, the Elder Epifanij. And if that spoken here is simple, you who read and listen must not rebuke, for the Lord's sake, our simple speech, as I love my native Russian tongue. I am not used to beautifying my speech with verses philosophic, as God listens not to our beautiful words but desires our deeds. Paul writes, 'Though I speak with the tongues of men and angels but have not love, I am nothing' [I Cor. 13:1]. Here is plenty for you to ponder: not in Latin, nor in Greek, nor in Hebrew, nor in any other tongue does the Lord seek our speeches, but he desires our love together with the other virtues. So I don't bother about eloquence or belittle my Russian tongue. But forgive me, sinful man that I am, and God will forgive and bless all you servants of Christ. Amen." It must be emphasized here, of course, that Avvakum is not advocating use of the vernacular in the liturgy during divine worship.

3.   The opening lines of the *Life* up to "Dionysios the Areopagite" are a deliberate revision of a very familiar prayer read at the beginning of the Psalter; the "good works" which, according to this prayer, ought to crown the reading of the psalms are here transformed into the deeds of Avvakum's life.

According to tradition, Dionysios the Areopagite was a disciple of the Apostle Paul and the first bishop of Athens. Around AD500, probably in Syria, some writings were forged in his name by an unknown Christian Neoplatonist. Because these works have had great influence upon the theological traditons in both the Eastern and Western churches, their author has come to be called Pseudo-Dionysios. As Avvakum's subsequent references to this authority indicate, he and his contemporaries were unaware of these problems of authorship. Avvakum obviously believed that references to Pseudo-Dionysios gave particular weight to positions taken by the Old Believers.

4.   *On the Divine Names* is the title of Pseudo-Dionysios' second book. Avvakum's remarks are based on its abstract discussion of the complex variety of attributive appellations for God, his essence being beyond comprehension. But Avvakum abandons the latter conviction by introducing a distinction between "connatural" and "consequent," that is, names which express God's essence and those that are partial but proceed logically from this essence.

5.   Although the usual meaning of the word *nepostojanen*, here translated as Omnipresent, is much closer to "Omnipotent," Avvakum's usage of it elsewhere indicates he had his own understanding of its meaning.

6.   Avvakum does not recall this passage perfectly; compare: "For the falling away of Truth is repudiation of self; Truth is connatural, and the falling away of Truth is the falling away of the connatural. If Truth is therefore connatural, the repudiation of Truth is the falling away of the connatural; God cannot fall away from the connatural, and that which cannot be, is not."

7.   Among several changes in the Creed, Avvakum here refers to the one which particularly incensed the Old Believers. Robinson discusses the confusion created in the Russian version of the Creed owing to diverse translations of an Old Greek word which could be read in context either as the noun 'lord' or the adjective 'lordly'; sometimes it was understood as 'the true' as well. This led in the 17th century to a combination of two translations for one word: "the true Lord." The reformers turned to the Greek text of the Greed as recorded in the actions of the Constantinople Council of 1592 (where Russia received its patriarchate) and produced a new translation which eliminated "the true." Unimpressed by claims regarding the authenticity of the liturgy of the corrupt Greek Church, the Old Believers defended the original reading in theological terms and by appealing to the authority of Holy Fathers, whose formulation of the Creed was congenial to their position. Such arguments vigorously pursued could indeed make this deletion appear heretical.

8.   This citation is a simplified version of a passage, not from Pseudo-Dionysios, but from a commentator on his works, Maksim the Confessor.

9.   The source of this dung simile is probably Phil. 3:8; it was popular among Old Believers, who had frequent cause to proclaim their rejection of worldly vanities in favor of their allegiance to heaven.

10.   According to tradition, Timothy was a disciple of the Apostle Paul, one of his most faithful co-workers, and the first bishop of Ephesus, where he was allegedly martyred under the Roman emperor Nerva. One legend identifies him as witness to the death of the Virgin Mary. There are references in the writings of Pseudo-Dionysios to his correspondence with Timothy regarding the ideas of Greek science. Timothy is indeed addressed by Pseudo-Dionysios in the manner indicated ("My child . . ."), but the specific remark cited by Avvakum is not found in his works.

11.   The vulgar word *bljad'*, here translated as "whoredom," was frequently used during the period of the schism to refer to heresy. The term "outward" (*vnešnjaja*) is used by Avvakum elsewhere (cf. his "Fifth Conversation: On Outward Wisdom"); the meaning conveyed goes beyond mere superficiality. Avvakum takes a very conservative position regarding the relationship between reason and truth. "Outward wisdom" he associates with foreign ideas, systematic knowledge, and philosophy; the pursuit of God through intellect comes of pride, and leads to certain damnation.

12.   "Apostle" refers to a book of readings used during worship and containing the Acts of the Apostles and their Epistles; this specific reading contains the passage found in 2 Thes. 2:10–12.
        Avvakum's *Life* contains many biblical quotations that usually contrast stylistically with their vernacular environment, especially in the narrative portions. I have used the King James Version wherever possible to strike a similar contrast with contemporary English.

13.   "City of the Sun" (*Solnečnyj grad*) was the Slavic translation of Heliopolis, the Greek name for one of ancient Egypt's major cities (Iunu or Onu), center for worship of the sun god Ra. In the Epistle to Policarp the presence of Dionysios and a disciple in this city is described; there they observed the solar eclipse that occurred during the Crucifixion, "contrary to nature" (the moon approached the sun from the east, not from the west as is always the case).

14.   The imagery, "turned into darkness . . . blood," has its source in the apocalyptic visions found in the book of Joel (2:31).

15.   This description of Dionysios' confusion is based upon an episode in *The Life of Dionysios the Areopagite*, wherein his reactions to the eclipse are described.

16.   Symbolic interpretation of the movements through the zodiac of the visible planets and the moon is the heart of this ancient astrological theory.

17.   Simeon, Archbishop of Tobol'sk and Siberia, came from Avvakum's Upper Volga area and took his final vows in the so-called Makar'evskij Yellow-Water Monastery, which Avvakum knew quite well. Simeon treated both Avvakum and Lazar, the latter's prisonmate at Pustozersk, with kindness when they were exiled to Tobol'sk (at different times). He attended the Moscow Council of 1654, which met in the early spring of that year to act upon liturgical reforms. He witnessed the eclipse after leaving the city, in part because of the plague spreading there. He returned to Tobol'sk in December 1654 and probably shared his impressions of the eclipse with Avvakum at that time.

18.   On 2 August (12 Aug., new style) 1654 a full eclipse of the sun occurred in Russia. Since Avvakum wrote his *Life* some 20 years later, he may have forgotten the precise times and sequence of events. In any case, he made two errors here, one of which enhances the prophetic impact of this celestial event: the eclipse occurred not "about two weeks" before St. Peter's Day but before the Feast of the Assumption (15 Aug.); and the eclipse happened during, not before, the plague, so the former was not an obvious omen of the latter.

19.   Avvakum misrepresents Pseudo-Dionysios here, perhaps unintentionally. The moon always "approaches" the sun from the west, so there is nothing contrary to nature here (see annotation 13).

20.   Nikon, more than any other man, was responsible for the liturgical reforms that led to the schism and made him Avvakum's most hated adversary. The lives of these spokesmen for the opposing camps seem almost fatefully intertwined. Nikon, of mixed Russian-Mordvinian blood, was born (1605) in the village of Val'demanovo, only a few miles from Avvakum's village of Grigorovo; during the late 1640's the two men acquired influence as members of the "Zealots of the Ancient Piety" (*Revniteli drevnego blagočestija*), otherwise known as the "Lovers of God" (*Bogoljubcy*). Unlike Nikon, however, Avvakum was not a member of the Tsar's inner circle of religious advisors. They were sent into exile in the Russian North simultaneously after decisions of the Ecumenical Council of 1666–67 went against them. Both were products of the religous vitality and fervor in the Russian Northeast which flared and faded as Russia moved toward the secular 18th century.
        Rising from peasant to Patriarch of All Russia, Nikon had a spectacular career by any standard. At age 12 he entered the Makar'evskij Yellow-Water Monastery, but left it at age 20 without taking his vows. He married and served for a time as a parish priest, but when his children died he convinced his wife to take the veil, while he became a monk in the small Anzerskij Skit on the White Sea. Later he moved to the Kožeozerskij Monastery, again near the White Sea, where his piety, intelligence, energy, administrative

talent, charismatic personality, and perhaps imposing stature (he was 6'– 6" tall) soon brought him to the attention of ecclesiastics in Moscow. He became after 1646 an energetic, effective member of the Lovers of God, and rose in a matter of six years to the Patriarchate, in part because of his great influence on the Tsar. It was only after his elevation that Nikon's ambition and lust for power became increasingly apparent. However, he announced six years later (1658) that he was laying down the burden of his office, and retreated to the Voznesenskij Monastery (this after a campaign of insults engineered by the Tsar). A quixotic attempt in 1664 to regain his past power failed. The Ecumenical Council of 1666–67, summoned in part to find a new patriarch and deal with Nikon, deposed him and sent him into exile. Legends quickly spread regarding his great works in his solitary exile; he accomplished not only healings but apparently built an island retreat in a lake with stones carried to the shore by hand. He died while returning to Moscow in 1681, in possession of a partial pardon from the imperial court.

21.   The image "vials of his wrathful fury" has its source in that most revered of eschatological books in 17th-century Russia, the Apocalypse (cf. Rev. 16:1). The plague raged in Moscow and other Russian cities from July to December, 1654; over half the population of Moscow perished (i.e., over 150,000 persons).

22.   This eclipse occurred 12, not 14, years after the first eclipse, on 22 June (2 July, new style) 1666. The Lovers of God and other religious zealots had long expected apocalyptic events in 1666 (as 666 is the number of the Beast of the Apocalypse), so this celestial event inevitably produced a strong impression. (Avvakum uses the old Russian calendar in his *Life*; the year 1666 was thus 7174, but he was certainly aware of the new calendar; see S. Zenkovsky, *Staroobrjadčestvo*, 97–98, 154, and J.H. Billington, 143–44). In addition, Avvakum notes the hour during which the eclipse began, for it recalls the Crucifixion and attendant eclipse, which also began in the sixth hour (Matt. 27:45). This time also coincided with the beginning of Matins in Russian churches, that is, worship using the defiled (reformed) liturgy.

23.   The verb "to shear" (*ostrič'*) is confusing for English speakers, since it implies the conferring of the tonsure upon a man entering holy orders. In Russian Orthodoxy precisely the opposite is meant: cropping of the head and beard symbolized the unfrocked cleric's loss of the image of God through great sin or heresy. (The verb *postrič'* was used in the sense of "tonsure.")
This is the first of several passages in which Avvakum refers to himself in the third person. Here this distancing is probably motivated by the cosmic dimensions of his Introduction: they dictate an appropriate humility.

The shift to first-person narration occurs in the very conclusion of this Introduction, as Avvakum moves to the narrative of his personal experiences.

24.   Avvakum was unfrocked and anathematized in the Moscow Kremlin's Cathedral of the Assumption on 13 May 1666. By order of Tsar Aleksej Mixajlovič he was imprisoned two days later in the Nikol'skij Monastery in Ugreša, near Moscow. The eclipse occurred some weeks after these events.

25.   The description of Joshua's great victory over the Amorites near the city of Gibeon is found in Jos. 10:12–13; the details regarding Joshua's symbolic pose and the sun's retreat are not found there, however. The second miracle is described in 2 Kings 20: 12–13 (4 Kings in the Russian Bible); again the details differ from Avvakum's description.

26.   Pseudo-Dionysios discusses three divine trinities of heavenly powers in his book *The Celestial Hierarchy*; in summary he says, "Mark you, as these are the ranks in trinity of the Powers of Wisdom: In the first trinity are the Thrones, also the Cherubim, and then the Seraphim; in the second trinity are the Principalities, the Powers, and Dominions . . . In the third trinity are the Virtues, the Archangels, and the Angels." Avvakum's exposition reverses the positions of Powers and Virtues in the second and third trinities.

27.   Cf. Ezek. 3:13.

28.   German, Patriarch of Constantinople, analysed the Alleluia in precisely these terms at the Ecumenical Council of 1666–67 in Moscow. Avvakum refers, however, to a Russian source, the encyclopedic *Alphabet* which contains a section entitled "On the Alleluia."

29.   St. Gregory, Bishop of Nyssa, was a leading Orthodox theologian in Asia Minor during the last decades of the fourth century and the younger brother of St. Basil the Great. He played a major role in the struggle against the Arian heresy. His works on theological problems, mysticism, and asceticism represent a balanced synthesis of the Hellenic (Platonic) and Christian traditions.

30.   St. Basil the Great, Bishop of Caesarea, was leader in a triad of Holy Fathers including his brother Gregory of Nyssa and their friend Gregory of Nazianzus, who together made fundamental and lasting contributions to Orthodox thought between   AD 360 and 390. He played a major role in the struggle against Arianism. Basil's works on asceticism and his preference for monasticism against eremitism as a community based upon the practice of brotherly love were important in shaping the great Orthodox monastic move-

ment; his *Longer Rules* and *Shorter Rules*, originally written for the monasteries under his supervision in Cappadocia, became standard for Orthodox monasticism, despite the modifications they underwent over time. It is uncertain whether he actually authored the entirety of the magnificent eucharistic prayers known as the *Liturgy of St. Basil*, one of the two liturgies established under canon law from the sixth century on (the other is the *Liturgy of St. John Chrysostom*).

31.   There is no commentary on the specific manner in which the Alleluia is to be chanted in the works of Pseudo-Dionysios nor in the commentaries of Maksim the Confessor.

32.   Cf. Isaiah 6:3.

33.   A lengthy debate was carried on in Pskov during the 15th century regarding the double versus the triple utterance of the Alleluia. Efrosin (d.1481) struggled with the clergy there for many years, and according to tradition finally journeyed to the Patriarch of Constantinople to gain support for the double utterance. His *Life*, written in the first decade of the 16th century by an unknown author and revised by Vasilij in 1547, contains a passage in which the original author (not Vasilij) describes his vision of the Virgin. The double utterance was also supported by Maksim Grek, and the resolutions of the Stoglav Council (1551) affirmed this practice. However, the Ecumenical Council of 1666–67 proclaimed the triple utterance, but without denying Efrosin's sainthood. Rather, it placed blame for the confusion on the "deceiving, lying" author of his *Life*. Avvakum's reference to the *Life* and this vision is thus a polemical rejection of the official liturgical position.

34.   In the Eastern Church the Father was regarded as the sole source of the Holy Spirit, whereas in Catholicism the Holy Spirit was understood as proceeding from both the Father and the Son. The original Nicene Creed agreed in its wording with the Eastern conception, but in the ninth century Charlemagne forced revision of this creed by adding "and the Son." This dispute thus had a long history, and Avvakum depended on it here in suggesting that a Roman Catholic heresy was evident in this reform.

35.   St. Athanasius (293–373), Bishop of Alexandria, was a statesman and Egyptian national leader as well as author of some of the earliest classics of Orthodox apologetics (*Against the Heathen*, *The Incarnation of the Word of God*, *Four Orations against the Arians*). His long defense of Orthodoxy against the Arian heresy contributed to the development of the doctrine of the Trinity, while his *Life of St. Antony* did much to spread the ascetic ideal both in the East and the West.

36.   Avvakum reproduces here with minor inaccuracies a creed taken from a book, *A Collection of Brief Instruction on the Articles of the Faith* (*Sobranie kratkija nauki o artikulax very*), published in Moscow in 1649. The statement immediately after this citation is from an article in the same book, "A Brief Exposition of the Faith" by Anastasius of Antioch and Cyril of Alexandria.

37.   The statement "and to his kingdom there is no end" was altered by the reformers to read, "will be no end." Avvakum and his colleagues considered this to be the Uniate heresy, which in their view asserted that Christ's kingdom had been interrupted and would be renewed at the Second Coming.

38.   Robinson notes (p. 216) that this title, *The Father's Council*, refers to a scene depicted in certain medieval icons; one, for example, shows Christ standing to the left of God the Father, who is blessing him in his mission of service to the world; between them is a throne on which there is an eight-cornered cross, a reed, and a lance (the Golgotha lance), and over it, the Holy Spirit in the traditional form of a dove (for parallels, see pp. 113–14).

39.   *Marguerite* (*The Pearl*) is a collection of St. John Chrysostom's sermons published in Moscow in 1641. It was one of the favorite books of Ivan Neronov, Avvakum's former confessor.

40.   The sentence, "Thus every man . . . the above-mentioned Athanasius," paraphrases both the beginning and the end of the Creed: He who "does not observe the faith . . . will perish forever"; "This is the catholic faith, and he who will not believe in it cannot be saved."

41.   Grigorovo is located to the southeast of old Nižnij-Novgorod, present-day Gor'kij, in the Bol'še-Muraškinskij Rayon of Gor'kovskaja Oblast. An old tax record book describes Grigorovo in the 17th century as follows: "The village consists of three groups of buildings, and between them there is a spring. In the village there is the wooden Church of Ss. Boris and Gleb," in which Avvakum's father served.

42.   In the first of the supplementary tales, Avvakum speaks at length about his 14-year-old brother Evfimej and the book of Efrem Sirin, published in 1647. If that episode happened in 1647 or 1648, then his father could not have died before 1632–33, when Avvakum was 11–13 years old (Avvakum was born in 1620 or 1621; see annotation 46).

43.   One copy of the *Life* adds the information that his mother wished

him to marry when he "was 17 years old, and she brought me a wife 14 years of age." Consequently, Avvakum married around 1638. His loyal wife Anastasija Markovna had a long but terribly difficult life, 1624–1710.

44.   The Russian word translated here as "feats of piety" is *podvig*. Like other medieval Russian writers, Avvakum uses it often, but it is difficult to translate consistently. For Avvakum it never implies a single feat but rather a life-style characterized by spiritual heroism. The term is bound up with his understanding of life as spiritual struggle: to be saved one must make a *podvig* of one's life.

45.   The "place" mentioned here was the village of Lopatišči (identified in the first supplementary tale), located somewhat further to the north than Grigorovo. Apparently Avvakum became a deacon in Lopatišči and remained there from 1642 to 1652.

46.   Robinson explains (p. 217) how it has been determined that Avvakum became an archpriest no later than March 1652. Since he became a deacon at age 21, a priest at 23, and an archpriest at 31 (no later than March 1652), he was born in either 1620 or 1621; we can be more precise if we assume his day of birth was June 29, as he was probably named on the eighth day of his life in honor of St. Avvakum, whose day is July 6.

47.   Avvakum ignores here his two years as a deacon and first three as a priest. Rather, he emphasizes the years since his first association with Vonifat'ev and the Lovers of God, which indeed led to his itinerent ministry. Since a confessor normally had only 15–20 spiritual children (i.e., persons who had chosen him as their confessor, their "spiritual father"), Avvakum takes justifiable pride in the size of his flock. They came from all classes of society, and the evidence indicates that Avvakum had great, even tyrannical, psychological and spiritual influence upon them.

48.   Sexual temptation of future saints was a hagiographical tradition, and Avvakum resists it in a traditional manner. For example, in the *Prologue* (a popular collection of edifying stories which came to Russia from Byzantium) there is a tale about an Egyptian hermit monk who responds to a similar tempatation by burning his fingers in an oil lamp. The Order for Confession directed confessors to demand detail regarding sexual transgressions from those come to confess, so Avvakum is not implying the young woman was in any way to blame for his lust. Indeed, the Order for Confession asserted that true repentance was impossible without tears, so her weeping is a sign of her sincerity.

49.   Avvakum uses the same image of swollen eyes in his *Book of Interpretations* to describe the tireless weeping of St. Andrej, the Fool in Christ. Vinogradov discusses the role of weeping in Avvakum's system of imagery in the article contained in this volume.

50.   Avvakum here uses a phrase from the Order for Confession in which ecclesiastics who lay excessive burdens on their flocks are condemned.

51.   "Eyes of the heart" is a literal translation from the Russian, which has its biblical source in Eph. 1:18. English translations of the Bible vary here (e.g., "eyes of understanding" [King James Version]; "inward eyes" [New English Bible]; "eyes of the heart" [Revised Standard Version]).

52.   It is probable that this Luka is the Luka Lavrent'evič discussed later in the *Life* (p. 95).

53.   Cf. Psalm 116:3 (Psalm 114 in the Russian Bible).

54.   Avvakum refers here to a large flintlock pistol with a smooth bore that came into use in Russia during the early 17th century. Military officers customarily armed themselves with a brace of these firearms.

55.   Prokopij was Avvakum's second son. His oldest son was named Ivan. Agrafena, his oldest daughter, was apparently his favorite child. (See annotations 109, 149, 153, and 189.) Regarding the eunuch, see Acts 8:26–39.

56.   Less is known about the biography of Archpriest Stefan Vonifat'ev than is the case with other important figures among the Lovers of God. Like Avvakum, who revered him, he was born in the area of Nižnij-Novgorod; he later became Archpriest of Moscow's Cathedral of the Annunciation and Tsar Aleksej Mixajlovič's personal confessor during the early period of his reign (1645–52), when the ideal of the Third Rome, of Holy Russia, dominated the latter's political and social ideas. Vonifat'ev's powerful influence upon the young Tsar unquestionably contributed to the atmosphere of energetic piety at court, and during these years he was the principal figure in the vital area of religious policy. He was especially close to Ivan Neronov (see following note), and he played a leading role in the inner circle of the Lovers of God. It is known that he was particularly sensitive and responsive to the suffering of the Russian masses, and that he attempted to ameliorate their condition by curtailing the abuses of the ruling classes. Some measure of the influence of his active piety on the Tsar can be seen in the latter's marriage; the traditional, semi-pagen, boisterous and scabrous customs associated with marriage

were replaced on Vonifat'ev's insistence by an atmosphere of reverence and high spiritual seriousness. The young couple retreated after the marriage, not to the traditional nuptial couch, but to a monastery to pray. After Nikon rose to power (1652), Vonifat'ev's influence waned, for he lacked the resolute ruthlessness necessary to oppose him. He protected his old friends to the extent possible after Nikon began arresting former associates among the Lovers of God, but in 1656 Vonifat'ev himself died under Nikon's surveillance in Iverskij Monastery on one of the islands of Lake Valdaj.

57.   Ivan Neronov, sometimes called "the Father of the Russian Reformation," was a seminal figure in the religious awakening that occurred in Russia toward the middle of the 17th century. He was born in 1590 or 1591 in the Monastery of St. Savior's, in the village of Lom near the northern Russian town of Vologda. The village, like many others in the area, grew up around this isolated, small monastery (*skit*) built by pioneering monks who desired the simple, elemental peace and austerity of the forests for their ascetic devotional life. Neronov must have grown up in contact with such men, perhaps with the monastery's founder, the Elder Ignatij. He acquired their ascetic fervor and simplicity, combining these qualities with a rich and sensitive spirit, a gift for preaching, and an indomitable love for others. Very early in his career Neronov distinguished himself in attempting to conform the life around him to the ideal Orthodox Christian model, to the end of saving men's souls; his denunciations of the impious nobility and of the depravity and drunkenness of his ecclesiastical superiors led to the kind of beatings that Avvakum knew so well. This, however, was the essence of the program of the future Lovers of God: to bring Russia into line with the precepts and ideals of Old Russian Orthodoxy, to make the Church penetrate and transform every corner of Russian life, so that Russia might become the Third Rome in fact. Like the other Lovers of God, Neronov did not wish to withdraw from the world like a monk to save his own soul, this despite his close association as a young man with Dionisij, Archimandrite of the St. Sergius-Trinity Monastery in Zagorsk, in the early 17th century the most important center of Russian religious and cultural life. Dionisij undoubtedly recognized Neronov's pastoral abilities and his potential as a teacher of ordinary people, and probably influenced his first major parish appointment in Nižnij-Novgorod (1630). Neronov's great success in this leading commercial center enhanced his reputation in Moscow as well, although he was also soon widely known as a troublesome moral pedagogue. Neronov was a revolutionary in his ministry, a preacher comprehensible to all in an age when the sermon was an almost forgotten art. The other Lovers of God followed his lead, and Avvakum speaks proudly of his own "preaching and teaching." In 1632 Neronov's outspoken denunciations of Russian preparations for war with Poland led to his exile in the far North,

but he returned to Nižnij-Novgorod not long after the death of Patriarch Filaret (1633). There and in Moscow he continued his efforts to cleanse and rejuvenate the Church and the private lives of its people; he was not without supporters, and in 1649 he became Archpriest of the Kazanskij Cathedral (St. Basil's) in Red Square. By 1651 he and his friends, the Lovers of God, were "at the helm of the Church," in Zenkovsky's apt phrase. Neronov protested vehemently and publicly against Nikon's initial reforms, and in 1653 was exiled once again to the North. In his letters he raised for the first time the spectre of the Antichrist in connection with Nikon's persecutions. He escaped his supervised exile and fled, first to Solovki, then back to Moscow, where Vonifat'ev and others concealed him. There he became the monk Grigorij. He continued to live as a fugitive, and in 1656 was condemned and anathematized in absentia by a Church Council organized by Nikon. During the next decade Neronov gradually became reconciled to the reforms, apparently owing to his fear of schism. Consequently, leadership of the Old Belief devolved automatically upon the fiery and uncompromising Avvakum. Although Avvakum deeply regretted Neronov's truce with the "apostates," he never condemned him publicly as did other Old Believers.

58.   The year was 1647, the period when Vonifat'ev and Neronov were working closely together. Tsar Aleksej Mixajlovič's great interest in religious reform suggests why they introduced Avvakum to him; as becomes clear in reading the *Life*, this meeting initiated many years of complex, difficult, and ambiguous relations between the two men.

59.   Avvakum is here referring to *skomoroxi*, itinerant minstrels with trained bears and other animals who provided ordinary Russians with a favorite form of entertainment during the Middle Ages. Such entertainments were condemned by the Church for their pagan origins and content, and for the impious carnival atmosphere they fostered. The use of musical instruments could hardly recommend the *skomoroxi* to churchmen, who viewed such devices as dead metal and wood, of this earth, associated with carnality, and alien to the only true living instrument, the unaccompanied human voice employed in divine worship. The Lovers of God took vigorous action against the *skomoroxi* and their audiences, for the Tsar gave full support to this repression, giving ecclesiastics the right to fine, imprison, and even to exile those who attended such frolics.

60.   Šeremetev (d. 1659) was a boyar and for many years a leading figure at the Russian court. He had been governor in Nižnij-Novgorod during the 1630's, so Avvakum had undoubtedly known of him long before this unfortunate confrontation.

61.   As was noted above, shaving of the beard was associated by churchmen with loss of the image of God. Although the practice had long been spreading through the upper classes, its heretical nature had recently been reaffirmed by the Church. Šeremetev's harsh treatment of Avvakum was not unexampled, for other zealous priests found that enforcement of such prohibitions was often resisted violently by local authorities. Matvej was Šeremetev's younger son and a close personal friend of the Tsar. He later became a talented military commander, but was killed in battle with the Swedes.

62.   Avvakum is apparently speaking about his brother Gerasim. Avvakum was the oldest brother, followed by Koz'ma, Gerasim, and Evfimej. Koz'ma served as a priest in Moscow, but left at the time of the plague (1654) and returned only in 1666. Gerasim served in both the Cathedral of the Annunciation and the Church of Dmitrij Selunskij by the Tver' Gates. As Evfimej was still young, Avvakum must have meant his second brother.

63.   Cf. Psalm 22:9 (21:10 in the Russian Bible).

64.   Filipp (1507–69) was the Boyar Fëdor Kolyčev before entering holy orders. He participated in a palace plot and subsequently fled to the Soloveckij Monastery, where he eventually became Father Superior. In 1566 he was elevated to Metropolitan of All Russia, but his opposition to Ivan the Terrible's *Opričnina* and denunciations of his atrocities finally led to his murder on Ivan's orders (he was smothered with a pillow). In 1591 his remains were removed to Solovki, but after his canonization in 1652 they were returned as relics to Moscow under Nikon's supervision and with great pageantry. As part of the ceremonies Tsar Aleksej publicly prayed to St. Filipp that he might forgive Ivan's sin.

The *Prologue* contains an aprocryphal tale about the death of Zacharias, father of John the Baptist and a priest in Jerusalem. When Herod ordered the death of all male children under two years of age, Zacharias' wife Elizabeth hid the baby John. Herod ordered Zacharias executed in the Temple, in the manner of a sacrificial animal. In his *Book of Conversations* Avvakum observes that Zacharias was beheaded.

Stefan was the first Bishop of Perm and a successful missionary among the Komi. His *Life* relates an episode in which he and a Komi sorcerer agree to test the truth of their conflicting religions by plunging into a river through a hole in its ice; the one returning from the bottom alive would be in possession of the true faith. The sorcerer ultimately avoided the test by fleeing. Avvakum obviously uses this story rather loosely in the present context.

65.   Avvakum's use of expressions such as "son of a whore" are not indicative of exceptional vulgarity for his time; the leading figures of his day frequently used such language, and in social and religious contexts that are unsettling even by our free-wheeling contemporary standards.

Šelepuga 'scourge' is a folkish form of *šelep*, a special type of whip used in administering religiously sanctioned punishment.

66.   These are the words of the Prodigal Son (Luke 15:18).

67.   Cf. Proverbs 3:34 and James 4:6 (*Poslanie Iakova* 'The Epistle of Jacob' in the Russian Bible).

68.   Avvakum fled to Moscow from Lopatišči for the second time no later than March 1652.

69.   Jur'evec was a small market town and still exists. In Avvakum's day it was surrounded by a stone wall and a ditch, in part excavated and in part natural (thus, the local people shout their threat, "We'll pitch his carcass in the ditch . . ."). Avvakum was in charge of the town's main church, to which ten other small churches were subordinate. There were also two small monasteries and two convents, also small.

70.   Avvakum's troubles in Jur'evec stemmed not only from his denunciations of the libidinous behavior of the local clergy. One of his major responsibilities was collecting the taxes due the patriarchal treasury. Among them was an impost on marriages consecrated by the Church. It turned out that the tax revenues Avvakum brought with him to Moscow exceeded the amount due from the city's inhabitants (i.e., in his zeal Avvakum apparently had taxed unsanctified unions, however temporary, along with genuine marriages). Thus, his parishioners may have called him a "crook" (*vor*) with reason.

71.   Avvakum's rescuer was Denis Krjukov; his "artillerymen" were no longer that in fact, as they had been converted by the 17th century into a local police force in Russian towns.

72.   Archpriest Daniil's problems and their origins were similar to Avvakum's. The local priests in Kostroma had allied with the common people and a group of *skomoroxi* and had beaten him repeatedly and severely, causing him to flee to avoid death. Avvakum arrived in Kostroma between 1–3 June 1652, approximately one week after these events.

73.   See note 64 regarding St. Filipp. Enhancing the prestige and sanctity

of the Kremlin's Cathedral of the Assumption (Uspenskij sobor) was part of the religious program pursued by Tsar Aleksej. Not only the relics of St. Filipp but those of the Patriarchs Germogen and Iov were brought to the cathedral at this time. Nikon left Moscow on 11 March 1652, and Patriarch Iosif died soon thereafter, on 15 April.

74.   Metropolitan Kornilij (d. 17 Aug. 1656) was certainly an acquaintance of Avvakum earlier, as he had been the Father Superior of the Makar'evskij Yellow-Water Monastery located near Nižnij-Novgorod. On 25 July 1652 Nikon was consecrated as patriarch by Kornilij through the laying on of hands.

75.   Although Avvakum quotes with considerable accuracy the salutation in the Tsar's letter, his addition of the phrase "of all Russia" was probably a deliberate error. Since 1589, when Russia received its own patriarchate, the phrase had not been included in any metropolitan's title; its presence here implies the Tsar wished to signal Nikon regarding his own favorite candidate for patriarch. Indeed, everyone soon realized that the Tsar would not begin the election in Nikon's absence, and his two letters to Nikon at this time do contain broad hints regarding his preferences. Thus, Avvakum is not actually misleading here, and such knowledge indicates he was privy through Kornilij and Vonifat'ev to the election process.

76.   Nikon moved quickly after his elevation to neutralize his former associates, the Lovers of God, whose influence had deprived Patriarch Iosif of any effective power. Although Nikon needed power to realize his vision of the Church's future, his ruthless and cynical tactics are to his permanent discredit.

77.   The Chamber of the Cross is the reception hall in the Patriarch's Palace, which is located in the Kremlin. Here the patriarch conducted his daily business and performed the Mass. Here Avvakum disputed with the leaders of the Church in 1666 after his second arrest and imprisonment, and here he and Nikon were both condemned in 1667. This large hall (approximately 42 X 62 feet), which has no central supports, was redecorated by Nikon in 1655 in hopes of overwhelming visitors with its splendor. Not only were former colleagues of the cloth often excluded, but agents of the Tsar were forced to cool their heels quite literally in the bitter Moscow winters while awaiting admittance. A contemporary, Pavel Aleppskij, writes: "Formerly boyars went in to speak with the patriarch without being announced by the doorkeepers.. . . But now we have seen with our own eyes how the Tsar's ministers and associates sit for a long time by the outer doors until Nikon allows them to enter. And they go in with extraordinary meekness and fear."

78.   The instruction was sent on 21 February 1653, the first day of Lent. Avvakum refers here to St. Basil's Cathedral (the familiar name in English) as the "Kazan' Church"; the Kazanskij sobor is the original name of the great cathedral in Red Square that has come to be known as the Cathedral of Vasilij the Blessed (Xram Vasilija Blažennogo) or the Cathedral of the Protection of the Holy Theotokos (Pokrovskij sobor).

79.   Discussions of Avvakum's possible assignment to this church almost certainly occurred during 1652, prior to Nikon's elevation.

80.   See note 56 concerning the renewal of preaching among the Lovers of God. Following the conclusion of divine worship they would "preach," that is, read and then elucidate in the vernacular the books of the Church Fathers and the Lives of the saints. Neronov's reputation as a preacher and teacher undoubtedly inspired Avvakum to emulate him. It is generally assumed that the experience gained and success achieved by Avvakum in his long career as a preacher had a profound influence on the style of his *Life*.

81.   Nikon began his reforms boldly – or stupidly – since obeisances and especially the technique of crossing oneself were matters of fundamental ritualistic importance. What is more, the Stoglav Council of 1551 had reaffirmed the traditional Russian manner of crossing oneself, with two fingers. Nikon took the unheard of step of announcing these changes at the beginning of Lent, the most revered fast, and on his own authority, without benefit of a Church council. The pious, conservative archpriests, who were accustomed to figuring prominently in all decisions affecting the Church, were shocked.

82.   An old center of learning, the Čudovskij (Miracle) Monastery is located in the Moscow Kremlin, and was founded in 1356. It was under the direction of the patriarch.

83.   In a letter to Vonifat'ev written from exile (13 July 1654), Neronov describes this event in slightly different terms: "In the year 7161 [1653], during the first week of Lent, a voice coming from the icon of the Lord spoke thus: 'Ioann, take courage and fear not, even unto death; it is thy bounden duty to strengthen the Tsar in my name, that Russia might not suffer in this day.' "

84.   Another leader born in the Upper Volga area, Pavel had only recently been elevated to the office of bishop (17 Oct. 1652). He was the only chief prelate to defend the old ritual, and at the Church Council of 1654, in the presence of both Nikon and Makarios, Patriarch of Antioch, he objected to

the changes made in the obeisances performed during the Prayer of Efrem Sirin (17 deep bows were replaced by four deep bows and 13 to the waist only). In both his position and personality Pavel was evidently viewed by Nikon as a serious threat. After the Council he addressed a letter to Paissios, Patriarch of Constantinople, in which he requested advice regarding his reforms and discussed the resistance of Bishop Pavel and Archpriest Neronov. In reply Paissios recommended excommunication. Pavel was arrested and exiled, first to the Paleostrovskij Monastery on Lake Onega, then to the Xutynskij Monastery near Novgorod. Later he was brutally flogged and burned by Nikon's agents. The official condemnation of Nikon at the Ecumenical Council of 1666–67 referred with extreme vagueness to Pavel's unlawful execution, stating that he had been flogged savagely but that the manner of his death was unknown; official admission of the burning of a bishop without trial could have endangered the reforms themselves, which Tsar Aleksej was determined to preserve at all costs. Perhaps this vagueness contributed to the rumors that circulated among the old-believing Don Cossacks during the 1780's, that Pavel had returned from exile to the Don area, to serve them as their special patriarch.

85.   These excerpts have not been preserved, but they are believed to be the first contribution to the polemical literature of the schism. During this period following his flight from Kostroma, Archpriest Daniil served with Avvakum under Neronov at St. Basil's Cathedral. Later the two archpriests wrote a petition requesting Neronov's release from exile and condemning Nikon in vigorous terms – an action that certainly hastened their own arrests. Years afterward Avvakum recalled his old friend: "And before the plague I used to go to St. Basil's, . . . and many a time I chanted Mass with this holy martyr, who suffered for the true faith from that wolf Nikon, the hellhound."

86.   This convent was founded in 1654 near the Church of the Suffering Mother of God (Cerkov' Strastnoj Bogorodicy), not far from present-day Pushkin Square. On this spot the Icon of the Suffering Mother of God was met by Muscovites in 1641 when it was brought from Nižnij-Novgorod.

87.   The ceremony of unfrocking a man in holy orders included divesting him publicly of his outer garment, symbolic of his consecrated state, together with the cropping of his head and beard. Compelling a prisoner to work in a monastery's bakery was a common ecclesiastical punishment.

88.   Temnikov is a small town, now in Mordovskaja ASSR (in the area of Saransk and Troitsk, north of Penza). Apparently Daniil, like Avvakum, had been driven from the town because of his efforts to curtail the pagan customs

of its citizens. He fled to Moscow and joined the Lovers of God. It would seem he later repented his resistance, for in 1670 he was again serving in Temnikov.

89.   Novospasskij was one of the principal monasteries in Russia during the 17th century. It was originally located in the Moscow Kremlin, but in the 15th century it was moved to Krutitsy.

90.   Rather like a biretta, a *skuf'ja* is a small peaked hat given to priests and deacons upon their consecration as a sign of their new spiritual state. The *skuf'ja* was thus much respected, and to be stripped of it was a signal disgrace. Adam Olearius, one-time Secretary of the Holstein legation in Russia and author of a remarkable description of the Muscovite state during the 1630's, observes that the *skuf'ja* was a sanctified object: "Anyone who strikes a priest and hits this hat or causes it to fall to the ground must be fined for this 'dishonor.' However, priests are still beaten . . . In order to protect this small hat in such a situation, it is first taken off, then the priest is thrashed to a fare-thee-well, and once again the hat is carefully placed on his head."

91.   The Simanov Monastery was one of the richest of Russia's monasteries during the 17th century. It was founded in the area immediately to the southeast of Moscow around 1370.

92.   The ancient Spasov Kamennoj Monastery is located on an island in Lake Kubinskoe, about 45 kilometers to the north of Vologda.

93.   Avvakum errs here slightly in that Neronov was sent not to this fortress but to the Kandalakšskij Roždestvenskij Monastery on the Kol'skij Peninsula.

94.   Cf. I Cor. 10:12.

95.   A slight variation on Matt. 24:24; the statement occurs during Christ's description of the end of the world and the Second Coming.

96.   Neledinskij was a high-ranking associate of Nikon, which indicates that considerable importance was attached to the arrest of the still youthful Avvakum. These events occurred on 21 August 1653, and they halted Avvakum's public defiance of the hierarchy. After he had returned to Moscow from accompanying Neronov into exile, Avvakum attempted to take the latter's place at St. Basil's by claiming it was Neronov's command. He was turned away, of course, and began to hold vigils in a shed attached to Neronov's

house. He apparently drew people away from St. Basil's, even though there was no canonical justification for worshiping in such a setting. Here and elsewhere in his writings, Avvakum omits this fact, thereby creating the impression that his arrest occurred in a church, not in a horse barn.

97.   The Andronikov or Spas-Andronikov Monastery (named after its first father superior) was founded around 1360; it is located on the Yauza River, in the outskirts of Moscow near the Rogožkaja zastava.

98.   Avvakum wished, of course, to bow to the east according to tradition.

99.   Avvakum here paraphrases Acts 10:10 in his contemporary Bible; the modern Russian Bible has altered the translation of this verse.

100.   Avvakum's description of this miracle resembles passages in Acts (5:19 and 12:7-9), wherein angels appear in prisons to assist the apostles.

101.   Login was a peasant by birth and one of the most intransigent of the Lovers of God. The story of the miracle involving his shirt (described in this same paragraph) apparently developed over time. Avvakum wrote a letter to Neronov (1653) after the shearing of Login and did not mention this event. In fact, he remarked that Login was dragged from church in his shirt (i.e., he did not throw it into the altar). Only later in writing his *Life* did Avvakum assert that Login cast his shirt at Nikon and afterwards was thrown "naked" into a cell.

102.   "He" is not expressed in the Russian original, only the masculine past-tense form of the verb. As Vinogradov observes, this is typical of Avvakum's references to Nikon, as if the latter's presence is so suffocatingly immediate in memory that no pronominal reference is necessary.

103.   Login's shearing occurred in the Kremlin's Cathedral of the Assumption, where Avvakum was later sheared as well, some 13 years later.

104.   Ferapont died in 1654, shortly after participating in Nikon's Church Council. He had been Archimandrite of this monastery since 1649, and one of his ex officio duties was to assist the patriarch, along with the three other Moscow archimandrites, when he was celebrating the Mass.

105.   During the third part of the liturgy (the "Liturgy of the Faithful"), the elements are brought from the credence table to the altar. A priest and a deacon exit from the sanctuary through the north gates of the iconostasis,

pass through the congregation, and enter the sanctuary once again through the Royal Gates (the central gates), the deacon being first to enter. The priest places the chalice on the altar, then takes the paten from the deacon, places it beside the chalice, and covers both with the communion cloth. Thus, Ferapont's failure to enter the Royal Gates before Nikon placed the paten on the altar is viewed by Avvakum as a "sundering" of the body of Christ, the body and blood being torn apart. Thus does he justify and magnify Login, whom heaven approved when his shirt fell in such a miraculous manner upon the elements. What is more, the anathema laid upon him is rendered invalid by the very fact that the Sacrament was defiled through this heretical error. However, Avvakum himself errs here in that he suggests the transubstantiation of the elements occurs before the ritual of transposition, not after they rest upon the altar as Church doctrine affirmed. This issue later cropped up in the polemics between Avvakum and the Deacon Fёdor during their imprisonment at Pustozersk.

106.   Avvakum remarks in his letter to Neronov (1653) that the Tsar was present during this Mass. Apparently both sovereigns were present, a circumstance explained perhaps by the fact that the date was September 1, the day set aside for the celebration of the New Year in old Russia.

107.   Avvakum's letter to Neronov describes in greater detail his first interrogation by the hierarchs, especially with regard to the petition which he and Daniil had sent to the Tsar requesting Neronov's release from exile. Although he was forced to walk through the streets to this inquiry "like a brigand," Avvakum boldly affirmed the petition's claim that " '[True] learning has disappeared in Russia, and the head has left the Church . . .' And I said to my judges, 'The head is Ivan [Neronov], but those destroying the ancient piety are swine.' " The Patriarchal Archdeacon Evfimij, "having contended with me and blasting me with mother curses, ordered me returned again to the Andronikov Monastery."

It was customary on 15 September for a procession to pass from the Kremlin's Cathedral of the Assumption to the eastern part of Moscow, to St. Nikita's church. Avvakum obviously felt his position to be humiliating, especially as many in the procession must have known him well.

108.   Semën Tret'jak Vasil'ev Bašmak was for many years a loyal government agent, working primarily in the fur trade. He came from the lower classes and was largely self-educated in religious matters. He became a staunch defender of the Old Belief, especially after he took the cowl. It is interesting that he advocated the use of vernacular Russian, undistorted by foreign models (i.e., Greek), well before Avvakum raised this particular banner.

109.   On 1 September 1653 Nikon ordered Avvakum and his family into exile, to the Lena River. However, on the 16th the Tsar eased the Archpriest's punishment by sending him only as far as Tobol'sk, the administrative center for Siberia. Besides his wife, Avvakum traveled with sons Ivan (9 yrs.), Prokopij (5 yrs.), newborn Kornilij, daughter Agrafena (8 yrs.), and his niece Marina. Travel to Tobol'sk and back to Moscow usually required 12 weeks in the winter; Avvakum's slow journey was caused by the muddy autumn roads and the obvious difficulties of traveling with small children. The family and their escort arrived in Tobol'sk during the last week of December 1653.

110.   Archbishop Simeon (see note 17) was an energetic administrator who did much to strengthen the Church in Siberia. He brought more priests into the region and obtained patriarchal approval in 1652 to appoint archpriests to both the regional ecclesiastical center, the Cathedral of St. Sofija in Tobol'sk, and to the city's Cathedral of the Ascension. The latter is the post to which Avvakum refers. An instruction from the Tsar also directed Simeon to give Avvakum ecclesiastical duties, as he was still a consecrated priest.

111.   Avvakum lived in Tobol'sk from December 1653 to 29 June 1655. Since these denunciations of crimes against the state were generally investigated quickly and ruthlessly, it is likely that the falsity of the accusations brought against Avvakum was apparent, and that the civil authorities were generally well disposed toward him.

112.   When Archbishop Simeon left for the Moscow Council of 1654, Struna was one of two officials left in charge of ecclesiastical administration in Tobol'sk. For whatever cause, Struna apparently entered the Church of the Ascension intent on arresting Anton. According to the Legal Code of 1649, rioting in a church was punishable by flogging. However, Avvakum was not justified in administering the punishment himself, for the Stoglav Council (1551) had reaffirmed the ecclesiastical law that made any cleric guilty of beating a believer or nonbeliever subject to excommunication. Thus, both Struna and Avvakum had grounds upon which to seek the conviction of the other.

113.   Because of Tobol'sk's importance as an administrative and military center, it had two "commanders" (*voevody*), a senior and a junior officer, who had chief responsibility in these areas. During Avvakum's residence there, V. I. Xilkov and I. I. Gagarin-Posnyj served in these posts.

114.   Metropolitan Pavel was one of the most vigorous opponents of the Old Believers. During the eight-year hiatus after Nikon's retirement he often

performed the patriarch's duties, and he was a principal organizer of the Ecumenical Council of 1666–67 that finally deposed Nikon. Although Pavel was apparently a decisive administrator, documents from the period are extremely partisan in their depictions of his life and work, and it is difficult to separate truth from fancies born of admiration or hatred. Avvakum's attitude toward him is predictable: "Why look to the Metropolitan Pavel? That one didn't live for his soul – he spent his time trading in pancakes and hotcakes, and as soon as he became a priestlet he learned to lick plates in all the nobles' houses." And of Pavel together with Ilarion Avvakum remarked, "I fought with those hounds like a hunting dog with borzois."

115.   Deacon Afanasij served in the Kremlin's Cathedral of the Assumption. His allegiance to Nikon was apparently heartfelt, for when the latter attempted to return to the patriarchal throne (1664) from his self-imposed retirement, Afanasij brought all his children to this cathedral to receive Nikon's blessing.

116.   Archbishop Simeon reported to Moscow that a woman and her daughter had petitioned him regarding the rape of the girl by her father, and that Struna had dismissed the peasant and ordered the women whipped "without mercy." The Archbishop chained Struna in the bakery of a monastery but the latter escaped, fled to the two local military commanders, and denounced not only Avvakum but the Archbishop as well for torturing him and for protecting "the exiled Archpriest." In addition, Struna complained about Avvakum's "violent words" and about his unlawful use of a bishop's crosier (not an archpriest's) as he walked about the streets of Tobol'sk. Avvakum's crosiers (he owned two) were sent to Nikon as evidence, and this had some bearing on his subsequent exile farther to the east.
    Struna's tactic is familiar: political denunciation of authorities who threaten punishment. He also took advantage of the continual political tug-of-war between the civil and ecclesiastical authorities in Tobol'sk over their respective jurisdictions. Even though Struna was subject to the ecclesiastical court, the commanders refused to return him to the Archbishop.

117.   Pëtr Beketov had served with honor in Siberia for many years, as Russia extended its area of influence and control ever to the east. He had recently arrived in Tobol'sk after a difficult and dangerous mission entrusted to him by Avvakum's future nemesis, Afanasij Paškov. His assignment as Struna's guardian was standard procedure, as informers customarily received protection while their denunciations were being investigated. His vitriolic and perhaps violent defense of Struna in church was not altogether unprovoked, for Struna was to be excommunicated and anathematized for a crime he did not commit in fact, that is, incest. Struna's judicial malfeasance was

not unusual in this place, and incest, as Robinson points out (p. 240), was so common there that it was not considered a serious offense. Nikon was sympathetic, and in 1656 he pardoned Struna. In addition, he soon denied Archbishop Simeon the right to celebrate the Mass, perhaps because of his collaboration with Avvakum in the Struna affair.

118.   In 1655 Tsar Aleksej Mixajlovič was away on his Polish campaign and Nikon had virtually a free hand in Moscow, as he was empowered to rule in the name of the Tsar's young son Aleksej as well as in his own. After the Church Council of 1655 had finally ratified his reforms, he acted swiftly, apparently in the conviction that he no longer had to await the results of the investigation of the charges brought against Avvakum by Ivan Struna. In the name of Aleksej he ordered Avvakum and his family on to the east, to the Lena river, as he had originally done before the Tsar intervened. That Nikon hoped for Avvakum's death in this wild, unsettled country can scarcely be doubted.

119.   Two of Avvakum's known brothers survived the plague (Gerasim and Koz'ma); Evfimij died together with another brother, whose name is unknown (see note 63).

120.   In 1653—64, Neronov warned the Tsar several times about the disasters that awaited Russia if Nikon's policies were continued. Avvakum is thus referring to events more than a year old. His statement of Neronov's prophecies echoes the manner of biblical passages such as Jer. 24:10 ("I will send the sword, famine, and pestilence") and Ezek. 14:21 (". . . I send my four sore judgments upon Jerusalem, the sword, and famine, and the noisome beast, and pestilence, . . .").

121.   The reference is obviously to the boat in Avvakum's vision. Thus, he manipulates into a metaphor the fact that travel by boat now became his principal means of transportation.

122.   The path covered by Avvakum's journey in the east is over 18,000 kilometers in length, that is, close to 20,000 versts. Daurija was the name used in the 17th century to denote the geographical area to the east of Lake Baikal which includes the basins of the Shilka, Argun, Seya, Amur (in part), Sungari, and Ussuri rivers. Avvakum remained in the western regions of this vast territory.

123.   Afanasij Paškov (d. 1664) was the great-grandson of Grigorij Paškevič, a Pole who came to Russia during the reign of Ivan the Terrible. Paškov's

long career included service at court, in the city of Moscow, and a military command in the Far North (in the area of the Mezen river) before he was sent to Yeniseisk as military commander (1660–65). There he set about walling the city, learning the best routes to China, building boats for military expeditions to the east, and enriching himself by any means and as quickly as possible. In 1655, I. P. Afinkov arrived as the new military commander of the city, bringing at the same time Paškov's appointment as commander in the "new land of Daurija." Paškov's task included the subjugation of the Daurian prince Lavkai and other local princes, collection of large tribute in furs, discovery of valuable metals (if any), and of arable lands in the river valleys. He was also to build in the East a church with two altars, one dedicated to Metropolitan Aleksej and the other to St. Aleksej, man of God (Aleksej was the name of the Tsar and his son). Archbishop Simeon was directed to send two priests and a deacon to serve in the East; he assigned Avvakum to one of these positions. Preparations for the expedition took more than a year (1655–56), as Paškov and Afinkov were feuding about the riotous behavior of the former's troops as well as over the problems of equipping them. Living in Yeniseisk during that year, Avvakum had ample opportunity to observe Paškov's savage treatment of those who displeased him, clergy included.

124.   A prame (also pram or praam) is a light-weight, flat-bottomed boat, traditionally propelled by sail or oars; it is thus similar in design to the *došćenik*, a type of boat widely used by Russian forces in Siberia. However, "prame" is not a precise translation, because the *došćenik* is larger, a good one being capable of carrying 30 persons or up to five tons of cargo.

125.   For a married woman to appear in public without her hair covered was considered a disgrace in Avvakum's day. A covered head was both emblematic of her husband's power and honorific, signaling her status as wife and mother. A woman's hair was also considered erotic. Anastasija Markovna's uncovered head thus distills the extreme danger and terror of this moment; presumably there were very few situations in life that would take precedence over covering her head.

126.   The Šamanskij Rapids are located on the Angara at a point where the river is divided by a rocky island. They are about three and one-half miles in length and extremely violent, with waves reaching 12–13 feet in height.

Paškov's effort to compel these widows to marry Cossacks was not necessarily an expression of morbid depravity, although this should not be discounted as a possibility. Baptized Russian women were in extremely short supply in Siberia, the result being that normal constraints in relations between the sexes almost completely disappeared. Women were bought and sold, forcibly married and divorced, and sent into exile with men. Paškov had been empowered by the Tsar to baptize native women and to give them in marriage. Such barbaric attitudes along with a pragmatic and cynical desire to keep his Cossacks happy probably figured in Paškov's motives here.

127.   The Long Rapids (approximately four and one-half miles in length) are also located on the Angara river. They are not especially dangerous for craft of the type used by Paškov. According to Čaleev, a Russian who traveled the length of the Angara in 1875, the river passes here between precipitous cliffs that have the appearance "of fantastic castles, towers, columns, and of the ruins of fortresses."

128.   Avvakum's laconic description of the lands around the Angara only hints at their rugged majesty and harshness. Avvakum apparently heard local legends about great snakes, for in fact only smaller species live in the area. However, the other fauna mentioned substantiate his memory of detail, as the birds and animals noted almost certainly reflect personal observation. It is likely that he refers here to the following fauna native to the Lake Baikal area: the grey goose, the red duck or *ogar'*, the Siberian raven, the white-collared or white-breasted Daurian jackdaw, the East-Siberian fish eagle, the Russian falcon, the Siberian gerfalcon, the mountain pheasant, the whooper swan, the Siberian roe deer, the Siberian forest deer, the elk, the wild boar, the Altai mountain goat, and the wolf.

129.   Avvakum's letter has not been preserved but his memory of it may be accurate, since the lines quoted are drawn from the "Order for Baptism" and slightly altered. Early in the service the priest proclaims: "Christ doth ban thee, devil, . . . Fear God, who sitteth above the Cherubim and gazeth into the abyss; before him the Angels and Archangels do tremble, together with the Thrones, Principalities, Virtues, Dominions, Powers, the many-eyed Cherubim and six-winged Seraphim; before him heaven and earth do tremble, and the sea and all that in them is." Avvakum's elliptical restatement of these lines substitutes "man" (i.e., Paškov) for "devil," a provocation the latter was almost certain to recognize. Indeed, in a message to the Tsar in which he attempted to justify himself and indict Avvakum, Paškov wrote: "On the 15th day of September, when I came to the Long Rapids, the exiled, unfrocked Priest Avvakumko [a belittling diminutive] wrote an anonymous, villainous letter with his own hand, suggesting . . . that there is no justice or truth to be found anywhere among our leaders, anywhere in their ranks. And he has made many other coarse speeches, wanting to spread dissension in my troop." He considered Avvakum deserving of death but "dared not" execute him without authorization from the Tsar. That Avvakum attacked leaders other

than Paškov in this letter is likely; Archbishop Simeon petitioned the Tsar regarding them: "They are kindly . . . to all orders of people, like foxes to chickens, and wolves to sheep."

130.   Although Avvakum had not yet been unfrocked and anathematized, Paškov could reasonably ask this question. Whereas Nikon had ordered him to deny Avvakum the right or opportunity to carry out priestly duties, Archbishop Simeon had sent him to the expeditionary force in place of an ordinary priest. Although Paškov enforced Nikon's temporary interdict, the Archpriest's influence spread among his Cossacks, as Avvakum suggests here in noting their sympathy. (At least some of these Cossacks were punished and expelled from Paškov's troop.) Obviously Avvakum was very far from submitting to Nikon's interdict, and this led inevitably to conflict with Paškov, who had good reason to avoid provoking Nikon's wrath by disobeying or failing to enforce his commands.

131.   The *čexan* ("command axe") was a single-bitted weapon used both in combat and as an emblem of rank. Despite Paškov's reputation for violence, his personal participation in Avvakum's flogging was an unacceptable breech of "propriety," even by the 17th century's savage standards. Paškov remained silent on this point in his report to the Tsar regarding Avvakum's punishment, but Archbishop Simeon denounced him vehemently in a letter to the Tsar (1658): "Afanasij Paškov . . . with his own hands beat Avvakum with his command axe. . . . He beat him about the head with his command axe and completely shattered his head; and from this flogging Archpriest Avvakum lay for a long time as if dead." Simeon also informed the Tsar that he had refused Paškov's request for another priest because "by nature he is a great brawler." Paškov's request for a deacon was met, however, and this indicates Simeon's tactics: in sending a deacon he did not appear uncooperative, but in refusing a priest he did not alter his original appointment of Avvakum to this position in Paškov's force; to do otherwise would not only show weakness at a time when he was clashing violently with the commanders in Tobol'sk, but it would place Avvakum in the extremely dangerous position of a common exile. Simeon's final comment ("Whether the Archpriest Avvakum is alive or not, I do not know") must have distressed not only the Tsar, who was not ill-disposed toward Avvakum personally, but even more the Empress and their older daughter, who greatly admired him. Some four years later Tsar Aleksej cited this event as his reason for stripping Paškov of his Siberian command.

132.   A man about to be flogged with the knout was customarily stripped to his thighs. Simeon stated in his letter to the Tsar that Avvakum received 60 blows, but Avvakum states elsewhere as well that he received 72 blows:

"The Commander beat me on my sinful face with his own hands, he tore the hair out of my head, and beat me on my spine with his command axe, then laid 72 blows on that same back with a knout" ("First Petition"). This was an extremely harsh punishment, as Nikon himself considered 50 blows to be a "merciless" flogging.

In the 17th century the knout consisted of a short wooden handle and a flexible leather shaft with a leather loop or metal ring at the end, to which was attached a wide, stiff rawhide "tail" bent lengthwise in such a way that the rough edges tore the skin and flesh. Sometimes the tail had sharp metal gouges attached to its striking end and edges. When blood caused a knout to lose the requisite degree of stiffness during a flogging, it was exchanged for a new one.

133.   Avvakum does not quote Job in a narrow literal sense here, but this anguished, rebellious prayer obviously echoes many passages in that biblical text (cf. 9:1–3, 32; 14:3; 16:9–21; 19:7; 23:1–7; chap. 31; 40:6–8). It is not certain that Avvakum's prayerful appeals to Christ for succor and strength during the flogging are the only appeals he made. In his letter to the Tsar, Paškov callously remarks that the Archpriest "said": " 'Brother Cossacks, don't do it!' – as if he, the villain, could place his hope in them."

134.   Cf. Acts 14:22.

135.   The Angara's Padun Rapids consist of seven cascades, of which three are the largest; the roar of the broiling water passing through them can be heard for miles around. At present the great Bratsk hydroelectric station is located at this point in the river. The word "gates" was a local term used to describe the navigable passages past the rapids (one of these passages was called "the old gates"). During the 19th century, Čaleev (see note 127) spoke to a local pilot, who repeated almost verbatim Avvakum's statement that (empty) boats must pass through these shallow passages and over flat rocks along the edge of the rapids or they will be "turned into splinters." Supplies obviously had to be carried manually.

136.   Cf. Heb. 12:5–8.

137.   The Bratskij fortress was located not far from the present-day city of Bratsk, near the confluence of the Angara and the Oka rivers. The fortress was established in 1631, shortly after Maksim Perfir'ev and Pëtr Beketov (see note 117) led the first Russian forces into the area (1628 and 1629 respectively). The original fortress was destroyed in 1654 by the Buryat Mongols, but Paškov rebuilt it at a new location closer to the confluence of the two rivers.

The northwest tower of the fortress still exists (it was moved to the village of Kolomenskoe near Moscow in 1959); according to tradition, Avvakum was imprisoned in precisely that structure. The tower is constructed of logs, roughly square in shape and about 23 feet high; it has two stories and is punctured here and there with small gun embrasures (see photograph, p. 62). Avvakum was imprisoned from approximately 1 October to 15 November, as St. Philip's Fast comprises the six weeks before Christmas. (In the third redaction of the *Life*, Avvakum indicates he was moved from the tower somewhat earlier, around 27 Oct.).

138.   Hostages were taken by Russian military leaders, usually from prominent families among native tribes, in order to force payment of "imperial taxes." Such taxes, or more accurately, tribute, consisted for the most part of furs.

139.   Ivan, the oldest of Avvakum's children, was 12 years of age in the winter of 1656–57.

140.   Paškov's force moved out early in May 1657. His original orders were to journey to the north of Lake Baikal and into Daurija. Paškov had decided before leaving Yeniseisk that his boats and supplies were too heavy for this northern route. So he continued up the Angara to Lake Baikal, crossed it, and proceeded up the Selenga river. The journey to the Xilok river through this tortuous, mountainous terrain required approximately two weeks. At the mouth of the Xilok, Paškov's force abandoned the large prames and built small, barge-like boats.

141.   Avvakum does not mean that he spent two summers on the Xilok. After moving up the Xilok to Lake Irgen, Paškov's troop abandoned their boats and carried their supplies over a long portage to the Ingoda river. The following spring and summer they moved down the Ingoda. As Avvakum makes vividly clear, this was a bitter, death-filled journey.

142.   The elevation of Lake Baikal is 1,525 feet above sea-level; that of Lake Irgen (one of several small lakes in a swampy upland separating the Lake Baikal and Amur river basins) is 3,640 feet. Paškov arrived at Lake Irgen during October 1657 and rebuilt the fortress there before beginning the winter portage to the Ingoda.

143.   Large numbers of logs were cut on the Ingoda and used in approximately 170 rafts, each carrying two or three persons downstream to the Shilka river. There the logs were used to build two forts, as there was little

timber for this purpose there.

Avvakum's journey was in its fourth year, as he claims: in summary, during the summer of 1655 he journeyed from Tobol'sk to Yeniseisk, where he wintered; during the summer and fall of 1656 he moved from Yeniseisk to the Bratskij fortress, where he spent the winter; during the spring, summer, and fall of 1657 he traveled from the Bratskij fortress to Lake Irgen; during the winter he hauled supplies over the portage to the Ingoda, and in the spring of 1658 struggled down this river.

144.   The phrase "fire and the rack" is not merely an exclamation; it refers to the inexpressibly inhuman practice of subjecting a victim simultaneously to firebrands and the rack. Avvakum later informed the Tsar that Paškov had "tortured" many people in Daurija, "flogged them with the knout, and broke their ribs, and burned them by fire," that one "was burned to death," that two "were sent naked beyond the river as food for the flies," that two "were hanged."

145.   What is called an "overdress" here (*odnorjadka*) has earlier been translated as "surplice" when referring to male ecclesiastics. Both sexes wore this long, loose garment with full sleeves over a kaftan. This one was probably very colorful and highly embellished, as the usual price for such a garment was 2–5 rubles.

146.   Paškov arrived at the mouth of the Nerča, a tributary of the Shilka, early in June 1658 and built a fort there to replace one earlier erected by Beketov and Urasov and destroyed by local tribes. The terrain in this general area is forest steppe and, in some areas, arid chernozem steppe. Avvakum later claimed that Paškov caused more than 500 people to starve to death. Robinson considers this figure to be only slightly exaggerated. Starvation began when needed supplies did not arrive from Yeniseisk.

147.   Avvakum probably means a "pine-bark porridge," the term he uses in his tale of the little black hen (p.68).

148.   It is unlikely that Paškov was seriously concerned about his people eating proscribed meat. Not religious but pragmatic reasons must have motivated his brutal punishments: without horses he could not fulfill his commission from the Tsar.

149.   These were Avvakum's youngest sons, Kornilij and the infant born on the way to Tobol'sk; the latter's name is unknown.

150.   This passage combines Jer. 9:1 with a line from the Service for the Presentation of Christ in the Temple, one of the 12 great Orthodox holidays (Feb. 2), known as Candlemas or Feast of the Purification of the Virgin in the Roman Catholic Church. The latter passage reads as follows: ". . . rain warm tears upon me that I might weep for my soul, which I have wickedly sullied."

151.   The term "Boyarina" is used here by Avvakum in a vernacular, honorific sense. This usage does not indicate actual social status, for these women are not of the same rank as, say, the famous Old Believer, the Boyarina Feodosija Morozova.

152.   One pood equals 36.11 lbs.

153.   Agrafena was living with her sisters Akulina and Aksin'ja, while her mother and brothers Prokopij and Ivan were imprisoned nearby in a covered pit. The third and youngest son Afanasij was apparently living with his sisters.

154.   Cf. Matt. 24:13 and Mark 13:13.

155.   It would seem that Avvakum reckoned this period from the time he left Tobol'sk to his departure either from the Nerča, or later from the fortress on Lake Irgen (1655 to 1661–62).

156.   This biblical citation (Matt. 27:24) was one of Avvakum's favorites, as he uses it rather often to describe energetic but futile actions.

157.   The story of Balaam is found in Num., chap. 22; the sources of the other two legends are unknown.

158.   This statement is frequently encountered in the Orthodox liturgy.

159.   *The Christian's Pilot* (*Kormčaja*) is a collection of ecclesiastical legislation and rules that came to Russia from Byzantium via Serbia at the beginning of the 13th century. It was published in Moscow in 1650 and again, with Nikon's emendations, in 1653. Avvakum apparently carried a copy of this very large volume (undoubtedly the first edition) into exile, for we later read that he gave it to a friend upon beginning his return to Russia (p.74).

160.   In the West the Eucharist was administered more frequently than in Russia, almost every week as compared to four times a year during the great

fasts. Confession in the Roman Church was not deemed necessary each time prior to communing, except when the believer was burdened with serious sins.

161.   The schism created serious problems in the continuing administration of Communion among Old Believers: Can a priest consecrated after the Nikonian reforms administer the Eucharist? (See Zenkovsky, *Staroobrjadčestvo*, especially 424–27.) That Avvakum gave advice concerning Communion in his *Life* is not surprising, as he was frequently queried on this issue.

162.   "Host" here translates *zapasnyj agnec*, communion bread consecrated in a church but used elsewhere. Generally Old Believers used bread consecrated only in unreformed churches, which meant it was increasingly difficult to obtain over time.

163.   This is a prayer recited by the priest and the deacon before the altar in the sanctuary prior to receiving the Sacrament.

164.   The "priest of darkness" refers to Sergij, an adherent of Nikon's reforms and Avvakum's opponent. He was the recognized ecclesiastic in Paškov's force, although Avvakum obviously did not admit his legitimacy.

165.   After Paškov's death in 1664, his wife Fekla Simeonovna moved into the Moscow Kremlin's Voznesenskij Convent, where she later took the veil and served as Mother Superior from 1673 to her death in 1685. Likewise, her daughter-in-law Evdokija Kirillovna took the veil in this convent prior to her death, and she was buried there by Avvakum.

166.   Initially this was a move from the fort on the Nerča to the fort on Lake Irgen in the spring of 1660.

167.   Avvakum had good reason to ascribe this hen's prodigious egg-laying powers to God's will, for they are well beyond the capacity of the best hens under ideal conditions.

168.   The reference here is to Evdokija Kirillovna.

169.   In the *Prologue* (see note 48), under the reading for Nov. 1, reference is made to the ability of these saints to heal all living creatures. In the folk tradition they are usually considered to be the protectors of fowl.

170.   As an adult Simeon was an important official in Rostov (a *stol'nik*, the rank immediately inferior to the boyars). In 1703 he participated in an

investigation of matters pertaining to the Old Belief in the Balaxonskij district, and his interesting observations were later included in a book dealing with this subject by Metropolitan Dmitrij of Rostov.

171.   Ecclesiastical law forbad sorcery of any kind, for in principle it was equivalent to worship of pagan divinities. Nevertheless, both the government and the church received reports from Siberia that not only the natives but Russians resorted to sorcerers, especially in healing the sick. Priests were required to ask women during confession whether they had visited sorcerers or brought them into their homes. Practitioners of sorcery were punished with flogging, exile, and death by fire.

172.   Paškov had two sons named Ivan.

173.   Priests could not perform any of their liturgical duties or pastoral duties involving ritual without first donning the stole, a long, narrow strip of cloth worn around the neck and falling from the shoulders.

174.   Here the phrase "God save you" (*Spasi Bog*) might be translated, perhaps with almost equal accuracy, as "Thank you" (modern Russian *spasibo*). In Avvakum's usage one can see that this phrase has already lost some of its religious coloration, so that the religiously unmarked translation is sometimes possible.

175.   Eremej was second in command in Paškov's expeditionary force, and he later rose high in the tsarist service. In 1667 he was sent by Aleksej Mixajlovič to search for silver ore near Vladimir; having the rank of *stol'nik* then, he next became the chief civil official (*voevoda*) in Tambov, then in Kozlov, then the official third in rank in Kiev. In 1676 he was appointed to the Kazan department with responsibility for official appointments.
        Eremej's force was certainly not large enough to conquer new territory to the east. The Mongols had been exacting tribute from the Buryat Mongols and from the Tungus, who were living in territories nominally under Russian control; the principal goal of Eremej's expedition was to strengthen the Russian hold on this source of wealth. The expedition took place during August and September 1661; its ultimate failure was due, according to Paškov, to 17 Yenisei Cossacks, who "plotting villainously" had betrayed Eremej one night by stealing arms and supplies and fleeing on rafts down the Ingoda.

176.   The Russian verb here (*šamanit'*) is formed on the noun *šaman*. The shaman was the central figure in the religions of most Siberian tribes,

for he was at once priest, healer, and prophet. Shamans among the Buryat Mongols and the Tungus often prophesied the outcome of important undertakings, preceding this with the sacrifice of an animal and sometimes basing their predictions on the pattern of fissures in the shoulder blade of a burned ram. Later descriptions of the behavior of a shaman exercising his prophetic powers substantiate the accuracy of Avvakum's remarks — the first such description on record. For example, the 19th-century scholar D. Banzarov wrote that the shaman first chants prayers in a sitting position, beating a drum with increasing force until, at the appropriate moment, he "rises, leaves the drum, and begins to dance, leap about, spin, beat himself, all the while chanting incantations and howling frightfully, so that foam flows from his mouth."

177.   The "sons of Zebedee" were the disciples James and John; cf. the Gospel according to St. Luke 9:54—56.

178.   Paškov speaks here the words of Judas the betrayer (Matt. 27:4). Avvakum's affirmation of God's patience and understanding echoes a prayer used in the sanctification of oil ("Quick to succor and slow to anger") and the Epistle of James (*Poslanie Iakova*) 1:19.

179.   Cf. the fourth commandment (Exodus 20:12).

180.   Grigorij may well have been a relative of Ivan Telnoj, who earlier had been driven out of Paškov's troop because of his sympathy for the Archpriest. Ivan Telnoj was from Berëzov, a town known for its skilled navigators. Another Telnoj from Berëzov is a likely choice for the helmsman of Paškov's own boat.

181.   Cf. Romans 14:8.

182.   Avvakum perhaps saw polar bears in the wild near Mezen, the place of his first exile in the Far North.

183.   Avvakum refers here to the entire period of his acquaintance with Paškov, 1655 to 1664, the year of the latter's death. The scarcely perceptible ambiguities present in Avvakum's depiction of Paškov only hint at what must have been an extremely complex relationship. It is probable that Avvakum's moral authority increased markedly in Paškov's eyes while they were still in Siberia, a perception that would surely be strengthened by Avvakum's warm reception in Moscow (Nikon was already in eclipse), while Paškov was in disfavor. Robinson repeats the suggestion that Paškov may even have

become Avvakum's spiritual child in Moscow (p. 255). This seems highly unlikely, unless it was merely a strategic move recognized as such by the Archpriest. A genuine victory of this sort would scarcely go unremarked in Avvakum's *Life*, especially as he habitually recalls the spiritual biographies of others, that is, their changes of heart regarding the Old Belief. It would appear the Tsar was prepared to visit any discomfort upon Paškov that would satisfy Avvakum; Paškov even attempted to buy Avvakum off. But the Archpriest did not want money. He had another dream in which piety and malice were marvelously conjoined: he wanted to make Paškov — a monk! Eventually there occurred a memorable scene in which Paškov cast himself at the feet and upon the mercy of the Archpriest. And Avvakum accomplished his long-desired goal. We have no evidence that becoming a monk hastened Paškov's sudden stroke and death. Avvakum later crowed triumphantly in a letter to his wife, written from prison at Pustozersk: "Do you remember how the Daurian beast plotted to destroy in every possible way that poor, unfrocked priest, which is to say, me, the Archpriest? . . . But in Moscow God placed him in my hands — stretching out, he lay before me like a dead man. Do you remember, wife, how he said to me, 'You have the power, do to me what you will!' And I tonsured and frocked him . . . Do you remember how I used to say to the Cossacks in Daurija during our journey, . . . and everywhere in the towns, 'I must tonsure Paškov!' "

184.   Paškov's replacement, I. B. Tolbuzin, journeyed around the north end of Lake Baikal; traveling on skis, he arrived first at the fort on the Nerča, and not finding Paškov there, he came to the fort on Lake Irgen on 12 May 1662. On 25 May Paškov left, heading back toward Lake Baikal, while Avvakum began his journey near the end of June. Owing to frequent attack by local tribes, it was generally very dangerous for Russians to travel along Siberian rivers without a heavily armed escort. The situation was much more serious in the spring of 1662, for a general uprising of the Bashkirs, Tatars, Chuvash, Kalmyks, Cheremis, and other tribes was occurring. It was led by Devlet-Kirei, who rose against Russia in hopes of resurrecting the Siberian kingdom of his grandfather, Kuchum Khan. The rebellion was provoked in large part by the lawlessness of the Russians and the onerousness of tribute payments, but it was rather quickly put down by the better organized Russian forces.

185.   See note 159.

186.   Execution by impalement was not an institution in Russia, but it was utilized in the 17th and early 18th centuries.

187.   The identity of this "servant of Christ," whom Avvakum addresses

several times, is unknown. Possibly he refers to the Afanasij to whom the Elder Epifanij addressed his *Life*.

188.   See Jos., chap. 2.

189.   Ksen'ja was the second child born to Avvakum and Markovna in Siberia (see note 153; Ksen'ja is a diminutive form of Aksin'ja).

190.   Avvakum is correct regarding the Canons: a priest was allowed to recite the Prayer of Purification for his wife and to baptize his own child if no other priest was available. We may assume that Avvakum's rival Sergij was in the neighborhood. He, however, was as acceptable to the Archpriest as the devil himself.

191.   Afanasij was Avvakum's youngest son; apparently he was born on the Mezen around 1665. Because of his tender years he was not imprisoned with his mother and two brothers in their pit in the earth (see note 153). He was well-schooled in the Old Belief nonetheless. In 1673 Avvakum wrote from Pustozersk, addressing his eight-year-old son first with a loving diminutive form of his name and following it with the formal and honorific patronymic: "Afanas'juško Avvakumovič, my little darling! You have comforted me!" It so happened that the local commander had questioned the boy regarding the conformation of the fingers, and in answer he had crossed himself in the old style. When threatened with imprisonment, the lad said defiantly, "God is strong, and I'm not afraid!" This answer touched not only his father but the commander, who praised the lad for his courage.

192.   To this point Avvakum has not made direct reference to Nikon's interdict. This defiant assertion of its spuriousness is important: it is part of the Archpriest's rationalization for assuming leadership in the Old Belief in the narration to follow.

193.   Pětr, Aleksej, and Iona were all metropolitans. Pětr (1305–26) moved the center of the Russian church from Vladimir to Moscow during the period that Grand Prince Ivan Kalita was consolidating the Muscovite state. Aleksej (1354–78), distinguished by his erudition, was the tutor of the young Dmitrij Donskoj. Iona was Metropolitan of Moscow from 1448–61. All were canonized. (Regarding Filipp, see note 64.) Representatives of both the official Church and the Old Belief appealed frequently to the authority of these metropolitons in the course of their doctrinal disputes.

194.   The Siberian stag sometimes attains a height of five feet at the shoulder and a weight of over 600 lbs. Having descended the Selenga to Lake Baikal, Avvakum encountered these Russians at its shallow mouth, where fish often school. Trappers pursued their prey during the winter, so fishing occupied much of their time during the summer. The boats were carried far away from the water owing to the frequent, violent storms in this area.

195.   In the third redaction Avvakum notes that he repaired the sail with a woman's sarafan. He and his party crossed Lake Baikal from the Selenga to the mouth of the Angara, a distance of 50–60 miles.

196.   Some of the highest mountains on Lake Baikal are located along Avvakum's route back to Russia; they reach heights of 5,000 feet above lake level. They are remarkable for their singular configurations, which indeed are reminiscent of medieval walled towns or monasteries.

197.   Avvakum was the first Russian writer to remark upon the flora around Lake Baikal as well as on the many varieties of fish in it. The types of fish he mentions specifically are of considerable commercial importance. For example, the Siberian sturgeon ranges in weight from 65–255 lbs., and in the past reached 450 lbs.; the amul salmon can exceed six lbs., while the whitefish may weigh 17–18 lbs. The large taimen salmon is more often encountered in the Selenga and Angara rivers, and the sterlet is found in the Angara, not in Baikal. The seals in Baikal reach a body weight of 280 lbs. In our time no sea lions live in the lake, but Robinson speculates (p. 258) that they may have been there in the 17th century. On the Mezen, Avvakum later saw Arctic sea lions, and his amazement over the size of those in Baikal lends credibility to his observations.

198.   Cf. Psalm 144:4 (143:4 in the Russian Bible). As Robinson observes, this psalm had immediate relevance to Avvakum's situation, and this may explain why he thought of it in this context. In the psalm the psalmist calls upon God for deliverance from "great waters" and "from the hand of strange children" (perhaps the Siberian tribes).

199.   The series of similes struck by Avvakum between man and beasts is traditional; for example, St. John Chrysostom remarks in his *Marguerite* (a book known to Avvakum; see note 39): "For when thou art angered, thou brayest like an ass, like a horse dost thou neigh at women; thou dost gorge thyself like a bear, fattening thy body like an ox . . . Thou ragest like a serpent . . . thou dost hate men like a lynx and provokest enmity like an evil devil."

The final line ("Forgive me, . . . ") is borrowed from the declaration of assurance made by priests prior to hearing confession, in which the penitent is told that his confessor is also a sinner.

200.   Cf. 1 Cor. 7:27.

201.   Avvakum refers here to the winters of 1662–63 and 1663–64.

202.   Avvakum's exile lasted approximately ten years and eight months, as he left Moscow in September 1653 and returned sometime between February and May 1664. His reckoning of the time required for the return to Russia at three years indicates he considered the first stage to have been the return to Lake Irgen from the Nerča (1660–61), and not the departure from the former. Once Avvakum and his family passed the confluence of the Ob and the Irtysh on their journey to the east, they indeed struggled against the current all the way to Lake Irgen, with the exception of their crossing of Lake Baikal. However, his journey from Tobol'sk to the fortress on the Nerča lasted not five but four years.

203.   Avvakum arrived in Tobol'sk near the end of June 1663. The town of Verxoturie marked the border of Siberia; in 1663 it was caught in the middle of the uprising of the Siberian tribes (see note 184).

204.   Komynin, a *stol'nik* in rank, was commander in Verxoturie during the period 1659–64. His close association with the Borovskij Pafnut'ev Monastery enabled him to give aid and comfort to Avvakum later when the Archpriest was imprisoned there.

205.   Fëdor Rtiščev (1626–73) was one of the most attractive personalities of his time; a close associate of Aleksej Mixajlovič and an influential figure at court, he was a energetic member in the inner circle of the Lovers of God prior to the elevation of Nikon. The evidence indicates he was a man who combined genuine learning and piety, a warm and vigorous personality, and an active concern for the welfare of others. As a young man he studied Greek under the tutelage of Kievan scholars. He later brought learned Kievan monks to Moscow and settled them on his estate near the city as well as in his home; he then organized a school in his house so that Muscovites might study Greek and Church Slavonic as well as rhetoric and philosophy. He was instrumental in bringing Ivan Neronov to Moscow in 1647 and establishing him at St. Basil's Cathedral (see note 57). Rtiščev's love of learning did not undermine his admiration for the ancient traditions, and when Nikon began to persecute his former colleagues Rtiščev tried to help them (for example, he concealed

Neronov from Nikon's agents "for many days"). Rtiščev seems to have judged others by himself, as he believed that men of good will can find some ground for compromise. That ground for him was love of the Church, and after Avvakum's return he hosted discussions between the two sides of the nascent schism in his own house in order to effect a reconciliation. (Avvakum remarks, "And I went to Fëdor Rtiščev's to wrangle with the apostates.") Undoubtedly his failure in this effort and the mounting violence and hatred among his ecclesiastical friends caused him much pain. What is more, his own family was split by the controversies (he was related to the Old Believers Feodos'ja Morozova [see note 219] and Spiridon Potëmkin, while his father judged and condemned Morozova). But Rtiščev's real accomplishments lay elsewhere. He was greatly admired and loved by common Muscovites, who benefited from his compassionate generosity. He built hospitals and homes for the aged in Moscow, ransomed Russian prisoners of war from the Turks, aided the starving, and opened his own land to poor city dwellers to use for gardens. During the Polish campaign of 1654–55, he organized medical aid for the wounded and sick and paid for it out of his own pocket. He was instrumental in increasing the government's support of hospitals and homes for the aged in several cities. His final thoughts before his death, according to his biography, were about his servants and serfs; the former he freed, and he adjured his children to treat the latter well, for "they are our brothers."

206.   The murmanka was an official parade hat; it had a high, flat crown with a fur band that had the appearance of ear flaps. It was normally made of velvet or brocade.

207.   Robinson is probably correct in stating that Avvakum's refusal to become the confessor of leading state functionaries and, above all, of the Tsar was the turning point in his career (p. 261). Acceptance of this position would certainly be contingent upon Avvakum's accepting the reforms. Refusal signaled his assumption of leadership in the Old Belief.

208.   Here Avvakum paraphrases Matt. 24:51.

209.   Avvakum refers to the preparation of the elements during the first part of the liturgy; this ritual had been altered by the reformers. The credence table stood to the left of the altar within the sanctuary (i.e., behind the iconostasis).

210.   In the third redaction of the Life, Avvakum identifies this body of water as Lake Šakšinskoe; about 7½ miles long and 3½ miles wide, it is located approximately nine miles from Lake Irgen. This area to the east of Baikal

receives very little precipitation in the winter, but the average January temperature is -13° F.

211.   Cf. Ex. 17:1–6.

212.   To "stand in the customary place" was a familiar ritualistic formula which has no specific meaning in this context, unlike "lifting my eyes to the east." The phrase is important nevertheless, for it suggests the Archpriest prays in the traditional manner no matter where he may be.

213.   This passage is a paraphrase of Amos 8:11.

214.   The evening psalms were read prior to the evening worship service, often in private. The Compline is the seventh and last of the canonical hours in Roman Catholicism; it is repeated at nightfall or before retiring. Thus it is not a precise translation for the *polunoščnica*, which was chanted at midnight or during the next hour. The Prime is the first of the canonical hours in the Western Church and corresponds closely in time to the Orthodox *čas pervyj*.

215.   In 1658 Paškov planted rather large crops of rye and barley on the Nerča. Because he was ignorant of the heavy spring rains that combine in this area with waters from melting mountain snows to cause severe flooding, he lost nearly the entire crop.

216;   Rodion Matveevič Strešnev (d. 1687) was a childhood friend of Aleksej Mixajlovič. He later was in the diplomatic service and led a Russian delegation in offical conversations with the Ukrainian leader Bogdan Xmel'nickij. He had the Tsar's special trust and served as an intermediary during the latter's conflicts with both Nikon and Avvakum.

217.   St. Simeon's Day: the date was 1 September 1664.

218.   Luk"jan Kirillov was Archpriest of the Cathedral of the Annunciation and the Tsar's confessor. Later his relations with Avvakum changed; the Deacon Fëdor writes: "I gave the Confessor the petition about Avvakum, about his freedom, and in a mighty rage he threw it in my face."

One hundred rubles was a great deal of money, equal, for example, to Arsenios the Greek's salary during the first two years of his work in the Church's printing house (see annotation 293).

219.   Feodos'ja Morozova née Sokovnina and her sister Evdok'ja were among the best-known representatives of the Old Belief during the early stages of the schism. They were born into the highest ranks of the aristocracy, and they moved freely in the inner circles of the Russian court (Morozova was a close friend and associate of the Empress). Married to a man already old and soon widowed, Morozova met Avvakum upon his return from Siberia and fell under the influence of his powerful personality. Although she had always known great wealth, her inclinations to asceticism and religious fanaticism rapidly came to dominate her behavior. Her household was reorganized in the manner of a convent, and its rooms were soon crowded with nuns and beggars. Morozova cared for the needy personally, cleaning the open sores of beggars, eating with them from the same pot, and walking the streets of Moscow in poor clothes, distributing alms and clothing made with her own hands to the poor. She practiced traditional mortifications of the flesh such as wearing a hair shirt, and, not surprisingly, she eventually took the veil in secret. Morozova's deep commitment to Avvakum and to the Old Belief aroused the ire of influential members of her family, but the pressure they brought to bear failed to alter her convictions.

In May 1666 Morozova was stripped of her hereditary land holdings, but they were restored to her after the Empress intervened on her behalf. During the period of Avvakum's second exile, trial, and imprisonment, she gave him constant moral and material support. In 1669 the Empress died, and Morozova lost her chief defender at court. When the Tsar remarried, she refused to fulfill her rightful – and obligatory – duties in the ceremonies. Soon thereafter (16 Nov. 1671) she and her sister were arrested, fettered, and cast into prison. Neither argument, nor bestial tortures including the rack, nor the death of her son, nor the loss of her vast wealth succeeded in bending Morozova. Her courageous resistance and terrible suffering understandably embroiled the court and deepened the schism, for the Muscovite masses loved her and were beginning to stir ominously. (V. I. Surikov's famous painting of Morozova being transported through Moscow on a drag sled, defiantly holding her hand aloft, her fingers in the traditional conformation, refers to this period of what came to be considered her passion.) Such audacity was not easily tolerated; she was swiftly condemned and a pit was prepared for her execution by fire. The Tsar's sister Irina pleaded with her brother, and Morozova received a temporary reprieve. She and her sister Evdokija were transported to Borovsk, imprisoned in harsh conditions, and starved. Evdokija died there in her sister's arms (11 Sept. 1675), while Morozova died on 2 November 1675. Avvakum's relations with Morozova were characteristically erratic. He rejoiced in and glorified her courage and loyalty to the Old Belief, and he cherished her martyrdom. His laments upon her death are still deeply moving to read. However, the few occasions that Morozova dared to disagree with him on minor issues evoked another kind of response: "And now this female is showing me how to succor Christ's flock! She herself lies there in the mud, and she's cleaning others off! She herself is blind and she's showing those with eyes the way! Get your wits about you!... Stupid, witless, ignorant woman, blind yourself with your weaving shuttle!" Or, "Why should I be surprised at you? A female is long on hair but short on brains!"

220.   Boyarina Miloslavskaja was among the close associates of the Empress and related to her by marriage as well.

221.   Nikon went into voluntary retirement in 1658, but technically he was still Patriarch. Avvakum's petition to the Tsar in 1664 was an effort to influence this complex, confused situation. Certainly the good will he had encountered at court gave him cause to believe his suggestions might have some effect.

222;   The "fool in Christ" (*jurodivyj*) was an important cultural type in medieval Russia. The term referred to people either mentally unbalanced or retarded, whose bizarre behavior was understood as an outward manifestation of the movements of mysterious spiritual forces to which they were privy. Thus, they were often respected as prophets and generally believed to be especially favored by God. Avvakum obviously distingushed such people from unfortunates suddenly become deranged; the latter were possessed by devils. Aleksej Mixajlovič apparently shared these views, for numbers of such fools were always living in and near his residences, fully supported by him. This may explain why Avvakum sent Fëdor to the Tsar with his letter; the chances that it would be received by the Tsar personally were improved by its bearer's "foolishness." Avvakum began to attract fools in Christ upon his return from Siberia, and one can scarcely doubt that they greatly enhanced the apocalyptic qualities of his public image and the impact of his preaching. Fëdor was his favorite, and Avvakum returns to him more frequently in his *Life* than any other representative of the Old Belief. So we know a good deal about their friendship, which began in Great Ustjug during Avvakum's return from Siberia and ended with Fëdor's execution by hanging at Mezen (March 1670), Avvakum's first place of exile in the Far North.

223.   The Red Terrace served as the parade entrance to the palace; it extended along the facade of the palace from the Cathedral of the Annunciation to the Hall of Facets. It was covered by a double-tent roof, a traditional design. Guards were always on duty there, and Fëdor was confined in their quarters beneath the Terrace.

224.   See note 114.

225.   Prior to his Siberian exile, Avvakum had drawn worshipers away from St. Basil's. The complaints against him then by priests were repeated now, but this time by prelates. Avvakum had succeeded in attracting large numbers of Muscovites, who abandoned their usual spiritual mentors. On 30 August 1664, an investigatory commission stated in its protocol that "Archpriest Avvakum has separated with his teaching many parishioners from the Church of St. Sofija, which stands beyond the Moscow river, in Sadovniki."

226.   Pëtr Mixajlovič Saltykov was an important administrator. At this time he was in charge of Ukrainian affairs, but he also played a role in ecclesiastical matters. He was given responsibility for guiding the investigation regarding the consequences of Nikon's sudden retirement.

227.   Mezen is a small town located on the right bank of the Mezen river, which flows northward into the White Sea. Avvakum and his family were sent from Moscow to Pustozersk on 29 August 1664. They traveled northward by boat along the Northern Dvina, then by crude "roads" through the forests to Mezen. On the way, in Xolmogor, the Archpriest had petitioned the Tsar that he and his family might be allowed to stay in Mezen, as the journey to Pustozersk in winter was very difficult and dangerous. Travel was possible only by reindeer and sledges, and he feared his children might perish in the bitter cold. When the family and their escort arrived in Mezen, the local peasants rebelled, refusing to turn over the money and sledges necessary to continue the journey to Pustozersk. In January 1665, Avvakum again appealed to the Tsar from Mezen, as Neronov had done on his behalf the previous month, referring to the "countless misfortunes" Avvakum had endured in Siberia, including the starvation deaths of two children. Avvakum was allowed to remain in Mezen, and he apparently lived there in relative freedom. He associated with the commander, argued with him, and treated his wife. According to tradition, he also served in the local church.

228.   Avvakum's return to Moscow (March 1666) was one element in Aleksej Mixajlovič's preparations for the Ecumenical Council of 1666–67. He was determined to protect the Nikonian reforms, to replace the quixotic and autocratic Nikon as patriarch, and to isolate and silence those in opposition. If entirely successful he would bring clarity to the murky situation in the Church, at the same time bringing under control those religious forces that were threatening to fragment Russian national life. Avvakum was initially allowed considerable freedom of movement in Moscow, and he spent two days with Morozova discussing the faith and how they should "suffer for

the Truth." He then went to the Kremlin's Cathedral of the Assumption and presented himself to "Metropolitan Pavlik" (a disparaging diminutive form of "Pavel"), showing that he had "voluntarily come to his torments."

229.   The Borovskij Pafnut'ev Monastery was founded in 1444; since the 16th century it had been a fortress surrounded by a stone wall with towers. It was widely respected and received special favors from the Tsar. Avvakum was imprisoned there from 9 March to 12 May 1666. Metropolitan Pavel directed Father Superior Parfenij to afflict Avvakum in an effort to compel his reconciliation with his enemies. However, Morozova was able to supply his with food and other necessities, and he did not yield.

230.   Paraphrase of Luke 9:55.

231.   The disputation with the bishops took place in the Chamber of the Cross on 13 May 1666 (see note 77). Later the same day Avvakum was defrocked in the Cathedral of the Assumption.

232.   The Deacon Fëdor (or Feodor in the traditonal ecclesiastical spelling) was one of the leading writers and teachers of the Old Belief. He was younger than Avvakum and had no direct connection with the Lovers of God or experience of the early struggles with Nikon. Like Avvakum, Fëdor was the son of a village priest, so he had first-hand knowledge of the life of the Russian masses. Largely self-educated, he was endowed with a sharp, logical intellect which caused him, perhaps inevitably, to clash with illogical Avvakum on doctrinal issues. When he was a young man, Fëdor was classified by his master N. I. Odoevskij as a common peasant despite his parentage, but he managed to escape this fate in some fashion, and in 1659 he became a deacon in the Kremlin's Cathedral of the Assumption. In this post he witnessed numerous clashes between Church leaders and their old-believer opponents. The first measure of the depth of Fëdor's commitment to the Old Belief was his initial public act in support of it; that is, in declaring himself he abandoned a promising career at a time when the old-believer leaders were being routed. Specifically, he submitted a petition to the Tsar's confessor Luk"jan regarding Avvakum, his future foe, that he be freed (March 1665; see note 218). He was arrested on 9 December 1665 during the repressions that preceded the Ecumenical Council. After Fëdor was imprisoned at Ugreša with Avvakum he recanted and reconciled himself to the reforms — but only briefly. His action here can only be attributed to hunger, exhaustion, and perhaps worry about his family, for when he was subsequently sent to the Pokrovskij Monastery, he escaped to his home, gathered his wife and children, and fled. After renewing his opposition, he was apprehended, arrested, and, after

having his tongue cut out, sent to Pustozersk to join Avvakum, Epifanij, and Lazar (Feb. 1668). After the death of the aged Archpriest Nikifor, these four became the famous, and notorious, prisoners of Pustozersk, whose prolific writings fueled the fires of schism until they died together in 1682.

Deacon Fëdor's fate was especially harsh at Pustozersk. After the initial period of concord during which he wrote *The Answer of the Orthodox* (see note 277), he began to argue with his fellow prisoners, especially with Avvakum. The latter's arrogant conviction that he was God's chief spokesman among Old Believers provoked him to genuine beastliness and − if Fëdor is to be believed − to fraud. When Fëdor completed a pamphlet summarizing his disputes with his enemies, he carried it to "Father Avvakum" to read, apparently under cover of night. Avvakum reported him to the guard for leaving his prison pit. As punishment Fëdor was severely beaten with cudgels, tied naked to a wall, and left to freeze there for almost two hours. According to Fëdor, his comrades watched from their own pits, laughing and mocking him. The guards seized Fëdor's notes and manuscripts and gave them to Avvakum, who made changes in them to introduce obvious errors and sent them to Old Believers elsewhere. To enhance his own stature in these exchanges Fëdor later related a miracle that allegedly occurred in 1677: the spring thaw flooded his pit, and his plight worsened when Avvakum convinced the guards to dig a furrow in the earth to funnel even more water in upon the hapless Deacon. But a prayer caused the water to disappear into the earth, "as into an abyss." Avvakum slipped into some of his heresies during his written disputes with Fëdor; their enmity apparently continued to their deaths together in a pit of flaming logs.

233.   The Patriarch's Court was located in the Kremlin, extending away from the northwest side of the Cathedral of the Assumption. Nikon enlarged the Court and constructed a new patriarchal residence there with passages connecting with the palace of the tsar.

234.   The Monastery of St. Nikola was located about nine miles to the northeast of Moscow, on the left bank of the Moscow river. According to traditon it was founded by Dmitrij Donskoj to commemorate the Russian victory over the Tatars at Kulikovo Field in 1380. It was situated near the village of Ostrovo, where the Tsar often retreated to rest. Consequently, Aleksej Mixajlovič often visited the monastery. The prisoners were sent there on 15 May 1666. Fëdor described their journey: "Having put me in a cart, they bore me past Kolomna to the Ugreša Monastery . . . through swamps and not by the road, so that no one could see by the familiar road where they were imprisoning us. And after a time, having traveled awhile, I looked around and saw − at a distance from me they were carrying Father

Avvakum. And when they brought us to the monastery, two streltsy took Father Avvakum under the arms, and wrapped his head with a cap sleeve, and led him into the monastery by the side gates, . . . and he didn't know where he was being put. And a lieutenant came up and ordered the streltsy to take me too, but they covered me from the top of my head to my legs with a bast mat. And . . . they put me in an empty tower, sealed the loop holes, and locked the doors." Avvakum wrote to Markovna by the light of a taper: "I'm locked up in a dark chamber at St. Nikola's in Ugreša; everything's been taken away from me, and my girdle taken off . . . Sometimes I'm given bread, sometimes cabbage soup. My poor [spiritual] children drive to the monastery, but they can't see me."

235.   Cf. Matt. 18:7 and Luke 17:1.

236.   The phrase "radiant Russia" (*svetlaja Rossija*) is a formula deriving from the tradition of Russia as the Third Rome: Rome and Constantinople had fallen, and Russia had become the third and last repository of undefiled Orthodoxy. Avvakum's statement here, which aims to explain the apparently unjust suffering of Old Believers, is borrowed almost verbatim from a letter by Avraamij, who was in frequent communication with the prisoners at Pustozersk (see note 252).

237.   Avvakum was confined at St. Nikola's from 15 May to 3 September 1666. Once again Morozova managed to supply him with necessities.

238.   In the third redaction of the *Life*, Avvakum specifies the date of this vision as Ascension Day (forty days after Easter); in 1666 this day fell on May 25th. Avvakum describes the vision in his Fifth Letter to the Tsar (1669). While praying that the Tsar would abandon the reforms, Avvakum "sank into forgetfulness . . . from his labors." And he saw the Tsar, and "on his belly there was a great ulcer, filled with much pus." The Archpriest "began to draw it together, sprinkling it with tears, and [his] belly was healed and whole." But "an ulcer larger than the first" appeared on the Tsar's back, and this one Avvakum was unable to heal completely. Clearly a complete "cure" depended on the Tsar himself, who must heal his own spirit by returning to the Old Ritual. Rumors of this vision began to spread much earlier, during the time of Avvakum's imprisonment at St. Nikola's.

239.   In a letter written sometime during 1678–79, Avvakum remarks: "The Tsaritsa Mar'ja was a good woman plain and simple, but the cunning bishops . . . envenomed the Tsar.. . . From their hearts they wrote out an order to burn me, but the late Tsaritsa didn't allow it." Lazar, Epifanij, and

Fëdor had their tongues cut out before their exile to Pustozersk, but Avvakum escaped this fate, undoubtedly owing to her intervention and the Tsar's ambivalent attitude toward him. One result of this argument between the Tsar and Tsaritsa over Avvakum may have been the Tsar's sudden departure for the village of Preobraženskoe the same day, without his wife; he remained there more than a week.

240.   Avvakum perhaps exaggerates Vorotynskij's allegiance to the Old Belief. He was the Tsar's first cousin and frequently accompanied him on both military campaigns and journeys. Almost certainly he spoke for the Tsar earlier in reprimanding Morozova during her torture, which he witnessed, at least in part: "What have you done? From what glory to what disgrace you have come! Who are you, and from what family? This is what must befall you, as you have received into your home the fools in Christ Kiprian and Fëdor, and you have angered the Tsar."

241.   Prince Ivan Ivanovič Xovanskij the Elder (1645–1701) was not altogether consistent in his support of the Old Belief. His flogging (around 1670) caused him to abandon the old rituals in his public life, and he rose in the state service in subsequent years. However, his real sympathies never changed, and he finally died in prison, having been implicated in the plot organized by the printer G. Talickij, who printed pamphlets aimed at fomenting rebellion against the "Antichrist," Peter the Great.

Isaiah was the butler of Boyar P. N. Saltykov. According to Semën Denisov, he convinced his master to stand firm in the Old Belief. The Tsar allegedly saw Saltykov crossing himself in the ancient manner and placed blame on the butler, who was arrested, interrogated, tortured, and finally burned.

242.   Evdok'ja suffered greatly on account of her small children. According to Avvakum: "One of Evdok'ja's daughters died during the time of her [mother's] torture. And three little children were left . . . She wrote to me from her dungeon, and greatly did she lament about them: 'Oh Father, Oh my light! Pray for my little children; nothing oppresses me as much as my children!' " Elsewhere he remarks, "The late Evdok'ja pestered me much on their account before her death. With her own hand she covered a whole scroll . . . and for a long time I had that scroll; I'd read it and weep." Evdok'ja's husband remarried, probably under pressure, before her death.

243.   Avvakum was taken from the Monastery of St. Nikola on 3 September 1666, and he arrived at the Pafnut'ev Monastery two days later to begin his second imprisonment there. He remained until 30 April 1667. By order

of the Tsar he was to be closely supervised; no one was to be admitted to see him, nor was he to be given writing materials. Nevertheless, Morozova managed to supply his needs.

244.   Smoking and trading in tobacco were criminal offenses punishable by death. Tobacco was of foreign origin and thus immediately suspect; the Old Believers referred to is as "the devil's incense." Musical instruments were forbidden in church, of course, where only the living human voice could rightfully lift up praise to God. Early in Aleksej Mixajlovič's reign, in 1649, six carriages of musical instruments were burned in Moscow. Associating the Greek hierarchs with either tobacco or musical instruments was another emblematic proof of their heretical views.

In mentioning the Metropolitan of Gaza, Avvakum has in mind the Greek Paissios Ligarid (1610—78), who was, judging from the available evidence, a cynical opportunist and adventurer. He left Orthodoxy, became a Roman Catholic, and was educated by the Jesuits in Rome, where he defended his doctoral dissertation. In 1657 he and several other Greek scholars were invited to Moscow by Nikon to assist in his reforms. It seems Nikon did not know that almost to a man they were morally suspect. Certainly he did not realize Ligarid had been defrocked and was under an interdict laid upon him by the Patriarch of Jerusalem for a series of serious crimes and misdemeanors. When Nikon lost his influence after his voluntary retirement, Ligarid swiftly turned against him by allying himself with the Tsar. Whereas Aleksej Mixajlovič now in effect governed the Church, Ligarid was responsible for fulfilling the purely ecclesiastical and spiritual duties associated with the patriarchal throne. He also was a major actor in the Ecumenical Council of 1666—67 (by this time Aleksej Mixajlovič had purchased Ligarid's forgiveness from the Patriarch of Jerusalem with lavish gifts). Ecclesiastical responsibilities did not hinder Ligarid from engaging in profitable activities such as money lending, accepting bribes, speculating in furs and precious stones, and operating as a middle-man in a variety of transactions. He also acquired large sums of money from the Tsar for "his eparchy" in Gaza before Aleksej Mixajlovič learned of his expulsion from that office. Apparently the Tsar needed the services of this disreputable but clever mountebank more than he needed moral rectitude in his principal ecclesiastical advisors. Ligarid was singularly successful in creating a pious impression, and this together with his attacks upon Nikon brought him favor in the eyes of Old Believers. This may explain the unusual restraint shown here by Avvakum in his criticism of this unsavory character.

245.   A paraphrase of Romans 14:4.

246.   Cf. Luke 6:26.

247.   Ilarion (d. 1673) grew up in a village near Avvakum's native place, Grigorovo, and as young men they were friends. But later he became a close associate of Nikon and strongly supported his arguments regarding the primacy of ecclesiastical power. Avvakum's antipathy is thus predictable. However, Ilarion was a man of some courage, for he objected vigorously during the Ecumenical Council to the extension of the Tsar's power. His continuing protests later brought him a temporary interdict. His stubborn and aggressive nature may explain why the Council selected him to read its verdict upon Nikon, his former associate and doctrinal mentor.

248.   The tale of Fëdor's escape from prison is modeled on a similar story involving the Apostle Peter, in Acts 12:7–10.

249.   Avvakum certainly refers here to tape worms, not intestines.

250.   The town Ustjug the Great is located on the left bank of the Suxona river. In the 1670's it consisted of approximately 1,000 households. Parties traveling into or from Siberia generally passed through it.

251.   During the decade 1653–63, eight editions of the Psalter containing Nikon's changes appeared. Because fire was understood as an agent of purification, the auto-da-fe was a customary way of destroying heretical materials. Of course, from the official perspective Fëdor's action was a serious crime.

252.   Avraamij, this "lover of weeping," proved to be one of the most tenacious and courageous of the spokesmen for the Old Belief. He was considered a fool in Christ, the only one of this particular group of Old Believers to leave a body of writings. After the trial and exile of Avvakum and his comrades to Pustozersk, Avraamij became the principal link between them and their followers in Moscow, and the ranking ideologist there as well. He was largely self-educated; in his early years, before he entered holy orders and abandoned the name Afanasij, he traveled about Russia from monastery to monastery making use of their libraries. After settling in Moscow he apparently met Avvakum and became one of his most loyal and outspoken followers. He was author of, among other things, *A Mighty Christian Shield of Faith Against the Armies of Heresy*; this compilation of old-believer writings, extracts from the patristic literature, and his own work developed an especially pessimistic eschatology. He was strongly inclined to view the year 1666 as the watershed between Moscow the Third Rome and the beginning of the reign of Antichrist. He openly denounced the Tsar as a "dishonorable heretic

and the new apostate of the Orthodox faith . . . and the new torturer and persecutor of the saints in Russia" (Nikon had retired). Such declarations could easily be viewed as treasonous summons to anarchy in troubled times, and Avraamij was eventually burned during the winter of 1671—72.

Avraamij's apocalyptic premonitions may belie what appears to have been his gentle and even good-humored nature. His description of his interrogation by Metropolitan Pavel (see note 114) is interesting in this connection: "And lo, my reasoning was most pleasing to Pavel; he could not remain sitting in his place, and having arisen, he came to me and graciously, from out of his humility, he began to bless me. He grasped me by the beard firmly, or better, yanked it. And in doing this, that holy man, troubling himself over me, tried my beard, whether it be strong or not, . . . to this end holding me so that I would not stagger from his blessing, thus falling and hurting myself on the floor. When he had tried my beard, he began to bless me with his right hand on my cheek, with some to spare, and with some to spare he blessed me on the nose too."

253.   Vinogradov discusses in his article Avvakum's use of baking imagery; this particular simile comparing the soul to bread fresh from the oven became popular among Old Believers when they were frequently facing death in the fire — and when they began to incinerate themselves.

254.   Avvakum was imprisoned in the Moscow guesthouse of the Borovskij Pafnut'ev Monastery. While there he was frequently visited by Morozova, and they were apparently allowed to converse freely with one another.

255.   On 2 November 1666 Paissios, Patriarch of Alexandria, and Makarios, Patriarch of Antioch, arrived in Moscow amidst great pomp and splendor for the beginning of the Ecumenical Council. The Greek Church lay prostrate before the Turks and was compelled to look to the northeast, to Orthodox Moscow, for support. This perhaps as much as the lure of rich gifts brought these prelates to Moscow. The Council began on 1 December 1666. After the condemnation of Nikon and the elevation of Ioasaf II, it turned to the matter of the schism, and on 13 May 1667 it anathematized the old rituals.

256.   The Deacon Fëdor uses the same image to describe the Russian prelates participating in the Council: "All the Russian bishops . . . began to bring many gifts to the patriarchs, gold, and silver, and sables, . . . and they began to stifle that court of justice with vanity, like cunning foxes stifle their scent with their tails."

257.   This is a paraphrase of Psalm 51:15 (50:16 in the Russian Bible).

258.   Palestine was an inclusive term used to denote all the southern and eastern Orthodox churches and peoples.

Avvakum's reference to the Poles and the Romans is an obvious device to discredit his opponents by associating them with Roman Catholicism, allegedly through their own words. It is possible, of course, that the Western inclinations of certain prelates might have caused one or more of them to refer to Western practices in the stormy debates about the Sign of the Cross. But such remarks, if made, are not reflected in the Proceedings of the Council.

259.   The conception of Moscow as the Third Rome is apparent in these remarks. It is the basis for both the contention and supporting argument which follow. Avvakum contends that the Old Believers are the sole repository of unsullied Orthodoxy. If they are indeed heretics as claimed, then earlier tsars and all the old Russian saints must have been heretics as well. Within the narrow confines in which theological argument was conducted in this era, there was no satisfactory response to this argument, and it therefore became dear to the hearts of the schismatic polemicists.

260.   These recognized authorities were especially valued by the Old Believers, because it was possible to argue on the basis of their writings, or writings attributed to them, that they taught Christians to make the Sign of the Cross with two fingers. Meletius died in 381, Theodoret's dates are approximately 386–457, and Peter was active during the second half of the 12th century. Maksim was greatly respected in Russia, and his writings made a deep impression on several leaders of the Old Belief. He was educated in Italy, but came to Russia in 1518 and remained there to his death in 1556.

261.   Avvakum refers to the Stoglav Council, which convened in February 1551. Although it failed to improve the quality of religious life in Russia – its principal goal – its resolutions were accepted as authoritative until the Council of 1666–67. Avvakum twice mentions Ivan the Terrible in these lines, emphasizing that the decisions of the Stoglav Council were binding upon both Church and State.

262.   After defeating the city of Kazan in 1555, Ivan the Terrible established the Kazan eparchy and made Gurij (c. 1500–63) its first archbishop. Varsonofij (1495–1576) was Gurij's close associate; both were canonized in 1595. While living with Ivan Neronov (see note 57) in Moscow, Avvakum served in "the Kazan Church" (i.e., St. Basil's, the church built by Ivan the Terrible and named for the holy fool to whom the victory over Kazan was credited); Avvakum therefore considered these saints his protectors. The term

"bearer of the Sign" (*znamenonosec*) refers to the highest rank of monastic ascetics, who wore large crosses on their mantles and cowls. Regarding Filipp, see note 64.

263.   Cf. Acts 18:6 and Luke 9:5. The statement "Better one . . . " has its source in the apocryphal book known in the Latin Bible and Greek manuscripts as The Wisdom of Jesus, Son of Sirach (16:3).

264.   It is likely that "Seize him!" echoes Luke 23:18 in the old Russian translation of the Bible used by Avvakum; the passage describes an event during the condemnation of Christ.

265.   Avvakum refers to the Greek prelate Dionysios, an archimandrite from the complex of monasteries on Mt. Athos. He came to Russia in 1655, and because of his fluency in Russian he served as translator for Patriarchs Paissios and Makarios in 1666–67. He was author of a tract which condemned old Russian rituals as heresies that had grown out of ignorance; it served as a guide for the Greek patriarchs during the Ecumenical Council, and was the basis for the third chapter of its Proceedings. Dionysios was an especially distasteful scoundrel, whose interests ranged from theology to sodomy. According to Deacon Fëdor, the Greek patriarchs were not prepared to condemn Lazar until Dionysios prevailed upon them, cynically reminding them that neither valuable gifts nor safe return to their native cities would be vouchsafed them should they refuse to comply with the wishes of their Russian hosts.

266.   A condensation of Heb. 7:26.

267.   A slightly rephrased citation of I Cor. 4:10.

268.   Evfimej was a man of considerable learning, having mastered Greek, Latin, Polish, and Hebrew, so Nikon installed him in 1652 as a proofreader in the Church's printing house. Evfimej's abrupt agreement with Avvakum here may reflect an important conflict that was already developing among the reformers. Evfimej later became an outspoken critic of Simeon Polockij's party, which was distinctly influenced by the Latin tradition; Evfimej represented the Greek tradition, which found abhorrent anything smacking of Rome. Polockij's book, *The Staff of Government* (*Žezl pravlenija*), had received the Council's approval as expressing the "pure silver of the Word of God," and this may have disposed Evfimej in Avvakum's favor.

269.   The Sparrow Hills are now called the Lenin Hills. They are located to the southwest of central Moscow and are the site for the new, monumental buildings of Moscow State University.

270.   Lazar became Avvakum's close friend and remained one of his staunchest supporters; he apparently became acquainted with the Archpriest in 1653, when he was in Moscow. He served as a priest in the town of Romanov-Borisoglebsk on the Volga, where he was an outspoken preacher of the Old Belief. Like Avvakum he had been exiled to Siberia (14 July 1661, to Tobol'sk). Although Robinson reports anecdotes about Lazar's drunkenness and "dirty stories" in the East (p. 281), he certainly continued his energetic preaching there, and he and Avvakum succeeded in keeping the Siberian churches in a state of unrest. In November 1665 he was brought back to Moscow to be tried, but was soon sent to Mezen while preparations for the Russian Council of 1666 continued. He was not returned to Moscow for the Russian Council, which tried and convicted him *in absentia*. When the Ecumenical Council began in December 1666, Lazar was brought before it; his trial there was to be the first step in the affirmation of the earlier convictions of the schismatics, this time by what those so disposed could call the highest court in Christendom. Lazar was not well-known in Moscow and he had been in exile for several years, so his hearing represented a cautious testing of the waters by the patriarchs. However, Lazar confounded their plans by abruptly demanding the ancient trial by fire: if he emerged from the flames unscathed, then the old rituals and books would stand vindicated. His trial was postponed, and he was condemned months later, in August 1667, along with Avvakum, Fëdor (*in absentia*), Epifanij, and Nikifor. Avvakum's special relationship with the royal family and Nikifor's advanced age saved them from the mutilation suffered by the other three, having their tongues cut out. (Fëdor underwent this punishment alone, when he was brought later to Moscow.) The punishment was subsequently repeated at Pustozersk, where Lazar also had his right hand chopped off. Lazar's literary activities were limited at Pustozersk to two lengthy letters addressed to the Tsar; he was by nature more a preacher and a martyr than a polemicist, and he ceased writing after 1668.

For all his toughness and endurance, the Elder Epifanij was a humble and retiring man. And despite his condemnation as a man dangerous to Church and State, his truest inclinations were to mysticism and private spiritual experience. Formerly he had been a monk at Solovki, but Nikon's reforms had driven him into the life of a hermit — a vocation that undoubtedly suited his temperment. During this period he associated with other anchoritic Old Believers in the area around the Onega river; he spent time, for example, with the Elder Kirill on Vidan'skoe island in the Suna river and with the well-known Elder Kornilij. While living with the latter he wrote (1665-66) a "book" dedicated to exposing the heresies in the Church, placing much of the blame on the Tsar (this book has not been preserved). He journeyed to Moscow with his work and gave it to the Tsar during the Council. He was arrested and convicted. His close association with Avvakum began soon thereafter. At Pustozersk he also wrote an autobiography, and Avvakum considered it a companion piece to his own (see Introduction and especially Robinson, pp. 52–60). The Archpriest's admiration and affection for Epifanij were unquestionably genuine; aside from Epifanij's obvious virtues, Avvakum may have been attracted to a man so radically different in personality who felt no desire to compete with him.

271.   See, for example, John 18: 13–14, 24, 28.

272.   The prisoners were taken to the Sparrow Hills on 17 June 1667, then moved into a horse barn in the Andreevskij Monastery, which was located at the base of the Hills. Nearby was the Savvin Settlement, in the immediate vicinity of the Convent of St. Savva, which had been joined since 1649 to the Novodevičij Convent.

273.   The Tsar made a sustained effort to convince Avvakum and his comrades to recant even after their conviction and excommunication, and these visits by Jurij Lutoxin, Artemon Matveev, and Dementej Bašmakov were only part of this effort. The failure of these negotiations must have disappointed Aleksej Mixajlovič, for the goals of the Ecumenical Council remained partially unrealized as long as these schismatics continued in their stubborn resistance. Not only was continuing religious turmoil likely, but it might very well intensify now that Old Believers were faced with a terrible decision: Should they leave the Russian Church to follow the spiritual path being blazed by their leaders?

Jurij Lutoxin was steward of the Tsar's estate near the village of Izmajlovo; he was one of the Sovereign's trusted agents.

Artemon Sergeevič Matveev (1625–82) was a boyar who enjoyed the Tsar's special trust. His wife was born in Scotland, an incidental fact that reflected his Western sympathies. In the mid-1660's the Tsar appointed him to lead some of the expeditions which searched out, scattered, and sometimes executed religious hermits in the Russian forests who, perhaps without exception, viewed the reforms as the work of the devil. During the Ecumenical Council, Matveev was assigned to serve the Greek patriarchs. Avvakum later described his arguments with Matveev and Simeon Polockij: "We were like drunkards when we separated; I couldn't even eat after all the shouting." By one of those twists of fate which occur with such preternatural frequency in Russian history, Matveev was arrested after the death of Aleksej Mixajlovič on charges of sorcery and conspiracy against the life of the new Tsar Fëdor; he was exiled to Pustozersk in 1677 and imprisoned near Avvakum and his comrades. Unlike those tireless ascetics, Matveev spent his three years at Pustozersk in constant laments to the Tsar regarding his innocence and his imminent demise from hunger. In 1680 he was moved to Mezen, where he continued in the same vein: "And what money we are given comes to a copeck and a half a day . . . But the enemies of the Church exiled to Mezen, Avvakum's wife and children, they are given two copecks a day for an adult and a copeck and a half for the little ones. But we are your servants and not enemies, neither of the Church nor of your kingly rule." Matveev was returned to Moscow early in 1682 and killed in the Kremlin during a revolt by the streltsy in May of that year.

Dementej Minič Bašmakov (1618–1705) was one of the Tsar's closest administrative associates. His chief responsibility was for the Chancellory of Secret Affairs, which often figured prominently in matters that were technically concerns of the patriarch and his administration. The principal function of this Chancellory was to keep the central administration under surveillance and to investigate cases of wrong-doing.

274.   Avvakum refers to the fall of Byzantium to the Turks in 1453.

275.   On 26 August 1667 Avvakum, Lazar, Epifanij, and Nikifor were exiled to Pustozersk by order of the Tsar. They left Moscow on 30 August and arrived in Pustozersk on 12 December. The Pustozersk fortress was established in 1499 at the mouth of the Pechora river. In 1679 there were 90 households there consisting of over 600 persons; there was also the commander's house, a customs house, and the prison. The land there is tundra — frigid, barren and treeless, inhospitable. According to Robinson, in 1961 only three houses remained standing there. For a time the exiles lived in the huts of local inhabitants and were allowed considerable freedom of movement.

276.   Avvakum has in mind his Fourth and Fifth Petitions to the Tsar. The former (1669) reported the death of Nikifor and requested that two of his sons be released from Moscow to live with their mother in Mezen; the latter (1669) he called his "final sorrow-laden supplication to you . . . from my dungeon, as from my grave."

277.   *The Answer of the Orthodox* was written in the name of all four prisoners at Pustozersk; it was a lengthy compilation of theological and polemical materials divided into the two parts indicated by Avvakum: a formal "answer" to the Nikonians and a discussion of the defilements wrought by the new books and attendant heresies. It was intended as a kind of manual,

a textbook and a guide for Old Believers everywhere in Russia. The text was sent to Mezen before September 1669. Deacon Fëdor requested Avvakum's son Ivan to have it copied "in a good hand" and to send it to the rebel monks at Solovki (see Introduction) and to Moscow, where it arrived in fact near the close of 1669. The new mutilations visited upon the prisoners at Pustozersk in April 1670 were in large measure reprisals for this intransigent, rebellious book. It had received, after all, the seal of approval from all four prisoners and thus stood for a time as the fundamental statement by revered Fathers of the faith on the new Old Belief — "new" because it was now formally condemned and rejected by an Ecumenical Council. Later, after Fëdor began to differ with Avvakum, Lazar, and Epifanij, Avvakum retracted his approval of some positions taken in *The Answer of the Orthodox*.

278.   Lazar wrote two prolix letters to the Tsar (Feb. 1668) in defense of the Old Belief. He requested the local authorities to have them delivered uncensored to Aleksej Mixajlovič. When Commander Ivan Neelov demanded to read them, Lazar refused. Written negotiations lasted almost two years, and by the time the letters were finally delivered (15 April 1670), Lazar having relented, the second mutilation of their author had occurred.

279.   Early in the 18th century a legend spread among Old Believers based on a tale told by Semën Denisov and Gavriil of Novgorod; it describes the aftermath of these executions in terms reminiscent of hagiography. Semën and Gavriil were traveling on business, and passing near Mezen they stopped and found the graves of the two martyrs enclosed in a small, covered log frame. The two men entered and began to chant a requiem, so filled with fear and foreboding that they dared not light a single candle. And then they noticed the paradisiacal odor emanating from the graves — a traditional hagiographical emblem of saintly sanctity.

280.   Cf. Matt. 26:75, Mark 14:72, Luke 22:62.

281.   Elagin had been the ranking official in Mezen between 1661–63, so he knew local conditions there. He was a reliable strong-arm man for the Tsar, as he had served in the royal bodyguard. His mission was important, because Mezen had become the principal communications link between Pustozersk and Moscow. By interrupting this correspondence Tsar Aleksej hoped to calm the restless capital and isolate the inflammatory Pustozersk schismatic leadership.

282.   Lazar's public mutilation took place on 14 April 1670. It may surprise readers to learn that these barbarous punishments had symbolic

significnace. Removing a heretic's tongue was a means of terminating his preaching of heresies, while chopping off part or all of his right hand might end their written propagation. In Russia the latter punishment also made the "heretical" crossing with two fingers impossible.

In response to this popular legend about Lazar's right hand, the official Church created another: in September 1682 Patriarch Ioakim allegedly discovered in the patriarch's sacristy an "ark" (i.e., similar to the Ark of the Covenant; see, for example, Jos. 3:14), wherein reposed the relics of St. Andrew; his right hand was conformed in the manner appropriate for making the Sign of the Cross with three fingers.

283.   The term "angelical image" translates *sxima*, a Greek borrowing which denoted the highest rank among monks; it was reserved especially for hermits. The rank had two degrees, and Epifanij had received the lesser before he left Solovki for the northern forests.

284.   Mutilation followed by regeneration of the amputated member(s) is an old hagiographical device, the obvious purpose of which is to demonstrate God's approval of the stand taken by any particular martyr.

285.   Cf. Acts 12:6.

286.   In characteristic medieval fashion Avvakum interprets this citation from his contemporary Bible as a metaphorical description of the relation between Christ, the "Heavenly Bridegroom" (a central Orthodox metaphor), and his Church. The passage is not found in the King James Version.

287.   Cf. Mark 16:15–16.

288.   Here again Avvakum suggests the official Church has been polluted by the Greeks, who have been defiled by the Islamic Turks. The wave of terror that enveloped Old Believers after 1667 gave Avvakum substantial grounds for invoking the Islamic notion of the holy war.

289.   Cf. Matt. 7:18.

290.   Cf. Dan. chap. 3. Feodos'ja Morozova and her sister Evdok'ja were incarcerated and later died in Borovsk (see note 219). The image of the Chaldean furnace is repetitious in Avvakum's writings (cf. Gudzij, ed., *Žitie*, p. 137). It must have acted powerfully on Old Believers, who were facing execution by fire and at times incinerating themselves.

291.   Cf. Prov. 22:28.

292.   Avvakum refers here to a number of specific changes introduced by the Nikonians. (1) A cross with four points (characteristic of Roman Catholic crosses) replaced the old eight-pointed cross. (2) Traditionally the altar was covered first by the antimension (with relics of saints sewn into it), and then by a frontal (*inditija*) that reached to the floor. During divine worship one more cloth was added, the so-called *liton*. Nikon directed that the frontal be placed on the altar first and that the antimension should cover it. (3) Prior to divine worship the priest traditionally recited two prayers of confession while standing behind the iconostasis within the sanctuary; they prepared him, an unworthy human being, to act as God's vessel in leading the Mass. (4) Avvakum's reference to baptismal prayers offered up to the devil is misleading. The new translation of the Service of Baptism contained at one point an extremely awkward syntactic structure which allowed one to understand the referent of the phrase "we pray to thee" (i.e., to God) to be the phrase following immediately, "cunning spirit." (5) The Council of 1666–67 had confirmed Nikon's order that the direction in which processions moved during marriage, Baptism, and consecration of churches be reversed.

293.   Arsenios the Greek was one of Nikon's closest associates; in his erratic religious life he did as much as any man to discredit the reforms. Arsenios was born in Turkish territory around 1610, but later made his way to Italy where he was educated by the Jesuits in Rome; he also studied in Padua and Venice. A man of considerable intellect, he possessed a good knowledge of philosophy, theology, and languages, as well as of medicine. For reasons unknown he returned to the East, to Constantinople, where he abandoned Roman Catholicism and became a Greek Orthodox monk. However, he soon left Orthodoxy for Islam, then returned to Orthodoxy during his wanderings in Wallacia and Moldavia. When his travels brought him to Poland he became a Uniat for a time. While there Arsenios lived at court and cured the king of a sickness, which apparently produced the letter of recommendation which he later carried with him to Kiev. In Kiev he managed to attach himself to the party of Paissios, Patriarch of Jerusalem, who was going to Moscow. When Paissios (who did much to incline the Tsar toward Greek practices) left Moscow in 1649, Arsenios remained behind as a teacher of rhetoric. However, information regarding his checkered past came to Moscow, and an immediate inquiry was instituted. He was declared a heretic and exiled to Solovki. There Arsenios explained to the Elder Martirij, a renowned holy man and Epifanij's erstwhile confessor, that his religious peregrinations resulted from his quest for knowledge – a notion completely alien to the

17th-century Muscovite religious mentality. Nikon met Arsenios in 1652 when he came to Solovki to transport the relics of St. Filipp to Moscow (see notes 64 and 73); apparently he was impressed by Arsenios' erudition. In addition, legend has it that the latter greeted Nikon by bowing before him and asking a blessing from "the Russian Patriarch," this prior to Nikon's election and elevation. In any case, Nikon needed talented, learned men who were utterly dependent on him, and so he soon brought Arsenios back to Moscow and in 1654 put him in charge of correcting the old books. Nikon's lack of strategic sense was perhaps never more apparent than here, for the conservatives were horrified, and later made much of the fact, that a declared heretic had been assigned to such duties. When Nikon retired, Arsenios quickly allied himself with his enemies, with Paissios Ligarid in particular (see note 244). But his career was already in eclipse owing to his notoriety, and in 1662 he was again sent into exile, to Solovki. It seems clear now that Arsenios was merely a functionary, an opportunist, and a coward who followed orders out of a desire, unguided by principle, to preserve and enrich himself. Many Old Believers grossly exaggerated his role in formulating and implementing the reforms.

294.   Paraphrase of Psalm 115:1 (113:9 in the Russian Bible).

295.   Cf. II Cor. 11:6.

296.   St. Efrem Sirin (d. 373) was a famous preacher and an important writer in the early Church. A book of his teachings was published twice in Moscow during 1649. Vonifat'ev, who made it his habit to bless others with this book, must have given it to Avvakum in 1647 or 1648, at the time of their first meeting.

297.   Evfimej died in 1654, at approximately 20 years of age.

298.   The reference is to the 17th of the 20 kathismata into which the Orthodox Psalter is divided (specifically, see Psalm 119:132 [118:132 in the Russian Bible]).

299.   Avvakum paraphrases here a prayer by Basil the Great used during exorcisms; he inserts into it Christ's command to a "foul spirit," as recorded in Mark 9:25.

300.   Cf. Mark 9:26.

301.   The great Russian stove, used for cooking and heating and providing spaces for sleeping, was located in the immediate left-hand corner as one entered a peasant hut. A space was often provided under the front of the stove for kittens, and there was a space at the back for puppies. Avvakum's devil, evidently a creature of meager proportions, most likely took refuge in one of these recesses.

302.   The Sundovik river, a tributary of the Volga, flows near Avvakum's native village of Grigorovo.

303.   Regarding Ilarion, see note 247. During the first part of the Orthodox service, the priest can remove pieces of communion bread for the health of those whose names have been made known to him.

304.   Ten streltsy had responsibility for transporting the schismatic leaders from Moscow to Pustozersk, and after arrival there they were assigned to guard duty.

305.   As part of his daily religious devotions each devout Christian repeated the Lord's Prayer at least three times, this in addition to before meals.

306.   Avvakum almost certainly intended a metaphoric level of meaning here beyond the literal, as the fish is an ancient Christian symbol.

307.   Two priests in Pustozersk, Grigorij and Andrej, were Avvakum's followers, and they continued to practice the old rituals. Avvakum indicates he provided the necessaries for this requiem (candles, incense, etc.) during the entire forty-day period following Kirill's death.

308.   The Prayer to Jesus was brought to Russia in the 15th century by the Greek Hesychasts, numbers of whom came from the Russian monastery on Mt. Athos. The Hesychasts' quest for inner peace and moments of transcendent illumination led them to treasure silence; long oral prayers were thus considered distracting. This brief utterance ("Lord Jesus Christ, Son of God, have mercy on me, a sinner") could be repeated in a single breath. According to the 13th chapter of the *Domostroi*, this prayer was helpful in combating the devil's cunning tricks.

309.   This is a slightly paraphrased version of a statement made by the Prodigal Son, which recurs in the *Life* (cf. Luke 15:18). Fetin'ja may have quarreled with the Archpriestess, but she was nevertheless so loyal to the family that she followed them into exile.

310.   The simile "like a cobweb" is biblical; it can be found in Psalm 38:12 in Avvakum's Bible (the modern Russian Bible has changed the translation of this passage).

311.   Paraphrase of John 13:8.

312.   Orthodox Russians were directed to abstain from sexual relations on the eve of any religious holiday or on Saturday nights (before the Sabbath); violation of this law was punishable by eight days of fasting (no milk or meat) and by 200 prostrations per day.

313.   The choir is located by the north and south gates of the iconostasis (the sanctuary always being at the east end of the church).

314.   The reference is to V. I. Xilkov (see note 113).

315.   The village of Lopatišči.

316.   Avvakum refers here to the final kontakion in the Canon of the Mother of God.

317.   Cf. Matt. 7:14.

318.   Anna has in mind iconic depictions of angels with white, undulating bands near their ears symbolizing their attendance upon the utterances of God.

319.   In old Russia it was believed that Satan made special efforts to snare the souls of men during this particularly important moment of the service.

320.   A priest could not confess his own wife nor could he give her extreme unction. Avvakum went to his church to get the breviary (*trebnik*), so that Markovna's confession might be conducted properly.

321.   Specifically these two lessons are found in Acts 15:12 and 19:17—18.

†

Notes to the Preface

1   F. M. Dostoevskij, *Dnevnik pisatelja* (3 vols.; Paris: YMCA Press, 194–), II, 302.

2   *The Life of the Archpriest Avvakum by Himself* (Hamden, Conn.: Archon Books, 1963), 26–27; this volume is a reprint of the original edition by the Hogarth Press, London, 1924. Mirsky has in mind untutored Russian as it was spoken during the first decades of this century. The Harrison-Mirrlees translation has been reprinted in a somewhat condensed form (less Avvakum's introduction and his "supplementary tales") in Serge Zenkovsky, ed., trans., and introd., *Medieval Russia's Epics, Chronicles, and Tales*, 2nd ed., rev. and enl. (New York: E. P. Dutton, 1974), 399–448. Zenkovsky has corrected many of the errors in the original edition.

3   G. P. Fedotov, introd. and ed., *A Treasury of Russian Spirituality* (New York: Harper and Rowe, 1965), 137–81.

4   *Žizneopisanija Avvakuma i Epifanija: issledovanie i teksty* (M.: AN SSSR, 1963). A photocopy of the holograph of the *Life* in its third redaction was recently published in the Soviet Union; the text is also printed in modern cyrillic. To compare this redaction with the second, see N. S. Demkova, N. F. Droblenkova, and L. I. Sazonova, eds., *Pustozerskij sbornik: avtografy sočinenij Avvakuma i Epifanija* (L.: AN SSSR, 1975). Translations of the *Life* into languages other than English known to me are *La vie de l'archiprêtre Avvakum, écrite par lui-même*, trans., introd., and notes by Pierre Pascal (Paris, 1938); *Das Leben des Protopopen Awwakum von ihm selbst niedergeschrieben*, trans., introd., and notes by Rudolph Jagoditsch, in *Quellen und Aufsätze zur russischen Geschichte*, 10 (1930); *Das Leben des Protopopen Awwakum von ihm selbst niedergeschrieben*, trans. and notes by Gerhard Hildebrandt (Göttingen: Vandenhoeck and Ruprecht, 1965); *Protopop Avvakum, Hayatim*, trans. Hihal Yulaza Talny (Istanbul, 1946) (Turkish trans.).

5   Serge Zenkovsky, *Russkoe staroobrjadčestvo* (Munich: Wilhelm Fink Verlag, 1970); see also Robert O. Crummey, *The Old Believers and the World of the Antichrist: The Vyg Community and the Russian State* (Madison: Univ. of Wisconsin Press, 1970).

6   N. S. Demkova, Žitie Protopopa Avvakuma: *tvorčeskaja istorija proizvedenija* (L.: Leningrad Univ., 1974).

7   "O zadačax stilistiki: nabljudenija nad stilem *Žitija protopopa Avvakuma*," *Russkaja reč'*, (Trudy Fonetičeskogo instituta praktičeskogo izučenija jazykov), no. 1 (1923), 195–293.

8   A. I. Issatschenko, "Vorgeschichte und Entstehung der modernen russischen Literatursprache," *Zeitschrift für slavische Philologie*, 37 no. 2 (1924), 245–49.

†

Notes to V. V. Vinogradov, "On the Tasks of Stylistics"

1   I accept the definition of C. A. Sechehaye: "Le symbole n'est pas un signe
    arbitrairement choise pour correspondre à une idée préexistante, mais
    la condition linguistique nécessaire à une opération psychologique,
    à savoir la formation d'une idée verbale"; *La stylistique et la linguistique
    théorique: Mélanges de linguistique offerts à M. Ferd. de Saussure*
    (Paris, 1908), p. 175.

2   I am aware of the defect in the stylistic analysis proffered here, the
    absence of any clear historical perspective in making judgments about
    the meaning of verbal signs. But nothing can be done about this until
    a large number of works are analyzed and until the history of the literary
    language's lexicon has received more attentive study.

3   In referring to his tale as "gabbling," Avvakum emphasizes his "heedless-
    ness of eloquence," setting himself the task as it were of stylizing popular
    speech. Some notion of the scornful, ironic, and comical connotations
    associated with the words "gabbling" (*vjakan'e*) and "to gabble" (*vjakat'*)
    in the mind of a seventeenth-century writer is provided by these citations
    from *Otrazitel'noe pisanie o novoizobretannom puti samoubijstvennyx
    smertej* (*A Reflection on a Newly Contrived Means of Self-Slaughter*)
    (Pamjatniki drevnej pis'mennosti, no. 8): "That peasant is a wood-
    chopper's gelding, he barks and swears at those better and more virtuous
    than himself, and he ignorantly sits in front of his masters and gabbles
    and bleats, 'I spit on everything!' " and, "Now there is still another
    teacher, the poor old monk who teaches according to the wood-demon's
    savage rule; the poor soul gabbles like a stray cat." [The author of the
    Otrazitel'noe pisanie was the Old Believer and Elder Efrosin; the work is
    a vigorous attack on the preachers of mass suicide by fire, who were
    active and successful among the conservative peasantry, especially during
    the 1680's. Trans.]

4   In the third redaction of the *Life* Avvakum develops this canine metaphor
    into a kind of leitmotif. In addition to further simple comparisons of
    himself to a dog, an entire episode is created on the basis of this image:
    "There was a chink in the wall. A little dog used to come every day and
    look at me . . . And I used to talk a bit with my little dog." This realized
    metaphor is then neutralized by a biblical reference which illuminates
    the experience as an episode from the life of a righteous man ("As the
    dogs licked the pus of Lazarus' ulcers at the gates of the rich man and
    brought him consolation . . . "), while emphasizing the antithetical
    attitude of people ("People walked past me far off, not daring to look
    at the prison"). Another time the comparison of his children to "little
    pups" (*kobelki*) evokes the same contrast: "Other people had dogs in

the harnesses, but I didn't have any; I only had my two sons Ivan and Prokopij. They were still little, and along with me, like little pups, they dragged the dogsled over the portages."

5   P.100; in Avvakum's *Book of Conversations* he states: "There's no reason for going to Persia to search after fiery furnaces; God gave us Babylon here˙at home, the Chaldean furnace is in Borovsk." Cf. the following from his article on the conformation of the fingers in making the Sign of the Cross ("O složenii perst"): "There's no reason for our going to Persia to suffer, Babylon's been laid up for us here at home."

6   Cf. the general commentary on the development of verbal representation of emotion in M. M. Pokrovskij, *Semasiologičeskie issledovanija v oblasti drevnix jazykov* (Moscow, 1895), p. 63; here one finds references to the works of Schneider and Bechtel. Cf. also A. Gruška, "Iz oblasti semasiologii, " *Filologičeskoe obozrenie*, vol. 11, 41–42.

7   [The epithets *milyj* and *milen'kij* are difficult to translate into English without introducing unfortunate connotations which vary depending on context. Consequently, several renderings are used here (and in the translation of Avvakum's *Life*). Similar problems arise with the epithets *bednyj* 'poor' and *gor'kij* 'bitter,' and with the latter's substantives *gorjun, goremyka* (discussed below). Trans.]

†

Notes to K. N. Brostrom, "Further Remarks on the *Life*"

1   D. S. Lixačëv argues that fabrication to literary or other ends was alien to medieval Russian writers; *Čelovek v literature drevnej Rusi*, 2nd ed. rev. (M.: Nauka, 1970), p. 108; and on page 114: "Everything that was not 'historical,' that did not exist in reality, was deceit, and deceit was from the devil."

2   Among Soviet scholars, the late Igor' Petrovič Erëmin argued this position frequently and forcefully with regard to medieval Russian writing generally. For example, in resisting the notion that "elemental Realism" or "Realistic elements" or "harbingers of Realism" can be found in this literature, he remarks: "A medieval Russian writer's depiction of life can have only a purely external resemblance to modern Realism, behind which there is hidden a profound inner difference. The depiction of life

in Old Russian literature is in many ways diametrically opposed to its depiction in the works of modern Realists"; "O xudožestvennoj specifike drevnerusskoj literatury" in *Literatura drevnej Rusi: étjudy i xarakteristiki* (M., L.: Nauka, 1966), 246–47.

3   For a summary statement of the Soviet Marxist understanding of Avvakum and the schism, see V. E. Gusev, "Protopop Avvakum, vydajuščijsja russkij pisatel' XVII veka" in *Žitie protopopa Avvakuma, im samim napisannoe*, ed. N. K. Gudzij (M.: GIXL, 1960), 8–22.

4   S. Matxauzerova has argued that a thematic dichotomy can be observed in Avvakum's use of aorist and imperfect forms in contrast to resultative participle forms. However, her argument is based on restricted data (Avvakum's "First Conversation") and does not work when applied to the *Life*; "Funkcija vremeni v drevnerusskix žanrax," *TODRL* (M., L.: AN SSSR, 1972), vol. 27, 227–35.

5   Dmitrij Čiževskij, *History of Russian Literature from the Eleventh Century to the End of the Baroque* (SP&R 12; The Hague: Mouton, 1960), p. 371.

6   Avvakum Petrov, "Beseda pervaja" in N. K. Gudzij, ed., *Žitie*, p. 127.

7   The term "fanaticism" reflects our modern perspective on these matters. As Lixačëv has observed, the doctrinaire preaching of a general point of view combined with the conviction that ideological opponents are agents of the devil (not victims of false ideas) was typical of medieval Russia's polemical literature. The writer's duty was not to discuss the Truth but to preach it and apply it to human experience. *Čelovek*, 133–34.

8   See Serge Zenkovsky, *Staroobrjadčestvo*, 352–54; Čiževskij, 370–71; Robinson, p. 21.

9   *The Icon and the Axe: An Interpretive History of Russian Culture* (N. Y.: Random House, 1970), p. 157.

10   Zenkovsky, *Staroobrjadčestvo*, 505–06.

11   Gudzij, ed., *Žitie*, p. 54.

12   Zenkovsky remarks that escape from Pustozersk was possible, as Cossacks imprisoned there managed to do so in a matter of weeks. Apparently Avvakum's sense of God's will for his life, his belief in the "one true path," was so strong that he never seriously considered this option. Neither did his comrades, as far as we know.

13   P. 100; in his "Beseda pjataja: o vnešnej mudrosti," Avvakum associates "external wisdom" with foreign ideas and with the prideful pursuit of God through intellect, and he contrasts it with "humble wisdom," with "humility, and unhypocritical love, . . . unsullied faith, fasting, . . . sober living." Gudzij, ed., *Žitie*, 138–40.

14   *O jazyke xudožestvennoj literatury* (M.: GIXL, 1959), p. 468.

15   Žitie protopopa Avvakuma: *tvorčeskaja istorija proizvedenija* (L.: Lenin-

grad Univ., 1974), p. 147.

16 *Poétika drevnerusskoj literatury* (L.: AN SSSR, 1967), p. 109.

17 Avvakum's frequent, spontaneous recourse to traditional ideas lessens the usefulness of A. N. Robinson's description of hagiographical "didactic illustration" in the *Life*. Although this notion clearly admits the possibility of metaphor, it also implies the conscious, deliberate shaping of experience to conform to particular ideas. At best the term is insufficiently flexible to describe Avvakum's manner of thinking; see *Žizneopisanija Avvakuma i Epifanija*, 64–71.

18 Lixačëv argues that "Realistic elements" in medieval Russiaň literature can be related to modern Realism essentially as indirect antecedents, although he also states that Realism as a method is not encountered here (*Poétika*, p. 127). For I. P. Erëmin's contrary opinion, see note 1.

19 Ernst Benz, *The Eastern Orthodox Church: Its Thought and Life* (Garden City, N. Y.: Doubleday Anchor, 1963), p. 6.

20 Robinson, p. 70.

21 Avvakum Petrov, "Prjanišnikovskij spisok" in Gudzij, ed., *Žitie*, p. 311.

22 Demkova, p. 146.

23 John Fennell and Anthony Stokes, *Early Russian Literature* (London: Faber and Faber, 1974), p. 237. (Chapter on 17th century by Stokes.) Avvakum, however, did not believe that this struggle was eternally unending. Like his contemporaries, he anticipated the end of the world and the ultimate triumph of Christ.

24 A touching and vivid illustration of this judgment involves Avvakum's two sons, who, imprisoned with their mother, denied the Old Belief under threat of execution (p. 95). Avvakum calls them to repentance and renewed commitment, and then compares them to the Apostle Peter, who also "made denial" but later returned to the true path. It is interesting that Avvakum relates two celestial omens of God's wrath early in the *Life* (38–39) to dates on the ecclesiastical calendar involving St. Peter (St. Peter's Day and the Fast of St. Peter). Could it be that this signaled for him a similar possibility for the Church, temporarily gone astray?

25 Zenkovsky discusses at some length (361–67) Avvakum's "optimism" concerning the restoration of the old ritual; he argues the pessimistic notion that the last apostasy had occurred and Russia was in the hands of the victorious Antichrist never figured prominently in his ideas. I believe this definition of Avvakum's optimism to be too narrow: both restoration and passive endurance promise victory and reward, one immediately in this world and the other after death. If we admit that general references to predestination may sometimes reflect eschatological ideas, then we may have to give more weight to their influence on

Avvakum's thinking than Zenkovsky does.

26 Avvakum's notion of the aggressive nature of evil requires no discussion. For details regarding the relevant imagery (grasping, clutching hands, burning and baking, attacks, etc.), see Vinogradov.

27 Avvakum was aware of his own inconsistency here, both in the *Life* and elsewhere in his works. An extreme example is encountered in his "Ninth Conversation"; there Avvakum relates the story of the poor, diseased Lazarus at the gates of the rich man, who later dies and suffers the torments of hell. From heaven Abraham addresses him as "child," and Avvakum adds the following aside: "I'm not Abraham, I wouldn't call him 'child.' You're a dog! ... I'd spit in his ugly mug and kick him in his fat gut!" Gudzij, ed., *Žitie*, p. 148;

28 "Beseda pervaja" in Gudzij, ed., *Žitie*, p. 127.

29 The principal biblical sources for this metaphor are the stories about Christ calming the stormy waters of the Sea of Galilee and his walking upon them to reassure his terrified disciples (Matt. 8: 23–27; 14: 22–33).

30 Zenkovsky makes a fundamental distinction between the Lovers of God (*Bogoljubcy*) and the Forest Elders (*Lesnye starcy*) on this point. The former wished to transform the religious life of all Russians while the latter fled the world and dedicated themselves to extreme asceticism; *Staroobrjadcestvo*, 133–55 and elsewhere.

31 *Žizneopisanija*, 79–80.

32 "Beseda pjataja" in Gudzij, ed., *Žitie*, p. 139; for another striking example, see "Beseda četvërtaja," ibid., p. 135.

33 Other references to the Beast of the Apocalypse in the writings of the Old Believers can be found in Zenkovsky, *Staroobrjadčestvo*, 263, 318. In the former Spiridon Potëmkin speaks of the "motley beast" (*zverju pëstromu*).

34 *Čelovek*, 104, 109; see also ibid., 13–14, for his discussion of the medieval "absolutization" of man in terms of good and evil.

35 Avvakum was not alone in this. For interesting commentary on this general problem in Russian literature during the 17th century, see Fennell and Stokes, 224–28, 249–50; and especially Lixačëv, *Čelovek*, 7–24.

36 *Poétika*, 221–22.

37 "O xudožestvennom realizme" in Ladislav Matejka, comp., *Readings in Russian Poetics* (Michigan Slavic Materials, 2; Ann Arbor: Univ. of Mich. Dept. of Slavic Langs. & Lits., 1962), p. 35.

38 Thus I disagree with Demkova's argument (147–54) regarding the stages in Avvakum's moral development. Like Lixačëv, she describes a kind of modernity in Avvakum's *Life* which, it seems to me, is not present in it.

39 See Benz, 20–25.

40 Gudzij, ed., *Žitie*, p. 54; see annotation 2.
41 Elsewhere in his works Avvakum makes this connection specific by referring to himself as a "living corpse," as being "buried alive," and in exclaiming "In my prison, like a coffin, what do I need? Just death!" Cited in D. S. Lixačëv, *Velikoe nasledie: klassičeskie proizvedenija literatury drevnej Rusi* (M.: Sovremennik, 1975), p. 300. See also Epifanij's use of this simile in Robinson, p. 197.
42 "Beseda pervaja" in Gudzij, ed., *Žitie*, p. 126.
43 See Zenkovsky, *Staroobrjadčestvo*, 116–17. Ju. N. Dmitriev argues that the medieval artist strove to transmit "archetypal beauty" in his work. Although Dmitriev overemphasizes earthly beauty in his argument, he retells a legend related by Simeon Polockij that captures the medieval tension between devilish ugliness and heavenly beauty. An artist painted the Virgin standing on a coarse, repulsive devil. The devil, angered, appeared to the artist in a dream and threatened him, but he was saved by the Virgin. Thus, true (spiritual) beauty is the product of a goodness against which the powers of hell cannot prevail. "Teorija iskusstva i vzgljady na iskusstvo v pis'mennosti drevnej Rusi," *TODRL* (M., L.: AN SSSR, 1953), IX, 109–10.
44 "Zametki o stile *Žitija* protopopa Avvakuma," *TODRL* (M., L.: AN SSSR, 1957), XIII, p. 273.
45 See, for example, Gudzij, ed., *Žitie*, 126–27, 319, and Robinson, p. 35.
46 Pp. 46–47. "Ispoved'–propoved' " is the title of Robinson's article on Avvakum in *Istoriko-filologičeskie issledovanija: sbornik statej k 75-letiju akad. N. I. Kondrata* (M., 1967).
47 See, for example, the introduction to the *Book of Conversations* (*Kniga besed*), in Gudzij, ed., *Žitie*, 123–24.
48 The single, partial deviation from this pattern is located in the final supplementary tale (p. 111), where Avvakum does not sin but is teased by a devil to illustrate the principle of hellish temptation.
49 Benz, 15–16.
50 This 13th chapter of Mark is rich in imagery and ideas which are reiterated in the *Life*.
51 Robinson notes in passing (p. 79) the manner in which Avvakum sometimes mixes antithetical emotional states (e.g., *I smex, i gore* 'We didn't know whether to laugh or cry'), in contrast to the traditional linear descriptions of emotions. As Robinson observes, this minor quirk is indicative of Avvakum's lack of interest in self-analysis.
52 Relevant here are Demkova's interesting comments (34, 70) regarding what we might call the *svod* mentality evident in successive redactions of Avvakum's and Epifanij's autobiographies: new materials were added to narrative written previously without any serious attempt to integrate

them in a way that would be considered logically coherent by a modern reader.

53 Gudzij, ed., Žitie, p. 198.

54 See especially 80–100.

55 Poétika, p. 308.

56 For some useful comments on this problem see Richard W. F. Pope, "But the Literature Does Not Fit the Theory: A Critique of the Teleological Approach to Literature," Slavic Review, 36 (1977), 667–75.

57 Such arguments often seem strained and unconvincing. For example, Lixačëv associates secularization with a retreat from the medieval categorical depictions of man (Čelovek, 12–13). Yet it is obvious that categorical depiction is not in itself alien to secularism; it is typical of the literature of the Enlightenment and, indeed, of Socialist Realism. Such characterization is likely to result when literature becomes the vehicle for a prescriptive, limited world view, whether religious or secular.

58 For an excellent discussion of this point see Serge A. Zenkovsky, "The Old Believer Avvakum: His Writings," Indiana Slavic Studies, 1 (1956), 13–18.

59 Fennell and Stokes, p. 228.

60 Zenkovsky, "The Old Believer Avvakum," 7–12.

61 Čelovek, ch. 4.

62 See Fennell and Stokes, 224–26, for an interesting discussion of this development.

63 The Idea of the Modern in Literature and the Arts (New York: Horizon Press, 1967), p. 34.

64 Gudzij, ed., Žitie, p. 200.

†

REFERENCES

As the literature on Avvakum is extensive, this listing includes only works cited in the course of argument. For a much more extensive compilation, see A. N. Robinson's edition of the *Life*.

Russian Texts of *The Life of the Archpriest Avvakum*

Demkova, N. S., Droblenkova, N. F., and Sazonova, L. I., eds. *Pustozerskij sbornik: avtografy sočinenij Avvakuma i Epifanija.* Leningrad: AN SSSR, 1975.
Gudzij, N. K., ed. *Žitie protopopa Avvakuma, im samim napisannoe.* Moscow: GIXL, 1960.
Robinson, A. N., ed. *Žizneopisanija Avvakuma i Epifanija: issledovanie i teksty.* Moscow: AN SSSR, 1963.

Translations of the *Life*

Harrison, Jane and Mirrlees, Hope, trans. *The Life of the Archpriest Avvakum By Himself.* Hamden, Conn.: Archon Books, 1963.
Hildebrandt, Gerhard, trans. and notes. *Das Leben des Protopopen Awwakum von ihm selbst niedergeschrieben.* Göttingen: Vandenhoeck and Ruprecht, 1965.
Iswolsky, Helen, trans. "The Life of the Archpriest Avvakum." *A Treasury of Russian Spirituality.* Edited by G. P. Fedotov. New York: Harper and Rowe, 1965, 137–81.
Jagoditsch, Rudolph, trans., introd., and notes. *Das Leben des Protopopen Awwakum von ihm selbst niedergeschrieben. Quellen und Aufsätze zur russischen Geschichte,* Vol. 10 (1930).
Pascal, Pierre, trans., introd., and notes. *La vie de l'archiprêtre Avvakum, écrite par lui-même.* Paris, 1938.
Talny, Hihal Yulaza, trans. *Protopop Avvakum, Hayatim.* Istanbul, 1946.

Secondary Sources

Benz. Ernst. *The Eastern Orthodox Church: Its Thought and Life.* Garden City, N. Y.: Doubleday Anchor, 1963.

Billington, James H. *The Icon and the Axe: An Interpretive History of Russian Culture.* New York: Random House, 1970.

Čiževskij, Dmitrij. *History of Russian Literature from the Eleventh Century to the End of the Baroque.* The Hague: Mouton, 1960.

Crummey, Robert O. *The Old Believers and the World of the Antichrist: The Vyg Community and the Russian State.* Madison: University of Wisconsin Press, 1970.

Demkova, N. S. Žitie protopopa Avvakuma: *tvorčeskaja istorija proizvedenija.* Leningrad: Leningrad University, 1974.

Dmitriev, Ju. N. "Teorija iskusstva i vzgljady na iskusstvo v pis'mennosti drevnej Rusi." *Trudy otdela drevnerusskoj literatury,* Vol. 9. Moscow, Leningrad: AN SSSR, 1957.

Erëmin, I. P. "O xudožestvennoj specifike drevnerusskoj literatury." *Literatura drevnej Rusi: étjudy i xarakteristiki.* Moscow, Leningrad: Nauka, 1966.

Fennell, John and Stokes, Anthony. *Early Russian Literature.* London: Faber and Faber, 1974.

Gusev, V. E. "Protopop Avvakum, vydajuščijsja russkij pisatel' XVII veka." *Žitie protopopa Avvakuma, im samim napisannoe.* Edited by N. K. Gudzij. Moscow: GIXL, 1960.

— — — — — —. "Zametki o stile Žitija protopopa Avvakuma." *Trudy otdela drevnerusskoj literatury,* Vol. 13. Moscow, Leningrad: AN SSSR, 1957.

Howe, Irving, ed. *The Idea of the Modern in Literature and the Arts.* New York: Horizon Press, 1967.

Issatschenko, A. I. "Vorgeschichte und Entstehung der modernen russischen Literatursprache." *Zeitschrift für slavische Philologie,* 37, no. 2 (1974).

Jakobson, Roman. "O xudožestvennom realizme." *Readings in Russian Poetics,* no. 2. Compiled by Ladislav Matejka. Ann Arbor: University of Michigan Department of Slavic Languages and Literatures, 1962.

Lixačëv, D. S. *Čelovek v literature drevnej Rusi.* 2nd ed. rev. Moscow: Nauka, 1970.

— — — — — —. *Poétika drevnerusskoj literatury.* Leningrad: AN SSSR, 1967.

— — — — — —. *Velikoe nasledie: klassičeskie proizvedenija literatury drevnej Rusi.* Moscow: Sovremennik, 1975.

Matxauzerova, S. "Funkcija vremeni v drevnerusskix žanrax." *Trudy otdela drevnerusskoj literatury*, Vol. 27. Moscow, Leningrad: AN SSSR, 1972, 227–35.

Pope, Richard. "But the Literature Does Not Fit the Theory: A Critique of the Teleological Approach to Literature. *Slavic Review*, 36 (1977), 667–75.

Robinson, A. N. "Ispoved'–propoved'." *Istoriko–filologičeskie issledovanija: sbornik statej k 75-letiju akad. N. I. Kondrata*. Moscow, 1967.

Vinogradov, V. V. *O jazyke xudožestvennoj literatury*. Moscow: GIXL, 1959.

—— ———. "O zadačax stilistiki: nabljudenija nad stilem *Žitija protopopa Avvakuma*." *Russkaja reč'*, no. 1 (1925), 195–293.

Zenkovsky, Serge. *Medieval Russia's Epics, Chronicles, and Tales*. 2nd ed. rev. and enl. New York: E. P. Dutton, 1974.

————. *Russkoe staroobrjadčestvo*. Munich: Wilhelm Fink Verlag, 1970.

————. "The Old Believer Avvakum: His Writings." *Indiana Slavic Studies*, no. 1 (1956), 1–51.